# A TRIM & TERRIFIC
# LOUISIANA
# KITCHEN

## AN EASY AND LIGHTER APPROACH TO SOUTHERN CUISINE

*Written by*
Holly Berkowitz Clegg

*Nutrient Analysis by*
Catherine M. Champagne, PhD, RD, LDN
Pennington Biomedical Research Center

*Artist*
Melanie DeJean Hansbrough

*Holly Berkowitz Clegg* is a graduate of Sophie Newcomb College. She attended the Cordon Bleu Cooking School in London. In Paris, she attended classes at the Cordon Bleu Cooking School and La Varenne.

This is Mrs. Clegg's fourth book. Her other books are:

*From A Louisiana Kitchen*

*From Mr. Bingle's Kitchen*

*The Devil's Food*

*Nutrient Analysis by*

Catherine M. Champagne, PhD, RD, LDN
Pennington Biomedical Research Center

*Artist*

Melanie DeJean Hansbrough

ISBN 0-9610888-3-4

Library of Congress Catalog Card Number 92-97408

| | | |
|---|---|---|
| First Printing | April 1993 | 5,000 books |
| Second Printing | June 1993 | 10,000 books |
| Third Printing | October 1993 | 10,000 books |
| Fourth Printing | February 1994 | 10,000 books |
| Fifth Printing | May 1994 | 10,000 books |
| Sixth Printing | September 1994 | 15,000 books |
| Seventh Printing | December 1994 | 10,000 books |

Printed in the USA by

# TABLE OF CONTENTS

# JUST A NOTE

I used to consider myself the queen of whipping cream and butter. I would hide my grocery cart when I saw all my new health conscious friends at the grocery store. However, I said it was o.k. for me to shop that way because I was a cook. Famous last words... I, too, have made adjustments in my life and in my cooking.

Surprisingly, these changes do not have to affect the taste of food. I promise! My intention of this book is to make one be more conscious of what they are eating while still enjoying their favorite foods. I have included easy everyday recipes where you can find the ingredients on your shelf. Most importantly, each recipe has been tested and analyzed to insure the quality is there. However, now you can enjoy these recipes without guilt and have an awareness of what you are eating. Yes, food can taste good yet be good for you!

Also, I am very excited to have discovered Healthcraft Waterless & Greaseless Cookware. Not only is it the perfect cookware to prepare all my low fat recipes, but it cleans with ease and maintains its appearance. For more information: 1-800-443-8079.

I want to thank Cathy Champagne and her staff for their expertise and guidance in the analysis of each recipe. Melanie Hansbrough has done a terrific job as my artist, and more importantly, as my backbone. Last, I want to thank my husband, Mike, and my three wonderful children Todd, Courtney, and Haley for their patience as I spent endless hours in my kitchen and on my computer. At least with this book nobody had to gain weight and could enjoy eating.

*Holly Berkowitz Clegg*

The concept of this book is food that is "good for you" can also be good to eat. To help interpret what the "good for you" means, the following notations about cholesterol and fat will help:

Ⓒ Cholesterol content less than or equal to 60 milligrams (mg) per serving. Many recipes achieve this goal even if they are not as low fat as recommended. It is suggested that the health conscious American consume no more than 300 mg of cholesterol per day as part of a heart healthy diet.

Ⓕ Fat approximately 30% or less of total calories. The American Heart Association suggests this level as the goal for the average American. While not every recipe in this collection will achieve this level, they can be combined with other recipes to achieve a total meal that will be 30% or less of total calories. The menus in the menu planning section are good examples of how this can be accomplished. One can have a higher fat entrée, when served with low and moderate fat vegetables, starches, and dessert, will achieve the desired fat level for the meal.

*Catherine M. Champagne, PhD, RD, LDN*
Pennington Biomedical Research Center

4

# MENUS

M. HANSBROUGH

## VEGETARIAN I

*Artichoke Soup, 45*

*Broccoli Stuffed Pasta Shells, 79*
*Honey Carrots, 102*
*Herbed Squash, 116*

*Poppy Seed Cake with Lemon*
*Filling, 193*

| Calories | Cholesterol (mg) |
|---|---|
| 796 | 40 |
| Fat (g) | % Calories from Fat |
| 21.9 | 24.8% |

## VEGETARIAN II

*Gazpacho, 53*

*Garden Pasta Medley, 75*
*Almond Asparagus, 98*
*Spinach Bread, 26*

*Pineapple Cake, 196*

| Calories | Cholesterol (mg) |
|---|---|
| 659 | 10 |
| Fat (g) | % Calories from Fat |
| 22.2 | 30.3% |

## BRUNCH FOR THE RITE OF SPRING

*Non Alcoholic Wine Cooler, 42*

*Herbed Biscuits, 27*

*Egg Soufflé, 38*

*Banana Pancakes, 40*

*Hot Fruit Compote, 41*

| Calories | Cholesterol (mg) |
|---|---|
| 637 | 98 |
| Fat (g) | % Calories from Fat |
| 16.5 | 23.3% |

## SOUTHWESTERN BRUNCH

*Tortilla Chips, 16*
*Salsa, 17*

*Egg and Green*
*Chili Casserole, 38*
*Hacienda Chicken, 154*
*Quick Cheese Grits, 39*

*Mango Salad, 72*

| Calories | Cholesterol (mg) |
|---|---|
| 778 | 190 |
| Fat (g) | % Calories from Fat |
| 17.7 | 20.5% |

## GREAT ITALIAN DINNER

*Caesar Salad, 69*

*Scampi Italian Style, 177*
*Perfect Pasta, 77*
*Herbed French Bread, 26*
*Eggplant Parmesan, 103*

*Tortoni, 215*

| Calories | Cholesterol (mg) |
|----------|------------------|
| 867 | 180 |
| Fat (g) | % Calories from Fat |
| 29.0 | 30.1% |

## SOUTH OF THE BORDER DINNER

*Mexican Corn Soup, 48*

*Mexican Chicken Casserole, 156*
*Southwestern Rice, 112*
*Cucumber Onion Salad, 68*

*Chocolate Layered Dessert, 211*

| Calories | Cholesterol (mg) |
|----------|------------------|
| 885 | 62 |
| Fat (g) | % Calories from Fat |
| 26.0 | 26.4% |

## TAILGATE PARTY

*Artichoke Squares, 12*

*Barbecued Chicken, 149*
*Marinated Slaw, 68*
*Baked Beans, 98*
*Spicy Corn Casserole, 120*

*Almost Better Than Sex Cake, 188*

| Calories | Cholesterol (mg) |
|----------|------------------|
| 985 | 141 |
| Fat (g) | % Calories from Fat |
| 31.2 | 28.5% |

## FORMAL ELEGANT EVENING

*Salmon Mousse*
*with Dill Sauce, 15*

*Raspberry Spinach Salad, 69*

*Garlic Grilled Pork*
*Tenderloin, 131*
*Fanned Baked Potatoes, 109*
*Honey Baked Onions, 105*
*Almond Asparagus, 98*

*Fantastic Trifle, 213*

| Calories | Cholesterol (mg) |
|----------|------------------|
| 1076 | 106 |
| Fat (g) | % Calories from Fat |
| 36.0 | 30.1% |

## NEW YEAR'S DAY

*Black-Eyed Pea and Rice Salad
served on a Cabbage Leaf, 66*

*Mustard Brisket, 122
Glazed Sweet Potatoes, 111
Garden Stuffed Tomatoes, 120*

*Blueberry Cobbler, 222*

| Calories | Cholesterol (mg) |
|----------|------------------|
| 1135 | 135 |
| Fat (g) | % Calories from Fat |
| 32.4 | 25.7% |

## KIDS' NIGHT IN ON PARENTS' NIGHT OUT

*Orange Mandarin Salad, 68*

*Meaty Cheesy Spaghetti, 94*

*Brownies, 203*

| Calories | Cholesterol (mg) |
|----------|------------------|
| 678 | 64 |
| Fat (g) | % Calories from Fat |
| 12.8 | 17.0% |

## CARIBBEAN NIGHTS

*Barbecued Pork Roast, 130
Roasted Sweet and White
Potatoes, 111
Spinach with Hearts of Palm, 119*

*Pineapple Dream Cake, 198*

| Calories | Cholesterol (mg) |
|----------|------------------|
| 729 | 108 |
| Fat (g) | % Calories from Fat |
| 22.3 | 27.5% |

## QUICK COOK MENU

*Easy Crab Soup, 44*

*Sirloin with Herbed Wine
Sauce, 123
Orange Glazed Carrots, 101
Potato Bake, 110*

*Chocolate Pudding Cake, 201*

| Calories | Cholesterol (mg) |
|----------|------------------|
| 875 | 188 |
| Fat (g) | % Calories from Fat |
| 23.6 | 24.3% |

# COCKTAIL BUFFET

*Crawfish Elegante, 181*

*Chicken Tarragon, 145*

*Red Pepper Dip
with Fresh Vegetables, 21*

*Cold Poached Salmon,
Dill Sauce, 16*

*Pork Tenders, 132*

*Marinated Shrimp, 12*

*Chocolate Fondue, 220,
served with Strawberries,
Bananas, and
Angel Food Cake Squares\**

*\*Not included in nutrient analysis.*

| Calories | Cholesterol (mg) |
|---|---|
| 915 | 491 |
| Fat (g) | % Calories from Fat |
| 17.8 | 17.5% |

# SOUPER SUPPER

*Tortilla Soup, 49
Caesar Salad, 69
Corn, Shrimp and Crabmeat
Soup, 47*

*Spinach Bread, 26*

*Mock Chocolate Éclair, 210*

| Calories | Cholesterol (mg) |
|---|---|
| 723 | 148 |
| Fat (g) | % Calories from Fat |
| 22.6 | 28.1% |

# SUMMER SALAD BUFFET

*Peach Soup, 53*

*Shrimp Pasta Salad, 57
Carrot Raisin Chicken Salad, 61
Tuna Salad, 62*

*Lemon Raspberry Muffins, 34*

*Praline Meringues, 206
Chocolate Chess Bars, 201*

| Calories | Cholesterol (mg) |
|---|---|
| 1050 | 306 |
| Fat (g) | % Calories from Fat |
| 26.5 | 22.7% |

# A SURE WINNER

*Marinated Crabmeat Salad, 65*

*Italian Shrimp, 174
Perfect Pasta, 77
Cheesy Spinach Casserole, 118
French Bread\**

*Chocolate Ice Cream Delight, 216*

*\*Not included in nutrient analysis.*

| Calories | Cholesterol (mg) |
|---|---|
| 1045 | 342 |
| Fat (g) | % Calories from Fat |
| 37.8 | 32.6% |

## CASUALLY CAJUN

*Crawfish Etouffée, 180*
*Green Bean Marinate, 104*
*Sweet Potato Rolls, 25*

*Bread Pudding*
*with Rum Sauce, 212*

| Calories | Cholesterol (mg) |
|----------|------------------|
| 690 | 235 |
| Fat (g) | % Calories from Fat |
| 14.3 | 18.7% |

## A CASUAL DINNER FOR FRIENDS

*Potato Soup, 50*

*Chicken Breasts Florentine, 154*
*Wild Rice and Peppers, 112*
*Broiled Tomato Half\**
*Whole Wheat Beer Bread, 24*

*Mocha Fudge Mousse Pie, 221*

*\*Not included in nutrient analysis.*

| Calories | Cholesterol (mg) |
|----------|------------------|
| 948 | 80 |
| Fat (g) | % Calories from Fat |
| 24.9 | 23.2% |

## FAMILY PLEASER

*Roasted Turkey Breast, 136*
*One Step Macaroni*
*and Cheese, 106*
*Green Bean Casserole, 104*

*Carrot Cake, 187*

| Calories | Cholesterol (mg) |
|----------|------------------|
| 686 | 118 |
| Fat (g) | % Calories from Fat |
| 17.7 | 23.2% |

## SPRINGTIME LUNCHEON

*Salmon Bisque, 48*

*Marinated Italian Tuna*
*Salad, 62*
*Sweet Potato Rolls, 25*

*Pretzel Strawberry Gelatin, 70*

| Calories | Cholesterol (mg) |
|----------|------------------|
| 559 | 42 |
| Fat (g) | % Calories from Fat |
| 15.5 | 25.0% |

M. HANSBROUGH

APPETIZERS &
DIPS

## ©Ⓕ ARTICHOKE SQUARES

1 (14-ounce) can artichokes,
  drained
½ cup chopped onion
1 clove garlic, minced
¼ cup water
1 egg
2 egg whites
¼ cup breadcrumbs

Pepper to taste
½ teaspoon dried oregano
Dash red pepper
½ cup grated zucchini
¾ cup shredded reduced fat
  Monterey Jack cheese
¼ cup shredded reduced fat
  Cheddar cheese

Chop artichoke hearts in food processor or finely by hand; set aside. Sauté the onions and garlic in water until tender; set aside. In small bowl, beat egg and egg whites until frothy. Stir in remaining ingredients, mixing until well combined. Transfer mixture into a 9x9x2-inch baking pan coated with no stick cooking spray. Bake at 350 degrees for 30 minutes. Cut into squares and serve. Yield: 25 squares.
*These are great warm, room temperature, or even reheated.*

**Nutritional Information Per Square:**

| Calories | Cholesterol (mg) | Fat (g) | % Calories from Fat |
|---|---|---|---|
| 26 | 9 | 0.6 | 21.4% |

## Ⓕ MARINATED SHRIMP

¼ cup olive oil
2 large cloves garlic, minced
1 tablespoon dry mustard
1 teaspoon salt
½ cup lemon juice
1 tablespoon red wine
  vinegar
1 bay leaf, crumbled
Dash cayenne

2 tablespoons chopped fresh
  parsley
1 small red onion, thinly
  sliced
2 tablespoons capers,
  drained
2 pounds cooked shrimp,
  peeled

In bowl, combine oil, garlic, dry mustard, salt, lemon juice, vinegar, bay leaf, and cayenne; mix well. Stir in remaining ingredients except shrimp. Add shrimp, tossing until well coated. Refrigerate for 2 hours. Drain marinade and serve shrimp with onions and capers. Yield: 10 servings.
*Always a hit and looks pretty in glass bowl.*

**Nutritional Information Per Serving:**

| Calories | Cholesterol (mg) | Fat (g) | % Calories from Fat |
|---|---|---|---|
| 99 | 143 | 2.0 | 18.5% |

# ⓒ ARTICHOKE AND RED PEPPER PIZZA

1 (10-ounce) can refrigerated
  pizza crust
5 cloves garlic
3 tablespoons olive oil,
  divided
2 red bell peppers, cut into
  ¼-inch strips
1 (2.5-ounce) jar sliced
  mushrooms, drained

1 teaspoon dried basil
1 (14-ounce) can artichoke
  hearts, drained and
  chopped
1½ cups shredded part skim
  mozzarella cheese
  (6 ounces)

Coat a 12-inch pizza pan with no stick cooking spray. Unroll dough and place in prepared pan, starting at center, press out with hands. Bake at 425 degrees for 5 to 8 minutes or until light golden brown. In food processor, mince garlic. Add 2 tablespoons olive oil, blending well. Spread garlic mixture over partially baked crust. In medium skillet, heat remaining 1 tablespoon olive oil and cook and stir red peppers until crisp tender, about 5 minutes. Layer peppers, mushrooms, basil, and artichokes over garlic mixture; top with cheese. Bake at 425 degrees for 10 minutes or until crust is golden brown and cheese is melted. Cut into small pieces. Yield: 12 slices.
*You might want to serve this as a meal so you can eat more.*

**Nutritional Information Per Slice:**

| Calories | Cholesterol (mg) | Fat (g) | % Calories from Fat |
|---|---|---|---|
| 121 | 8 | 6 | 44.6% |

# ⓒ CRABMEAT MOLD

½ cup light mayonnaise
1 bunch green onions,
  chopped
¼ cup finely chopped onions
1 tablespoon lemon juice

1 tablespoon Worcestershire
  sauce
Salt and pepper to taste
2 pounds lump crabmeat
1 pound white crabmeat

Combine all ingredients except crabmeat in a bowl. Pick through crabmeat and add to mixture. Carefully fold in the crabmeat. Transfer to a 6-cup fish mold coated with no stick cooking spray. Refrigerate until served. Yield: 25 people at cocktail party.
*What can be better than eating plain crabmeat! For variation: substitute 1 pound small peeled, cooked shrimp for 1 pound white crabmeat.*

**Nutritional Information Per Serving:**

| Calories | Cholesterol (mg) | Fat (g) | % Calories from Fat |
|---|---|---|---|
| 68 | 56 | 2.6 | 34.4% |

# ⓒ MARINATED CRAB FINGERS

⅓ cup safflower oil
¼ cup vinegar
1 tablespoon lemon juice
2 large cloves garlic, pressed
2 green onions, sliced
2 tablespoons Worcestershire
    sauce

¼ cup chopped parsley
1 tablespoon white wine
½ teaspoon pepper
½ teaspoon sugar
1 pound fresh crab fingers

Combine all ingredients except crab fingers in a bowl, mixing well. Pour dressing over crab fingers in a shallow 2-quart dish. Cover with plastic wrap and refrigerate overnight. Turn crab fingers several times to keep completely covered. Serve with some of the dressing poured over them. Yield: 6 to 8 servings.
*Make ahead and serve with ease the next day.*

## Nutritional Information Per Serving:

| Calories | Cholesterol (mg) | Fat (g) | % Calories from Fat |
|---|---|---|---|
| | *(with marinade dressing)* | | |
| 78 | 9 | 7.0 | 80.6% |
| | *(without marinade dressing)* | | |
| 15 | 9 | 0.9 | 50.4% |

# ⓒ ⓕ CRAB ROLL UPS

¼ cup fat-free mayonnaise
Salt and pepper to taste
3 green onions, chopped
½ cup shredded low fat Swiss
    cheese

½ (4-ounce) can chopped
    green chilies, drained
1 cup white crabmeat
6 medium flour tortillas

Combine mayonnaise, salt and pepper, green onions, Swiss cheese, and chilies together in bowl. Fold in crabmeat. Soften tortillas in microwave for 30 seconds covered with wet paper towel. Place filling on one end of tortilla and roll up jelly roll style. Place rolled tortillas, seam side down, in microwave dish and cook for 1 minute. Cut each tortilla into 5 pieces. Serve warm. Yield: 30 roll ups.
*Delicious and quick if you are in a pinch.*

## Nutritional Information Per Roll Up:

| Calories | Cholesterol (mg) | Fat (g) | % Calories from Fat |
|---|---|---|---|
| 41 | 5 | 1.0 | 21.3% |

# ©Ⓕ SALMON MOUSSE WITH DILL SAUCE

2 envelopes unflavored
   gelatin
¼ cup cold water
½ cup boiling water
½ cup non fat plain yogurt
1 tablespoon lemon juice
1 tablespoon grated onion
½ teaspoon hot pepper sauce
½ teaspoon paprika

Salt and pepper to taste
1 (14.75-ounce) can red
   salmon, drained, skin
   discarded, and bones
   picked
2 tablespoons chopped
   capers
½ cup evaporated skimmed
   milk, chilled

Soften gelatin in cold water in small bowl. Add boiling water and stir until gelatin is dissolved; cool. Add yogurt, lemon juice, onion, hot pepper sauce, paprika, and salt and pepper to taste; mix well. Refrigerate until consistency of unbeaten egg whites. Add salmon and capers mixing well. In chilled mixing bowl, beat cold evaporated milk at high speed until stiff peaks form. Fold into salmon mixture. Pour into a 6-cup mold coated with no stick cooking spray. Refrigerate until congealed. Unmold and serve with Dill Sauce (see recipe below). Yield: 10 servings.

## Dill Sauce

1 cup non fat plain yogurt
¼ teaspoon sugar
2 tablespoons lemon juice
1 tablespoon grated onion

Salt and pepper to taste
1 tablespoon dried dill weed
½ cup grated, peeled, and
   seeded cucumber

Mix all ingredients together. Stir and refrigerate.

## Nutritional Information Per Serving:

| Calories | Cholesterol (mg) | Fat (g) | % Calories from Fat |
|---|---|---|---|
| 94 | 17 | 2.8 | 27.0% |

# ⓒⓕ COLD POACHED SALMON WITH DILL SAUCE

2 cups water
1 cup dry white wine
1 carrot, diced
1 stalk celery, chopped
1 onion, sliced

½ tablespoon black
   peppercorns
1 (2-pound) fresh salmon
   fillet

In large poacher or pan, combine all ingredients except salmon. Bring to a boil. Lower heat, cover, and cook for 15 minutes. Add salmon fillet. Cover and cook over low heat until salmon is done, approximately 15 to 20 minutes. Cool in stock. When cool, remove from stock and remove skin from salmon; chill for several hours or overnight. Serve with Dill Sauce (see recipe below). Yield: 10 servings.

**Dill Sauce**
1 cup non fat plain yogurt
1½ tablespoons white
   vinegar
1½ tablespoons Dijon
   mustard

3 tablespoons light brown
   sugar
2 teaspoons dried dill weed

Mix all ingredients together in small bowl. Refrigerate before serving; best if refrigerated overnight.
*This dip is great with fresh vegetables also.*

**Nutritional Information Per Serving:**

| Calories | Cholesterol (mg) | Fat (g) | % Calories from Fat |
|---|---|---|---|
| 139 | 32 | 3.6 | 22.9% |

# ⓒⓕ TORTILLA CHIPS

12 whole wheat flour
   tortillas

Water

Brush each tortilla with water. Cut tortillas into eight wedges and place on baking sheet coated with no stick cooking spray. Bake at 425 degrees for 3 minutes, turn, and continue baking 3 minutes longer or until crisp. Repeat until all tortillas have been cooked. Yield: 12 servings.
*Make as many of these as desired and store in bags.*

**Nutritional Information Per Serving:**

| Calories | Cholesterol (mg) | Fat (g) | % Calories from Fat |
|---|---|---|---|
| 73 | 0 | 0.5 | 5.6% |

## Ⓕ CRAWFISH PROVENÇALE

2 tablespoons light
   margarine
1 large onion, chopped
2 cloves garlic, minced
½ pound mushrooms, sliced
1 pound crawfish tails,
   rinsed and drained
½ cup white wine

1 cup chopped tomatoes
1 cup chopped green onions
1 teaspoon dried basil
2 tablespoons chopped
   parsley
Salt and pepper as desired
4 to 6 artichoke bottoms

In large pan, melt margarine and sauté onion, garlic, and mushrooms until vegetables are tender and liquid is thick. Add crawfish tails and white wine, cooking about 10 minutes over a low heat. Add tomatoes, green onions, basil, and parsley. Heat through. Season with salt and pepper. Spoon crawfish mixture over artichoke bottoms. Yield: 4 to 6 servings.
*This dish can be served over pasta also.*

### Nutritional Information Per Serving:

| Calories | Cholesterol (mg) | Fat (g) | % Calories from Fat |
|---|---|---|---|
| 158 | 135 | 3.3 | 19.0% |

## Ⓒ Ⓕ SALSA

3 green onions, chopped
2 cloves garlic, minced
1 (28-ounce) can whole
   tomatoes, drained and
   chopped

2 tablespoons finely chopped
   jalapeños
¼ cup chopped fresh cilantro
1 teaspoon dried oregano
¼ teaspoon cumin

Combine all ingredients. Serve with homemade tortilla chips or as a topping for chicken or fish. Yield: 2 cups.
*This is a wonderful salsa recipe and fresh tomatoes can be substituted when available (5 tomatoes). (Serve with Tortilla Chips, page 16 or with Keebler Munch 'em crackers.)*

### Nutritional Information Per Tablespoon:

| Calories | Cholesterol (mg) | Fat (g) | % Calories from Fat |
|---|---|---|---|
| 6 | 0 | 0.1 | 10.5% |

# Ⓒ MUSHROOMS STUFFED WITH CRAWFISH

36 fresh medium mushrooms
1 onion, chopped
½ bunch green onions,
   chopped
¼ cup chopped green bell
   pepper
¼ cup light margarine
1 cup breadcrumbs,
   approximately

½ teaspoon white pepper
¼ teaspoon red pepper
½ teaspoon garlic powder
Salt and pepper to taste
1 pound crawfish tails,
   rinsed and drained
2 tablespoons olive oil
1 tablespoon sherry

Wash mushrooms and remove stems. Chop stems; set aside. Sauté onions, green onions, and green pepper in margarine in skillet until tender. Add breadcrumbs, chopped mushroom stems, seasonings, and crawfish tails. Mix together and cook over low heat for 15 minutes, stirring occasionally. Add olive oil and sherry. Place mushrooms in metal colander over pot of boiling water. Cover with lid. Cook mushrooms for about 5 minutes. Remove and submerge in ice water. Drain and stuff. Yield: 36 mushrooms.
*These are worth the effort!*

**Nutritional Information Per Serving:**

| Calories | Cholesterol (mg) | Fat (g) | % Calories from Fat |
|----------|------------------|---------|---------------------|
| 44 | 22 | 1.7 | 35.2% |

#  HEARTY STUFFED ARTICHOKES

1 onion, chopped
3 cloves garlic, minced
½ pound ground turkey
½ pound extra lean ground
  beef
1½ cups Italian breadcrumbs

⅓ cup grated Romano cheese
2 teaspoons dried basil
1 tablespoon lemon juice
⅓ cup olive oil
3 whole artichokes
3 tablespoons olive oil

In large pan, sauté onion, garlic, turkey, and beef until onion is tender and meat is done. Remove from heat. Drain any excess fat. Add remaining ingredients except 3 tablespoons olive oil. Mix well. Trim the stems off the artichokes with a sharp knife. Snip off the pointed tops of the leaves with scissors. Holding the artichokes firmly with one hand, turn them leaves-down and pound on a flat surface to force open leaves. Turn leaves-up again and rinse quickly under cold running water. Shake to remove excess moisture. With fingers open the leaves more to make room for the stuffing. Stuff the reserved mixture into the spaces inside the open leaves. Sprinkle each artichoke with 1 tablespoon olive oil. Place artichokes in pot with 1-inch lightly salted water. Bring to a boil, lower heat, cover, and cook about 1 hour or until leaves pull off easily and are tender on the inside. Watch to make sure there is always water in pot, and, if necessary; add more water. Yield: 3 artichokes.

**Nutritional Information Per ⅓ artichoke:**

| Calories | Cholesterol (mg) | Fat (g) | % Calories from Fat |
|----------|------------------|---------|---------------------|
| 287 | 33 | 16.2 | 50.8% |

#  GUACAMOLE

1 large avocado, peeled,
  pitted, and mashed
Salt and pepper to taste
1 clove garlic, minced

¼ teaspoon chili powder
1 teaspoon lemon juice
2 teaspoons minced onion
¼ cup non fat plain yogurt

Put mashed avocado in small bowl and season with salt and pepper, garlic, chili powder, and lemon juice. Stir in onion. Cover with yogurt to keep mixture from darkening. Just before serving, stir well. Refrigerate. Yield: 1½ cups.
*If you have the urge for guacamole, this recipe is the one.*

**Nutritional Information Per Tablespoon:**

| Calories | Cholesterol (mg) | Fat (g) | % Calories from Fat |
|----------|------------------|---------|---------------------|
| 15 | <1 | 1.3 | 76.1% |

# SHRIMP SPREAD

1 pound cooked peeled
  shrimp
1 (8-ounce) package light
  cream cheese, softened
¼ cup fat free mayonnaise
1 bunch green onions, thinly
  sliced

1 tablespoon chopped
  parsley
1 tablespoon lemon juice
1 teaspoon Worcestershire
  sauce
¼ teaspoon hot sauce
Salt and pepper to taste

Chop shrimp coarsely; set aside. In bowl, combine remaining ingredients, mixing well. Add shrimp. Yield: 16 servings.
*Serve with crackers. For a special appetizer, fill cherry tomatoes with shrimp mixture.*

**Nutritional Information Per Serving:**

| Calories | Cholesterol (mg) | Fat (g) | % Calories from Fat |
|---|---|---|---|
| 82 | 76 | 3.2 | 35.2% |

# ⓒ GARBANZO SPREAD

1 (15-ounce) can garbanzo
  beans, drained
2 tablespoons olive oil
½ cup finely chopped onion
½ cup finely chopped green
  onions
⅓ cup finely chopped parsley

3 cloves garlic, minced
2 tablespoons sesame seeds,
  toasted
2 tablespoons fresh lemon
  juice
½ teaspoon dried oregano
Salt and pepper to taste

Place garbanzo beans in food processor to mash. In skillet, heat olive oil and cook onions, green onions, parsley, and garlic until tender. Blend into mashed garbanzo beans. Add toasted sesame seeds, lemon juice, oregano, and salt and pepper. Refrigerate. Yield: 2 cups.
*This dip has a Greek flair. Serve with pita triangles or carrot sticks.*

**Nutritional Information Per Tablespoon:**

| Calories | Cholesterol (mg) | Fat (g) | % Calories from Fat |
|---|---|---|---|
| 28 | 0 | 1.4 | 44.1% |

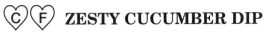

##  ZESTY CUCUMBER DIP

1 cup non fat plain yogurt
1 (.7-ounce) package Italian
   dressing mix
½ cucumber, seeded, peeled,
   and chopped

1 tomato, seeded and
   chopped
3 green onions, chopped
1 tablespoon lemon juice

Combine yogurt and dressing mix until well combined. Stir in remaining ingredients. Refrigerate until ready to serve. Serve with chips. Yield: 2 cups.

**Nutritional Information Per Tablespoon Serving:**

| Calories | Cholesterol (mg) | Fat (g) | % Calories from Fat |
|---|---|---|---|
| 7 | <1 | <0.1 | 3.8% |

##  RED PEPPER DIP

1 red bell pepper, roasted
   (see recipe for
   instruction on roasting)
1 tablespoon olive oil
1 (12-ounce) container 1%
   cottage cheese

2 cloves garlic, minced
1 tablespoon lemon juice
⅛ teaspoon white pepper
Dash hot pepper sauce

To roast: Slice red pepper in half; core and seed. Brush with olive oil. Broil until soft, about 20 minutes, turning once. Place peppers in paper bag and let steam for 10 minutes to loosen skin. Remove skin (skin should be removed easily with paring knife). Cut into pieces. Place in food processor along with other ingredients; blending until very smooth. Yield: 8 to 10 servings.
*Serve in hollowed out green or red pepper with fresh vegetables. If you ever want to roast peppers, use method above.*

**Nutritional Information Per Serving:**

| Calories | Cholesterol (mg) | Fat (g) | % Calories from Fat |
|---|---|---|---|
| 39 | 2 | 1.7 | 38.7% |

# ⓒ SPINACH DIP

1 (10-ounce) package frozen
   chopped spinach
⅔ cup light mayonnaise
1 cup non fat plain yogurt
1 teaspoon seasoned salt

½ teaspoon dried dill weed
Juice of half lemon
½ cup chopped parsley
½ cup chopped green onion

Thaw, squeeze, and drain chopped spinach. Blend spinach with remaining ingredients in bowl. Refrigerate. Recipe is best when made a day ahead. Serve with fresh vegetables or with your favorite Keebler reduced fat cracker such as Townhouse Crackers. Yield: 3 cups.
*There are short cuts to this recipe with a mix, but this one is by far the best. If desire lower fat content, substitute fat free mayonnaise.*

**Nutritional Information Per Tablespoon:**

| Calories | Cholesterol (mg) | Fat (g) | % Calories from Fat |
|---|---|---|---|
| 13 | 1 | 0.9 | 65% |

# ⓒⒻ CRAWFISH DIP

¼ cup light margarine
¼ cup flour
2 cloves garlic, minced
1 bunch green onions,
   chopped
1 small onion, chopped
1 (10¾-ounce) can 99% fat
   free cream of mushroom
   soup

1 (10-ounce) can chopped
   tomatoes and green
   chilies
1 teaspoon Worcestershire
   sauce
Salt and pepper to taste
1 pound crawfish tails, rinsed
   and drained

In skillet, melt margarine, add flour, and mix well. Sauté all vegetables until tender, stirring constantly, to prevent sticking. Add mushroom soup and chopped tomatoes and green chilies; mix well. Add seasonings. Gently stir in crawfish tails. Cook until dip is thoroughly heated. Serve warm with melba rounds. Yield: approximately 4 cups.

**Nutritional Information Per Tablespoon:**

| Calories | Cholesterol (mg) | Fat (g) | % Calories from Fat |
|---|---|---|---|
| 15 | 5 | 0.5 | 29.6% |

M. HANSBROUGH

# BREADS & BRUNCH

## ⓒⒻ BEER BREAD

3 cups self-rising flour  
⅓ cup sugar  
1 (12-ounce) can light beer  
   (room temperature)

2 tablespoons light  
   margarine, melted

Combine all ingredients mixing until just moistened. Pour batter into a 9x5x3-inch loaf pan coated with no stick cooking spray and dusted with flour. Bake at 350 degrees for 50 minutes. Serve warm. Yield: 16 slices. *This quick bread is too good for words, and you can eat it without guilt!*

**Nutritional Information Per Serving:**

| Calories | Cholesterol (mg) | Fat (g) | % Calories from Fat |
|---|---|---|---|
| 111 | 0 | 0.9 | 7.6% |

## ⓒⒻ WHOLE WHEAT BEER BREAD

2 cups self-rising flour  
1 cup whole wheat flour  
1 teaspoon baking powder  
4 tablespoons honey

1 (12-ounce) can light beer,  
   room temperature (never  
   opened)

Combine dry ingredients. Stir in honey and beer. Pour batter into a 9x5x3-inch loaf pan coated with no stick cooking spray and dusted with flour. Bake at 350 degrees for 40 to 45 minutes. Yield: 16 servings. *This wonderful recipe can be included at last minute with ease.*

**Nutritional Information Per Serving:**

| Calories | Cholesterol (mg) | Fat (g) | % Calories from Fat |
|---|---|---|---|
| 102 | 0 | 0.3 | 2.7% |

# ⓒⒻ SWEET POTATO ROLLS

| | |
|---|---|
| 1 cup cooked mashed sweet potatoes (about 1 large) | 1¼ cups warm water |
| 3 tablespoons light margarine, melted | 1 egg |
| | 1 teaspoon salt |
| 1 package rapid rise yeast | 3 tablespoons sugar |
| | 5 cups flour |

Blend potatoes with melted margarine. Dissolve yeast in ½ cup warm water. Combine potatoes with egg, salt, sugar, and yeast mixture. Add flour alternately with remaining ¾ cup warm water, mixing until well combined. Turn onto a well floured board and knead. Place in bowl coated with no stick cooking spray; cover. Allow to rise for 1 hour in warm place. Remove to board and roll to one-inch thickness and cut into round circles with cutter or glass. Place on baking sheet coated with no stick cooking spray and let rise in warm place for 30 minutes or until doubled in size. Bake at 425 degrees for 15 to 20 minutes. Yield: 24 rolls. *These rolls are hard to resist as they come out of the oven, and no one will ever guess the secret ingredient.*

**Nutritional Information Per Roll:**

| Calories | Cholesterol (mg) | Fat (g) | % Calories from Fat |
|---|---|---|---|
| 129 | 9 | 1.2 | 8.4% |

# ⓒⒻ CORN BREAD

| | |
|---|---|
| 2 cups white cornmeal | 1 teaspoon baking soda |
| 1 cup flour | 2 cups low fat buttermilk |
| ½ cup sugar | 3 tablespoons canola oil |

Combine dry ingredients. Mix buttermilk and oil; stir into dry mixture. Mix well. Pour batter into a 9x5x3-inch loaf pan coated with no stick cooking spray and dusted with flour. Bake at 350 degrees for 55 minutes. Serve hot. Yield: 16 servings.
*This corn bread melts in your mouth.*

**Nutritional Information Per Serving:**

| Calories | Cholesterol (mg) | Fat (g) | % Calories from Fat |
|---|---|---|---|
| 153 | 1 | 3.1 | 18.4% |

# ♡Ⓒ SPINACH BREAD

2 (10-ounce) packages frozen
  chopped spinach
⅓ cup light margarine,
  melted
4 cloves garlic, minced
¼ teaspoon hot sauce

1 teaspoon Worcestershire
  sauce
1 loaf French bread
1 (8-ounce) package part
  skim mozzarella cheese,
  shredded

Cook spinach according to directions of packages. Drain very well.
Combine margarine with garlic, hot sauce, and Worcestershire sauce.
Mix with spinach, stirring well. Slice French bread in half lengthwise.
Spread spinach mixture on top of each half of French bread. Sprinkle
with shredded mozzarella cheese. Place under broiler until cheese is
melted and slightly browned. Yield: 14 slices.
*To freeze, wrap each half in plastic wrap and then foil.*

**Nutritional Information Per Slice:**

| Calories | Cholesterol (mg) | Fat (g) | % Calories from Fat |
|---|---|---|---|
| 168 | 9 | 5.7 | 30.7% |

# Ⓒ Ⓕ HERBED FRENCH BREAD

2 tablespoons light
  margarine, melted
1 teaspoon finely chopped
  parsley
½ teaspoon Worcestershire
  sauce

¼ teaspoon dried basil
⅛ teaspoon garlic powder
1 small loaf French bread,
  split in half

Combine all ingredients in bowl except bread; stir well. Lightly brush
each half with margarine mixture. Broil in oven until lightly browned
or put back together, wrap in foil and bake at 350 degrees for 10
minutes. Yield: 6 to 8 servings.
*You will want to double this recipe over and over again.*

**Nutritional Information Per Serving:**

| Calories | Cholesterol (mg) | Fat (g) | % Calories from Fat |
|---|---|---|---|
| 162 | 0 | 2.4 | 13.4% |

## ⓒ HERBED BISCUITS

3 tablespoons light
    margarine
1 (10-ounce) package
    refrigerated biscuits
2 cloves garlic, minced
1 tablespoon chopped
    parsley

1 teaspoon dried basil
½ teaspoon dried oregano
2 tablespoons grated
    Parmesan cheese
1 tablespoon sesame seeds

Melt margarine in 9-inch round cake pan in oven. Separate biscuits and cut each into four pieces. Stir all remaining ingredients into margarine in pan. Arrange pieces of biscuits next to each other in margarine. Bake at 400 degrees for 15 minutes or until tops are brown. Immediately invert biscuits onto platter and serve. Yield: 4 to 6 servings.
*Can prepare ahead and refrigerate covered. Bring to room temperature before baking. Fantastic!*

**Nutritional Information Per Serving:**

| Calories | Cholesterol (mg) | Fat (g) | % Calories from Fat |
|---|---|---|---|
| 174 | 1 | 7.2 | 36.9% |

## ⓒⓕ APPLE BREAD

1 egg
4 egg whites
1½ cups light brown sugar
½ cup low-fat buttermilk
½ cup canola oil
1 tablespoon vanilla
1 cup old fashioned oatmeal
1 cup whole wheat flour

1½ cups flour
½ cup non fat dry milk
1 teaspoon baking powder
½ teaspoon baking soda
1 teaspoon cinnamon
2 tart cooking apples, cored,
    peeled, and chopped
⅔ cup raisins

In large bowl, beat egg, egg whites, sugar, buttermilk, oil, and vanilla until smooth. In another bowl, combine oatmeal, whole wheat flour, flour, dry milk, baking powder, baking soda, and cinnamon. Stir in chopped apples and raisins. Add egg mixture to flour, stirring only until combined. Pour into two 9x5x3-inch loaf pans coated with no stick cooking spray and dusted with flour. Bake at 350 degrees for 45 minutes or until a cake tester inserted into center comes out clean. Yield: 2 loaves with 16 slices each.
*Breads freeze well and this is a good one.*

**Nutritional Information Per Serving:**

| Calories | Cholesterol (mg) | Fat (g) | % Calories from Fat |
|---|---|---|---|
| 148 | 7 | 4.2 | 25.7% |

# BANANA RAISIN BREAD

1½ cups flour
1 teaspoon baking soda
1 cup sugar
½ teaspoon salt
3 to 4 bananas, mashed
   (about 1½ cups)

2 eggs
1 teaspoon vanilla
½ cup safflower oil
¾ cup non fat plain yogurt
⅔ cup raisins

In bowl, combine all dry ingredients. In another bowl, whisk together bananas, eggs, vanilla, and oil. Fold yogurt into banana mixture. Add raisins. Pour banana raisin mixture over dry ingredients and pour batter into a 9x5x3-inch loaf pan coated with no stick cooking spray and dusted with flour. Bake at 350 degrees for 50 to 60 minutes. Cool in pan. Yield: 16 slices.

*This is so good you will keep wanting more.*

**Nutritional Information Per Serving:**

| Calories | Cholesterol (mg) | Fat (g) | % Calories from Fat |
|---|---|---|---|
| 202 | 27 | 7.7 | 34.2% |

# BANANA BREAD

½ cup light margarine
⅓ cup sugar
½ cup light brown sugar
3 medium bananas, mashed
1 teaspoon vanilla
1 teaspoon lemon juice
2 cups flour

1 tablespoon baking powder
1 teaspoon baking soda
1 teaspoon cinnamon
½ cup chopped pecans,
   toasted
4 egg whites, beaten until
   frothy

In mixing bowl, cream margarine and sugars. Stir in bananas, vanilla, and lemon juice. Combine flour with baking powder, baking soda, and cinnamon; add to banana mixture. Stir in pecans. Fold in egg whites and pour into a 9x5x3-inch pan coated with no stick cooking spray and dusted with flour. Bake at 350 degrees for 45 to 50 minutes or until done. Yield: 16 servings.

*Always a favorite.*

**Nutritional Information Per Serving:**

| Calories | Cholesterol (mg) | Fat (g) | % Calories from Fat |
|---|---|---|---|
| 176 | 0 | 5.4 | 27.4% |

## Ⓒ Ⓕ BLUEBERRY BREAD

2 cups flour
1 cup sugar
1 teaspoon baking powder
¼ teaspoon baking soda
¼ teaspoon salt
2 tablespoons light
    margarine, melted

¼ cup hot water
½ cup orange juice
1 tablespoon grated orange
    rind
1 egg, beaten
1 cup blueberries

Combine all dry ingredients in bowl. In another bowl, mix melted margarine, hot water, orange juice, orange rind, and egg. Fold dry ingredients into orange juice mixture. Fold in blueberries. Pour batter into a 9x5x3-inch loaf pan coated with no stick cooking spray and dusted with flour. Bake at 350 degrees for 50 to 60 minutes. Remove bread from pan and spread with Glaze (see recipe below). Yield: 16 slices.

**Glaze**
2 tablespoons orange juice          2 tablespoons honey
½ teaspoon grated orange
    rind

Bring all ingredients to a boil in a saucepan and boil for 1 minute or bring to boil in microwave. Spread over bread.
*Those fresh blueberries in the summer will make you repeat this recipe often.*

**Nutritional Information Per Serving:**

| Calories | Cholesterol (mg) | Fat (g) | % Calories from Fat |
|----------|------------------|---------|---------------------|
| 139 | 13 | 1.2 | 7.9% |

## ©Ⓕ LEMON BERRY BREAD

⅓ cup canola oil
⅔ cup sugar
2 tablespoons lemon extract
4 egg whites
1½ cups flour
1 teaspoon baking powder

½ cup nonfat milk (2½
  tablespoons nonfat dry
  milk and ½ cup water)
1 cup fresh blueberries
2 tablespoons grated lemon
  rind

In a large bowl, mix oil, sugar, lemon extract, and egg whites. In another bowl, combine flour with baking powder. Add flour mixture to sugar mixture alternately with milk, stirring just until blended. Fold in blueberries and lemon rind. Pour batter into a 9x5x3-inch loaf pan coated with no stick cooking spray and dusted with flour. Bake at 350 degrees for 40 to 50 minutes or until a wooden toothpick inserted in center comes out clean. Immediately poke holes at 1-inch intervals on the top of the bread and pour Lemon Glaze (see recipe below) over. Yield: 16 servings.

**Lemon Glaze**
½ cup sugar                    ½ cup lemon juice

In a small saucepan, combine sugar and lemon juice, heating until sugar is dissolved.
*This bread is a real treat whenever you have it. Hint: When blueberries are not in season, leave them out for a delicious lemon bread.*

**Nutritional Information Per Serving:**

| Calories | Cholesterol (mg) | Fat (g) | % Calories from Fat |
|----------|------------------|---------|---------------------|
| 164      | <1               | 4.8     | 26.3%               |

## ©Ⓕ ORANGE WALNUT BREAD

1 cup whole wheat flour
2 cups flour
½ cup sugar
½ cup light brown sugar
3½ teaspoons baking powder
1½ cups skim milk

3 tablespoons canola oil
2 egg whites
2 tablespoons grated orange
  rind
1 tablespoon orange extract
½ cup chopped walnuts

Combine all ingredients and beat only until well combined. Pour batter into a 9x5x3-inch loaf pan coated with no stick cooking spray and dusted with flour. Bake at 350 degrees for 1 hour or until inserted toothpick comes out clean. Yield: 16 servings.

**Nutritional Information Per Serving:**

| Calories | Cholesterol (mg) | Fat (g) | % Calories from Fat |
|----------|------------------|---------|---------------------|
| 199      | <1               | 5.3     | 23.9%               |

# ⓒⒻ CRANBERRY ORANGE BREAD

2 cups flour
1½ teaspoons baking powder
½ teaspoon baking soda
¼ teaspoon salt
1 cup sugar
2 tablespoons shortening
¾ cup orange juice

1 egg, beaten
1 tablespoon grated orange rind
½ teaspoon almond extract
1½ cups cranberries, coarsely chopped

Combine flour, baking powder, baking soda, salt, and sugar in bowl. Combine shortening, orange juice, egg, orange rind, and almond extract in small bowl. Add orange juice mixture to dry ingredients, stirring just until dry ingredients are moistened. Fold in cranberries. Pour batter into a 9x5x3-inch loaf pan coated with no stick cooking spray and dusted with flour. Bake at 350 degrees for 45 to 50 minutes or until done. Yield: 16 slices.

*A great holiday bread! For pecan lovers, add ½ to 1 cup chopped pecans.*

**Nutritional Information Per Serving:**

| Calories | Cholesterol (mg) | Fat (g) | % Calories from Fat |
|---|---|---|---|
| 140 | 13 | 2.1 | 13.6% |

# ⓒ ZUCCHINI BREAD

¾ cup whole wheat flour
¾ cup flour
½ teaspoon baking soda
½ teaspoon baking powder
1 teaspoon cinnamon
2 egg whites
⅓ cup sugar
⅓ cup light brown sugar

⅓ cup canola oil
1 teaspoon vanilla
1 cup shredded zucchini, unpeeled
½ cup crushed pineapple, in its own juice
⅓ cup raisins
⅓ cup pecans, toasted

In a large bowl, mix whole wheat flour, flour, baking soda, baking powder, and cinnamon. Add egg whites, sugars, oil, and vanilla. Mix thoroughly. Fold in zucchini, pineapple, raisins, and pecans. Pour batter into a 9x5x3-inch loaf pan coated with no stick cooking spray and dusted with flour. Bake at 350 degrees for 40 to 45 minutes. Yield: 16 servings.

**Nutritional Information Per Serving:**

| Calories | Cholesterol (mg) | Fat (g) | % Calories from Fat |
|---|---|---|---|
| 148 | 0 | 6.3 | 38.2% |

# Ⓒ CINNAMON CRESCENTS

¼ cup light brown sugar
¼ cup chopped pecans
1 teaspoon cinnamon
2 cups biscuit baking mix

1 tablespoon sugar
½ cup cold water
3 tablespoons tub margarine

Combine brown sugar, pecans, and cinnamon in small bowl; set aside. In another bowl, mix baking mix, sugar, and water until soft dough forms; beat vigorously 30 seconds. Roll mixture into a ball with hands dusted with baking mix so dough will not stick. Knead 1 minute. Pat or roll dough into a circle. Cover with margarine and brown sugar mixture. Cut into 8 wedges. Roll up, beginning at wide edges to point. Place crescents on ungreased baking sheet; shape into semi-circle. Bake at 425 degrees for 10 minutes or until golden brown. Cool slightly; drizzle with Glaze (see recipe below). Yield: 8 crescents.
*You will impress everyone at breakfast with these crescents.*

**Glaze**
½ cup powdered sugar
1 tablespoon tub margarine

¼ teaspoon vanilla
1 tablespoon water

Mix all ingredients together, adding more water until smooth.

**Nutritional Information Per Serving:**

| Calories | Cholesterol (mg) | Fat (g) | % Calories from Fat |
|---|---|---|---|
| 236 | 0 | 8.9 | 33.8% |

# Ⓒ Ⓕ PINEAPPLE BRAN MUFFINS

1 egg
2 tablespoons light
 margarine, melted
2 tablespoons honey
¾ cup low fat buttermilk
¼ cup whole wheat flour
⅓ cup flour

¼ cup sugar
1½ cups all-bran cereal
¼ teaspoon salt
¼ teaspoon baking soda
¼ teaspoon cinnamon
¼ cup crushed pineapple,
 drained

In mixing bowl, mix egg, margarine, honey, and buttermilk until blended. Add flours, sugar, bran, salt, baking soda, and cinnamon. Mix only until blended. Stir in pineapple. Spoon batter into muffin papers in muffin pans, filling only three-fourths full. Bake at 400 degrees for 15 to 20 minutes or until center bounces back. Yield: 12 muffins.

**Nutritional Information Per Serving:**

| Calories | Cholesterol (mg) | Fat (g) | % Calories from Fat |
|---|---|---|---|
| 99 | 18 | 1.8 | 16.1% |

© Ⓕ **CHUNKY WHOLE WHEAT
APPLE MUFFINS**

1½ cups flour, divided
½ cup peeled, chopped
   baking apples
½ cup whole wheat flour
⅓ cup light brown sugar
1½ teaspoons baking powder
½ teaspoon cinnamon

¼ teaspoon salt
½ cup skim milk
3 tablespoons canola oil
2 egg whites, lightly beaten
⅓ cup chopped pecans
⅓ cup golden raisins

Combine ½ cup flour and apple in small bowl, tossing to coat; set aside. Combine remaining 1 cup flour, whole wheat flour, and next 4 ingredients in bowl; make a well in center of mixture. Combine milk, oil, and egg whites in a bowl; stir well. Add milk mixture, apple mixture, pecans, and raisins to flour mixture, stirring just until dry ingredients are moistened. Spoon batter into muffin pans coated with no stick cooking spray, filling two-thirds full. Bake at 400 degrees for 20 minutes. Remove muffins; cool. Yield: 12 muffins.

**Nutritional Information Per Serving:**

| Calories | Cholesterol (mg) | Fat (g) | % Calories from Fat |
|---|---|---|---|
| 174 | <1 | 5.8 | 29.8% |

© **BRAN MUFFINS**

3 cups all bran natural fiber
   cereal
1½ cups boiling water
1 cup sugar
2 eggs
2 cups low fat buttermilk

½ cup canola oil
1½ cups flour
1 cup whole wheat flour
1 teaspoon cinnamon
2½ teaspoons baking soda

In a large bowl, measure all bran cereal. Pour boiling water over and let sit for 2 minutes. Add sugar, eggs, buttermilk, and oil, stirring until mixed. In another bowl, combine flour, whole wheat flour, cinnamon, and baking soda. Add to bran mixture, mixing only until well combined. Pour batter into paper lined muffin tin. Bake at 400 degrees for 20 minutes. Yield: 3 dozen muffins.
*This batter will keep in refrigerator up to six weeks. Keep in covered container. If desired, can add raisins and pecans.*

**Nutritional Information Per Serving:**

| Calories | Cholesterol (mg) | Fat (g) | % Calories from Fat |
|---|---|---|---|
| 107 | 12 | 3.7 | 30.8% |

## Ⓒ CRANBERRY PINEAPPLE MUFFINS

1 cup flour
½ cup whole wheat flour
½ cup quick cooking oatmeal
¼ cup sugar
2 teaspoons baking powder
¼ teaspoon salt
½ teaspoon cinnamon
¼ cup light margarine
1 egg, beaten

1 cup skim milk
1 cup fresh cranberries,
    coarsely chopped
½ cup unsweetened crushed
    pineapple, drained
½ cup chopped pecans
1 tablespoon sugar
¼ teaspoon cinnamon

Combine first 7 ingredients; mix well. Cut in margarine with a pastry blender or fork until mixture resembles coarse crumbs. Make a well in center of mixture. Combine beaten egg and milk; add to dry ingredients, stirring just until moistened. Gently fold in cranberries, pineapple, and pecans. Spoon batter into muffin pans that have been coated with no stick cooking spray, filling three-fourths full. Combine 1 tablespoon sugar and ¼ teaspoon cinnamon. Sprinkle evenly over muffin batter. Bake at 400 degrees for 20 to 25 minutes or until golden brown. Remove immediately from pans. Yield: 12 muffins.

**Nutritional Information Per Muffin:**

| Calories | Cholesterol (mg) | Fat (g) | % Calories from Fat |
|---|---|---|---|
| 163 | 18 | 5.8 | 32.2% |

## ⒸⒻ LEMON RASPBERRY MUFFINS

2 cups flour
⅔ cup sugar
3 teaspoons baking powder
1 cup skim milk
⅓ cup canola oil
1 teaspoon lemon extract

1 egg
2 egg whites
1½ cups fresh or frozen
    raspberries (if frozen, no
    syrup)

In large bowl, combine flour, sugar, and baking powder, mixing well. In small bowl, combine milk, oil, lemon extract, egg, and egg whites, blending well. Add to dry ingredients, stirring just until ingredients are moistened. Carefully fold in raspberries. Line muffin pan with papers and fill ¾ full with batter. Bake at 425 degrees for 18 to 23 minutes or until golden brown. Cool 5 minutes; remove from pan. Yield: 12 to 16 muffins.

*A great muffin for raspberry lovers.*

**Nutritional Information Per Muffin:**

| Calories | Cholesterol (mg) | Fat (g) | % Calories from Fat |
|---|---|---|---|
| 154 | 14 | 5.1 | 30.1% |

## ⓒⒻ RASPBERRY MUFFINS

1½ cups flour
¼ cup sugar
¼ cup light brown sugar
2 teaspoons baking powder
1 teaspoon cinnamon
2 egg whites

½ cup tub margarine
½ cup skim milk
1 cup fresh raspberries or
   frozen unsweetened
   raspberries
1 teaspoon grated lemon rind

In medium bowl, combine flour, sugars, baking powder, and cinnamon. In another bowl, mix egg whites, margarine and milk until blended. Stir in flour mixture just until moistened. Fold in raspberries and lemon rind. (If frozen raspberries are used, they must be thawed and well drained). Spoon batter into muffin cups coated with no stick cooking spray. Sprinkle top with Pecan Topping (see recipe below). Bake at 350 degrees for 20 to 25 minutes or until lightly browned. Yield: 12 muffins.

*You will want these muffins at any time of the day.*

**Pecan Topping**
⅓ cup light brown sugar
¼ cup chopped pecans
¼ cup flour

1 tablespoon tub margarine
½ teaspoon cinnamon

In small bowl, combine brown sugar, pecans, flour, margarine and cinnamon. Mix with fork until crumbly.

**Nutritional Information Per Muffin:**

| Calories | Cholesterol (mg) | Fat (g) | % Calories from Fat |
|---|---|---|---|
| 189 | <1 | 5.5 | 26.1% |

## ©Ⓕ TROPICAL MUFFINS

1 cup flour
1 cup whole wheat flour
⅓ cup light brown sugar
2 teaspoons baking powder
½ teaspoon baking soda
1 cup plain non fat yogurt

2 egg whites
¼ cup safflower oil
2 teaspoons coconut extract
1 cup crushed pineapple, in
    its own juices, well
    drained

In bowl, combine flours, sugar, baking powder, and baking soda. Combine yogurt, egg whites, oil, and coconut extract. Mix into flour mixture stirring just until blended. Fold in drained pineapple. Spoon batter into muffin cups coated with no stick cooking spray. Bake at 400 degrees for 20 to 25 minutes. Yield: 12 muffins.

*You will want these delicious muffins at other times besides breakfast!*

**Nutritional Information Per Muffin:**

| Calories | Cholesterol (mg) | Fat (g) | % Calories from Fat |
|---|---|---|---|
| 149 | <1 | 4.8 | 29.2% |

## ©Ⓕ APRICOT MUFFINS

¾ cup whole wheat flour
¾ cup flour
½ cup light brown sugar
2 teaspoons baking powder
1 teaspoon cinnamon
¼ teaspoon salt

1 (6-ounce) package dried
    apricots, chopped
⅓ cup white raisins
2 egg whites
½ cup skim milk
½ cup apricot nectar
¼ cup canola oil

Combine first eight ingredients together; set aside. In small bowl, mix egg whites, milk, apricot nectar, and oil. Add to apricot-flour mixture, stirring until only combined. Do not overmix; batter will be lumpy. Spoon batter into paper-lined muffin tins, filling about ⅔ full. Bake at 400 degrees for 30 minutes. Yield: 12 to 15 muffins.

*Great with a tart flavor.*

**Nutritional Information Per Muffin:**

| Calories | Cholesterol (mg) | Fat (g) | % Calories from Fat |
|---|---|---|---|
| 151 | <1 | 3.9 | 23.3% |

# Ⓕ CRABMEAT EGG CASSEROLE

6 slices whole wheat bread
1½ cups water
1 tablespoon light margarine,
   melted
1 onion, chopped
½ cup chopped green bell
   pepper
½ cup chopped celery
2 cloves garlic, minced
8 ounces reduced fat sharp
   Cheddar cheese,
   shredded

1 (8-ounce) can sliced water
   chestnuts, drained
1 pound lump crabmeat,
   picked for bones
1 egg
2 egg whites
½ cup fat free mayonnaise
Salt and pepper to taste
Several dashes hot pepper
   sauce

Place bread in bowl with water. Let stand 15 minutes. In skillet coated with no stick cooking spray, melt margarine and sauté onion, green pepper, celery, and garlic until tender. Add shredded cheese to bread and water mixture, stirring together. Carefully stir in sautéed vegetables, water chestnuts, and crabmeat. In mixing bowl, beat egg, egg whites, mayonnaise, and seasonings. Combine with crabmeat mixture, mixing well. Transfer into a 2-quart baking dish and bake at 350 degrees for 30 to 40 minutes. Yield: 10 servings.
*Crabmeat lovers will enjoy this delicious brunch dish.*

**Nutritional Information Per Serving:**

| Calories | Cholesterol (mg) | Fat (g) | % Calories from Fat |
|---|---|---|---|
| 190 | 72 | 4.0 | 19.0% |

## FRIED EGGS AND ASPARAGUS

6 asparagus spears
1 egg
Salt and pepper to taste

1 teaspoon grated Parmesan
   cheese

Trim asparagus spears and steam in ¼ cup water, covered, in microwave for 5 minutes or until tender. In frying pan coated with no stick cooking spray, fry an egg until done. Place egg on plate and season with salt and pepper. Cover with steamed asparagus spears and top with Parmesan cheese. Yield: 1 serving.
*Steam asparagus spears ahead to save time. This is a great combination for a special breakfast.*

**Nutritional Information Per Serving:**

| Calories | Cholesterol (mg) | Fat (g) | % Calories from Fat |
|---|---|---|---|
| 104 | 213 | 5.7 | 49.6% |

## Ⓕ EGG AND GREEN CHILI CASSEROLE

1 (8-ounce) package reduced
    fat Monterey Jack cheese,
    shredded
1 (8-ounce) package reduced
    fat Cheddar cheese,
    shredded
2 (4-ounce) cans chopped
    green chilies, drained

1 bunch green onions,
    chopped
5 eggs
7 egg whites
3 tablespoons non fat plain
    yogurt
1 tomato, thinly sliced

Coat a 3-quart glass baking dish with no stick cooking spray. Combine cheeses, green chilies, and green onions; spread on bottom of dish. Beat eggs and egg whites together with yogurt. Pour over cheeses, making a space with fork so eggs will go through to bottom. Refrigerate overnight. Place in cold oven, and bake at 350 degrees for 15 minutes. Add sliced tomatoes along top of casserole and continue baking for 15 to 20 minutes longer or until done. Serve hot. Yield: 12 servings.

**Nutritional Information Per Serving:**

| Calories | Cholesterol (mg) | Fat (g) | % Calories from Fat |
|---|---|---|---|
| 153 | 97 | 4.8 | 28.2% |

## Ⓕ EGG SOUFFLÉ

7 slices whole wheat bread,
    crusts removed
1 red bell pepper, seeded and
    chopped
1 bunch green onions,
    chopped
6 ounces reduced fat sharp
    Cheddar cheese,
    shredded
6 ounces reduced fat
    Monterey Jack cheese,
    shredded

5 eggs
4 egg whites
3 cups skim milk
2 tablespoons light
    margarine, melted
1 teaspoon dry mustard
Several dashes hot pepper
    sauce
1 teaspoon Worcestershire
    sauce
Salt and pepper to taste

Line bottom of a 3-quart or 13x9x2-inch baking dish with slices of bread. Cover with chopped red peppers and green onions. Sprinkle with shredded cheeses. In bowl, mix remaining ingredients, and pour liquid with seasonings over cheeses. Refrigerate for 6 hours or overnight. Bake at 350 degrees for 45 minutes to 1 hour. Yield: 12 servings.
*This is great to use for brunch because it can be made ahead.*

**Nutritional Information Per Serving:**

| Calories | Cholesterol (mg) | Fat (g) | % Calories from Fat |
|---|---|---|---|
| 176 | 96 | 5.5 | 28.2% |

## ©Ⓕ QUICK CHEESE GRITS

4 cups water
1 cup skim milk
½ teaspoon salt
1½ cups quick grits
3 tablespoons light
    margarine
4 ounces "lite" pasteurized
    processed cheese spread

6 ounces reduced fat sharp
    Cheddar cheese,
    shredded
1 tablespoon Worcestershire
    sauce
¼ teaspoon garlic powder
¼ teaspoon red pepper

In saucepan, bring water, milk, and salt to a boil. Add grits, reduce heat, and cook approximately 5 minutes, stirring occasionally. Add margarine, cheeses, Worcestershire sauce, garlic powder, and red pepper. Stir until margarine and cheeses have melted. Yield: 12 servings. *If not serving immediately, reheat, and add milk to make creamy if needed.*

**Nutritional Information Per Serving:**

| Calories | Cholesterol (mg) | Fat (g) | % Calories from Fat |
|---|---|---|---|
| 148 | 7 | 3.3 | 20.2% |

## ©Ⓕ BANANA PUFF

2 eggs, separated
¼ cup sugar
1 cup non fat plain yogurt
2 tablespoons light
    margarine, melted
1 teaspoon vanilla

½ teaspoon butter flavoring
¾ cup flour
2 teaspoons baking powder
1 teaspoon baking soda
¼ teaspoon cinnamon
1 banana, diced

In mixing bowl, beat egg yolks, sugar, yogurt, and margarine until blended. Add flavorings. Combine dry ingredients, and beat into egg mixture until all ingredients are moistened. In another bowl, beat egg whites until stiff. Carefully fold into batter. Fold in bananas. Spread batter into a 9-inch round cake pan coated with no stick cooking spray and dusted with flour. Bake at 400 degrees for 20 to 25 minutes. Serve immediately. Yield: 8 servings.
*A wonderful compliment to any brunch. It is best served warm.*

**Nutritional Information Per Serving:**

| Calories | Cholesterol (mg) | Fat (g) | % Calories from Fat |
|---|---|---|---|
| 134 | 54 | 2.9 | 19.5% |

# BANANA PANCAKES

¾ cup whole wheat flour
½ cup flour
2 teaspoons baking powder
1 tablespoon sugar

Dash salt
1¼ cups milk
1 tablespoon canola oil
¾ cup chopped banana

In bowl, combine flours, baking powder, sugar, and salt. Add milk and oil. Stir until combined; batter will be lumpy. Stir in banana. Cook pancakes on griddle or in pan coated with no stick cooking spray. Serve with light syrup. Yield: 12 pancakes.
*A super pancake!*

**Nutritional Information Per Pancake:**

| Calories | Cholesterol (mg) | Fat (g) | % Calories from Fat |
|---|---|---|---|
| 78 | <1 | 1.4 | 16.5% |

# WAFFLES

3 egg whites
1 cup whole wheat flour
1 cup flour
1 tablespoon light brown
   sugar

1 teaspoon baking soda
2 teaspoons baking powder
2 cups low fat buttermilk
1 teaspoon vanilla
¼ cup canola oil

In mixing bowl, beat egg whites until frothy. Combine dry ingredients together. Fold in dry ingredients and remaining ingredients into egg whites. Pour batter into center of heated waffle iron. Yield: five 8-inch waffles.

**Nutritional Information Per Waffle:**

| Calories | Cholesterol (mg) | Fat (g) | % Calories from Fat |
|---|---|---|---|
| 339 | 3 | 12.5 | 33.3% |

 **BISCUITS**

1 cup flour
1½ teaspoons baking powder
⅛ teaspoon baking soda
⅛ teaspoon salt

2 tablespoons light
   margarine
½ cup non fat plain yogurt
1 teaspoon honey

Combine flour, baking powder, baking soda, and salt in bowl; cut in margarine with pastry blender or fork until mixture resembles coarse meal. Add yogurt and honey, stirring just until dry ingredients are moistened. Turn dough onto floured surface and knead 4 times. Roll dough to ½-inch thickness; cut with cutter about 2½-inches wide. Place on ungreased baking sheet. Bake at 425 degrees for 10 minutes or until golden. Serve hot. Yield: 8 servings.
*When these are right out of the oven, they are the best!*

**Nutritional Information Per Serving:**

| Calories | Cholesterol (mg) | Fat (g) | % Calories from Fat |
|----------|------------------|---------|---------------------|
| 81 | <1 | 1.5 | 17.1% |

## HOT FRUIT COMPOTE

1 (29-ounce) can "lite" sliced
   peaches
1 (16-ounce) can "lite" pear
   halves, sliced
1 (16-ounce) can "lite"
   apricot halves, sliced
1 (16½-ounce) can pitted
   Bing cherries

1 (20-ounce) can pineapple
   chunks, in its own juice
2 bananas, sliced
1 tablespoon lemon juice
4 tablespoons cornstarch
1 cup light brown sugar
½ teaspoon curry
6 tablespoons light
   margarine, melted

Drain peaches, pears, apricots, cherries, and pineapple chunks. Sprinkle bananas with lemon juice. Mix all fruits together with bananas. Transfer to a 3-quart glass baking dish. In small bowl, combine cornstarch, brown sugar, and curry. Sprinkle over fruit. Drizzle melted margarine over top of dish. Bake, covered, at 350 degrees for 30 minutes. Uncover, and bake for another 15 minutes or until bubbly. Yield: 12 to 15 servings.

**Nutritional Information Per Serving:**

| Calories | Cholesterol (mg) | Fat (g) | % Calories from Fat |
|----------|------------------|---------|---------------------|
| 206 | 0 | 2.4 | 10.7% |

# Ⓒ CEREAL MIXTURE

3 tablespoons honey
3 tablespoons light
  margarine
3 tablespoons peanut butter

3 cups cereal (assorted
  shredded wheat, corn
  bran chex)

In microwave, combine honey, margarine, and peanut butter and heat until smooth. Toss with cereal, coating well. Spread on cookie sheet and bake at 175 degrees for 1½ hours. Yield: approximately 3 cups, or six ½-cup servings.
*Double this recipe and store in a jar. Great snack for everyone.*

**Nutritional Information Per Serving:**

| Calories | Cholesterol (mg) | Fat (g) | % Calories from Fat |
|---|---|---|---|
| 181 | 0 | 7.5 | 37.3% |

# Ⓒ Ⓕ NON ALCOHOLIC WINE COOLER

2 (12-ounce) cans carbonated
  sugar-free lemon-lime
  drink
1 (12-ounce) can sugar-free
  ginger ale

1 tablespoon apple cider
  vinegar
1 lime or lemon, thinly sliced

Combine all ingredients. Refrigerate and serve. Yield: approximately 36 ounces, or six 6-ounce servings.

**Nutritional Information Per 6 Ounces:**

| Calories | Cholesterol (mg) | Fat (g) | % Calories from Fat |
|---|---|---|---|
| 62 | 0 | 0.1 | 0.8% |

M. HANSBROUGH

SOUPS

## Ⓕ SEAFOOD GUMBO

¾ cup flour
1 tablespoon minced garlic
2 onions, chopped
2 green bell peppers,
  chopped
2 stalks celery, chopped
2 tablespoons chopped
  parsley
9 cups water
1 (14½-ounce) can whole
  tomatoes, crushed

3 bay leaves
Juice of half lemon
1 teaspoon dried thyme
¼ teaspoon red pepper
4 whole cloves
Salt and pepper to taste
1 pint claw crabmeat
2 pounds shrimp, peeled
2 pounds trout, cut into
  pieces
1 cup chopped green onions

Place flour on baking sheet and bake at 400 degrees for 20 to 30 minutes, stirring every 7 minutes, or until flour is brown (color of pecan shells). Works well in toaster oven. While flour is browning, coat a large pot with no stick cooking spray and sauté garlic, onion, peppers, celery, and parsley until tender. Gradually stir in browned flour (roux); stirring. Gradually add water, tomatoes, and seasonings. Bring to boil; lower heat and cook for 15 minutes. Add crabmeat, shrimp, and fish cooking for another 20 minutes. Add green onions, cooking until all seafood is done. Discard bay leaf and cloves before serving; serve over rice. Yield: 10 to 12 servings.

*There is not much that can beat this gumbo with all the fresh seafood. Freezes well.*

**Nutritional Information Per Serving:**

| Calories | Cholesterol (mg) | Fat (g) | % Calories from Fat |
|---|---|---|---|
| 220 | 153 | 4.2 | 17.0% |

## Ⓕ EASY CRAB SOUP

1 onion, finely chopped
¼ cup light margarine
1 (14½-ounce) can reduced
  fat chicken broth
½ cup water

1 (12-ounce) can evaporated
  skimmed milk
1 pound lump crabmeat
3 green onion stems, finely
  sliced

In saucepan, sauté onions in margarine until tender. Add broth and water. Simmer for 20 minutes on low heat and add milk. Stir well and fold in crabmeat. Garnish with green onion stems. Yield: 4 servings.

*A quick version when in a pinch!*

**Nutritional Information Per Serving:**

| Calories | Cholesterol (mg) | Fat (g) | % Calories from Fat |
|---|---|---|---|
| 273 | 118 | 8.9 | 29.5% |

# Ⓕ CHICKEN AND SAUSAGE GUMBO

⅔ cup flour
3 onions, chopped
4 cloves garlic, minced
2 green bell peppers,
    chopped
2 stalks celery, chopped
10 cups water
1 (14½-ounce) can stewed
    tomatoes

3 to 4 pounds skinless,
    boneless chicken breasts,
    cut in pieces
½ teaspoon dried thyme
¼ teaspoon red pepper
1 pound lite sausage
1 bunch green onions,
    chopped

Place flour on baking sheet and bake at 400 degrees for 20 minutes. Stir every 5 minutes. Flour should be very brown. (Works well in toaster oven). Set aside. In large, heavy pot coated with no stick cooking spray, sauté vegetables until tender. Add browned flour (roux), stirring constantly. Gradually add water, tomatoes and chicken. Bring to boil, lower heat, and simmer for 1 hour. While gumbo is cooking, boil sausage in water in a pot until done. Slice in 1-inch slices and add to gumbo. Cook an additional 20 minutes. Add green onions cooking 10 more minutes. Skim any fat from surface of gumbo. Serve over rice. Yield: 10 to 12 servings.
*This recipe makes a browned flour roux which does not have oil; yet, the flavor is there. Freezes well if there is any left.*

**Nutritional Information Per Serving:**

| Calories | Cholesterol (mg) | Fat (g) | % Calories from Fat |
|---|---|---|---|
| 255 | 101 | 5.2 | 18.4% |

# Ⓒ Ⓕ ARTICHOKE SOUP

3 (14-ounce) cans artichoke
    hearts, drained
3 (10¾-ounce) cans 99% fat
    free cream of mushroom
    soup

1 cup skim milk
2 cups chicken broth
½ cup dry white wine
Dash cayenne

Place artichokes in food processor and purée. Combine remaining ingredients in bowl and add to processor. Blend until well combined. Transfer to pot and heat over low heat to serve. Yield: 6 to 8 servings.
*A quick soup that will become one of your favorites.*

**Nutritional Information Per Serving:**

| Calories | Cholesterol (mg) | Fat (g) | % Calories from Fat |
|---|---|---|---|
| 135 | 2 | 3.1 | 20.8% |

# Ⓒ ONION SOUP

1 tablespoon light margarine
1 tablespoon olive oil
5 large yellow onions, thinly
  sliced
1 teaspoon sugar
3 tablespoons flour
2 (14½-ounce) cans beef
  broth

2 (14½-ounce) cans chicken
  broth with ⅓ less salt
½ cup white wine or
  Vermouth
6 tablespoons shredded
  Swiss cheese

In large pot, coated with no stick cooking spray, melt margarine and olive oil. Add onions, cover and cook slowly for 15 minutes. Uncover, add sugar. Cook, stirring, until onions are golden brown, about 30 to 40 minutes. Sprinkle flour over onions, stirring. Add beef and chicken broths, and white wine. Simmer soup partly covered for 30 minutes. To serve, pour soup into individual bowls and sprinkle with cheese. Yield: 6 servings.

*Now you can enjoy this old favorite!*

**Nutritional Information Per Serving:**

| Calories | Cholesterol (mg) | Fat (g) | % Calories from Fat |
|----------|------------------|---------|---------------------|
| 192 | 13 | 8.4 | 39.3% |

# Ⓕ SEAFOOD CHOWDER

2 tablespoons margarine
1 onion, chopped
2 cloves garlic, minced
⅓ cup flour
1 (14½-ounce) can reduced
  fat chicken broth
1 cup skim milk

¼ pound medium, peeled
  shrimp
½ pound white crabmeat
¼ teaspoon white pepper
Dash hot pepper sauce
1 tablespoon lemon juice
1 small bunch green onions,
  sliced

In pot, melt margarine and sauté onion and garlic until tender. Stir in flour and gradually add chicken broth and milk. Add seafood and remaining seasoning except green onions. Cook shrimp until done, stirring often. Before serving, garnish each bowl with green onions. Yield: 6 servings.

**Nutritional Information Per Serving:**

| Calories | Cholesterol (mg) | Fat (g) | % Calories from Fat |
|----------|------------------|---------|---------------------|
| 179 | 91 | 6.0 | 30.1% |

# Ⓕ CORN, SHRIMP, AND CRABMEAT SOUP

1 red onion, chopped
4 stalks celery, chopped
1 green bell pepper, chopped
2 cloves garlic, minced
1 (16-ounce) bag frozen sweet
   corn
1 (10-ounce) can chopped
   tomatoes and green
   chilies
1 (6-ounce) can tomato paste
1 pound shrimp, peeled

1 pound claw crabmeat
1 tablespoon Worcestershire
   sauce
Salt and pepper to taste
¼ teaspoon red pepper
2 cups reduced fat chicken
   broth
2 cups water
1 bunch green onions, thinly
   sliced

Coat a large pot with no stick cooking spray and sauté onion, celery, green pepper, and garlic until tender. Add corn, tomatoes and green chilies, tomato paste, shrimp, crabmeat, and seasonings. Add chicken broth and bring to boil, lower heat, and cook for 1 hour, adding water as needed to keep the consistency soupy. Add green onions, simmer for 15 minutes. Yield: 8 servings.

*This soup can be the meal itself, especially on a cold night.*

**Nutritional Information Per Serving:**

| Calories | Cholesterol (mg) | Fat (g) | % Calories from Fat |
|----------|------------------|---------|---------------------|
| 211      | 135              | 3.3     | 14.0%               |

# Ⓒ Ⓕ CRAB SOUP

2 tablespoons light
   margarine
2 cloves garlic, minced
⅓ cup chopped onions
2 tablespoons flour
1 teaspoon dry mustard
¼ teaspoon white pepper
Dash hot pepper sauce

1 tablespoon Worcestershire
   sauce
3 cups hot skim milk
1 tablespoon sherry
4 green onion stems, thinly
   sliced
1 cup white crabmeat

In saucepan, melt margarine and sauté garlic and onions until tender. Stir in flour, dry mustard, pepper, hot sauce, and Worcestershire sauce. Gradually add hot milk, stirring constantly, until a smooth soup results. Add sherry and green onions. Carefully fold in crabmeat. Yield: 2 to 4 servings.

**Nutritional Information Per Serving:**

| Calories | Cholesterol (mg) | Fat (g) | % Calories from Fat |
|----------|------------------|---------|---------------------|
| 155      | 35               | 3.8     | 22.1%               |

## ⓒ MEXICAN CORN SOUP

1 pound zucchini, coarsely
  shredded
1 bunch green onions, thinly
  sliced
2 cloves garlic, minced
2 tablespoons light
  margarine
1 (7-ounce) can diced green
  chilies

1 (16-ounce) package frozen
  corn, thawed
4 cups chicken broth
½ teaspoon dried thyme
Salt and pepper to taste
1 cup shredded reduced fat
  Monterey Jack cheese

Sauté zucchini, onion and garlic in margarine until tender. Stir in green chilies. Add corn, chicken broth, thyme, and salt and pepper to taste. Bring to boil and then reduce heat. Cook until corn is tender, about 10 minutes. Gradually pour soup in food processor to purée. Return to saucepan and stir in cheese. Cook over low heat, stirring frequently, until cheese is melted and mixture is combined. Do not boil after cheese has been added. Serve with tortilla chips if desired. Yield: 6 servings.

*Do not let the color of this soup fool you as the flavor is good.*

**Nutritional Information Per Serving:**

| Calories | Cholesterol (mg) | Fat (g) | % Calories from Fat |
|---|---|---|---|
| 205 | 17 | 9.3 | 40.6% |

## ⓒⒻ SALMON BISQUE

½ pound fresh salmon fillet
  or steak
2 tablespoons light
  margarine
1 bunch green onions,
  chopped
2 cloves garlic, minced

⅓ cup flour
4 cups skim milk
½ cup tomato purée
2 tablespoons dry sherry
1 teaspoon dried dill weed
Salt and white pepper to
  taste

Poach salmon in 1-inch of water until done. Cool, flake, and remove any bones; set aside. In large pot, melt margarine and stir in green onions and garlic, cooking until tender. Blend in flour. Cook, stirring constantly, for a few minutes. Gradually add milk, stirring until thickened. Add flaked salmon, tomato purée, sherry, dill weed, and salt and pepper to taste. Simmer, covered, for 15 minutes. Yield: 6 to 8 servings.

*This bisque is absolutely delicious!*

**Nutritional Information Per Serving:**

| Calories | Cholesterol (mg) | Fat (g) | % Calories from Fat |
|---|---|---|---|
| 140 | 15 | 3.7 | 23.5% |

# ⓒ TORTILLA SOUP

2 (10¾-ounce) cans reduced
  fat chicken broth
½ cup chopped celery
1 teaspoon chili powder
1 tablespoon olive oil
1 tomato, peeled, and seeded,
  chopped

¼ cup chopped onion
3 cloves garlic, minced
1 teaspoon chopped parsley
½ cup tortilla chips
4 tablespoons shredded
  reduced fat Cheddar
  cheese

In pot, bring chicken broth, celery, and chili powder to boil. In small pan, heat olive oil and sauté tomato, onion, garlic, and parsley until tender. Add to broth. Add tortilla chips boiling until soft. Serve into bowls and top with shredded cheese. Yield: 2 to 4 servings.
*A great first course to a Mexican meal.*

**Nutritional Information Per Serving:**

| Calories | Cholesterol (mg) | Fat (g) | % Calories from Fat |
|---|---|---|---|
| 109 | 2 | 6.0 | 49.5% |

# ⓒ GREEN ONION AND MUSHROOM SOUP

3 large bunches green onions
1 pound fresh mushrooms
3 tablespoons light
  margarine
Salt and white pepper to
  taste

⅛ teaspoon cayenne pepper
3 tablespoons flour
5 cups chicken broth
1 cup water
⅓ cup non fat plain yogurt
2 green onions, thinly sliced

Coarsely chop 3 bunches green onions. Chop ¾ pound of the mushrooms; set aside. In large pot coated with no stick cooking spray, melt margarine. Add green onions, salt and white pepper, and cayenne. Reduce heat, cover, and cook for 10 minutes, stirring occasionally. Add flour. Gradually stir in chicken broth and water cooking until soup comes to a boil. Reduce heat, and cook for 10 minutes longer. Add chopped mushrooms and heat one minute. Purée the soup in food processor (in batches if necessary). Slice the remaining ¼ pound mushrooms. In small pan coated with no stick cooking spray, sauté the sliced mushrooms until tender. To serve soup: ladle into bowl and top with yogurt, sautéed mushrooms, and sliced green onions. Yield: 8 servings.
*This is an outstanding soup which everyone will enjoy.*

**Nutritional Information Per Serving:**

| Calories | Cholesterol (mg) | Fat (g) | % Calories from Fat |
|---|---|---|---|
| 111 | 2 | 4.1 | 33.4% |

## ©Ⓕ POTATO SOUP

6 cups peeled and sliced red
   potatoes
4 cups sliced onions
1½ to 2 quarts water (just to
   cover potatoes and
   onions)
Salt and pepper to taste

4 teaspoons powdered
   chicken broth or 5
   bouillon cubes
1 cup skim milk
1 bunch green onions, finely
   sliced

Bring potatoes and onions to boil in water. Reduce heat and simmer, partially covered, for 45 minutes. When potatoes are tender, transfer with onions and water to food processor in batches and process until smooth. Return to pot and add remaining ingredients except green onions, cooking until thoroughly heated. Top with green onions and serve. Yield: 12 servings.

*Everyone wanted this recipe for potato soup.*

**Nutritional Information Per Serving:**

| Calories | Cholesterol (mg) | Fat (g) | % Calories from Fat |
|---|---|---|---|
| 95 | <1 | 0.5 | 4.6% |

##  BEEFY VEGETABLE AND BARLEY SOUP

2 pounds lean round steak,
   ½-inch thick
1 onion, chopped
3 stalks celery, chopped
1 bay leaf
2 tablespoons chopped
   parsley
2 cups water

1 (46-ounce) can cocktail
   vegetable juice
1 red potato, peeled and cut
   in small cubes
½ cup barley
1 large carrot, sliced
1 (10-ounce) package frozen
   mixed vegetables

Cut meat into 1-inch cubes. Coat a large heavy pot with no stick cooking spray. Add meat, cooking until browned, stirring often. Add onion, celery, bay leaf, parsley, and 2 cups water. Bring to a boil, lower heat and simmer covered 45 minutes. Add vegetable juice, potato, and barley. Cook 30 minutes and add carrot and mixed vegetables. Cover, and cook over low heat 30 minutes or until meat is tender and barley is done. Yield: 6 to 8 servings.

**Nutritional Information Per Serving:**

| Calories | Cholesterol (mg) | Fat (g) | % Calories from Fat |
|---|---|---|---|
| 257 | 68 | 5.0 | 17.4% |

# ⓒⒻ SPLIT PEA SOUP

2 cups dried split peas
5 slices turkey bacon, cut
    into pieces
1 onion, chopped
½ cup chopped celery
4 cups chicken broth
    (approximately)

1 bay leaf
2 cups sliced carrots
1 potato, peeled and diced
Salt and pepper to taste
½ teaspoon dried thyme

Soak peas in water to cover overnight. In large pot sauté turkey bacon, onion, and celery until tender. Add peas in water and remaining ingredients. Bring soup to boil, lower heat, and cook, covered for 1½ to 2 hours or until peas are very soft. Stir occasionally. If soup gets too thick, thin with additional broth or water. Remove bay leaf before serving. Yield: 6 servings.
*Good on a winter evening.*

**Nutritional Information Per Serving:**

| Calories | Cholesterol (mg) | Fat (g) | % Calories from Fat |
|----------|------------------|---------|---------------------|
| 323 | 7 | 4.0 | 11.0% |

# ⓒⒻ MINESTRONE SOUP

1 cup dried white beans
4 cloves garlic, minced
2 stalks celery, chopped
1 onion, chopped
1 (10-ounce) can chopped
    tomatoes and green
    chilies
1 (14½-ounce) can whole
    tomatoes, chopped
3 (14½-ounce) cans chicken
    broth with ⅓ less salt
1 cup water

¼ cup red wine
1 tablespoon dried oregano
1 tablespoon dried basil
Salt and pepper to taste
2 bay leaves
1 red potato, peeled and
    diced
½ pound fresh green beans,
    cut diagonally into thirds
2 carrots, peeled and diced
⅓ cup elbow macaroni

Soak white beans for 6 hours in 1 quart of water; pour beans with soaking liquid into a pot. Bring to a boil and add garlic, celery, and onions. Cook 1½ hours or until beans are tender. Add chopped tomato and green chilies, chopped tomatoes with juice, chicken broth, water, red wine, and seasonings. Heat to boiling; add potato, green beans, carrots, and macaroni. Reduce heat to simmer and cook 30 to 45 minutes or until vegetables are tender. Yield: 6 to 8 servings.

**Nutritional Information Per Serving:**

| Calories | Cholesterol (mg) | Fat (g) | % Calories from Fat |
|----------|------------------|---------|---------------------|
| 190 | 2 | 2.2 | 10.2% |

# ⓒⓕ VEGETARIAN CHILI

1½ cups chopped onions
1½ teaspoons minced garlic
¼ cup water
3 (1-pound) cans red kidney
   beans, rinsed and
   drained
1½ cups tomato juice
1 (4-ounce) can chopped
   green chilies, undrained

1 large ripe tomato, cut in ¼-
   inch pieces
1¼ teaspoons chili powder
Salt and pepper to taste
1 teaspoon cumin
½ cup shredded reduced fat
   Cheddar cheese

In large pot, sauté onion and garlic in water. Cover, and cook 10 minutes, stirring, until onion is tender. Stir in remaining ingredients except cheese. Cook for 5 to 10 minutes until hot. Serve in bowls with shredded cheese. Yield: 6 servings.

**Nutritional Information Per Serving:**

| Calories | Cholesterol (mg) | Fat (g) | % Calories from Fat |
|---|---|---|---|
| 195 | 2 | 1.5 | 7.1% |

# ⓒ CHEESY SOUP

3 tablespoons liquid
   margarine
½ cup chopped onion
½ cup finely chopped carrots
½ cup finely chopped green
   bell pepper
¼ cup finely chopped celery
3 tablespoons flour
¼ teaspoon dry mustard

3½ cups chicken broth
½ pound reduced fat sharp
   Cheddar cheese,
   shredded
1½ cups skim milk
Salt and white pepper to
   taste
4 tablespoons chopped green
   onions

In pot melt margarine and sauté onion, carrot, green pepper, and celery until tender. Blend in flour and dry mustard; gradually add chicken broth, mixing until well blended. Bring to a boil and cook until slightly thickened, stirring frequently. Reduce heat and simmer for 10 minutes. Slowly add shredded cheese and cook until melted. Add 1 cup skim milk. Add the remaining ½ cup milk only if soup is too thick. Heat and season to taste. Before serving, sprinkle with green onions. Yield: 4 servings.
*Serve at lunch with a salad or sandwich.*

**Nutritional Information Per Serving:**

| Calories | Cholesterol (mg) | Fat (g) | % Calories from Fat |
|---|---|---|---|
| 340 | 14 | 14.1 | 37.4% |

#  GAZPACHO

| | |
|---|---|
| 8 tomatoes | ½ cup chopped green bell |
| 1 slice whole wheat bread | peppers |
| 2 tablespoons olive oil | ½ cup chopped cucumber, |
| 1 tablespoon red wine | peeled |
| vinegar | ¼ cup chopped onion |
| Salt and pepper to taste | ½ cup chopped celery |
| 1 clove garlic, minced | 2 teaspoons chopped parsley |

Peel and quarter tomatoes. Remove crust from bread and tear into small pieces. Place tomatoes, bread, oil, vinegar, salt and pepper, and garlic in food processor. Add water to cover (about ½ to 1 cup depending on size of tomatoes) and blend well. Stir in remaining ingredients. Chill in refrigerator before serving. Yield: 8 servings.
*The flavor improves the longer it is refrigerated so make ahead.*

**Nutritional Information Per Serving:**

| Calories | Cholesterol (mg) | Fat (g) | % Calories from Fat |
|---|---|---|---|
| 71 | <1 | 3.9 | 49.9% |

#  PEACH SOUP

| | |
|---|---|
| 1½ pounds peaches, peeled, | 1 cup pineapple juice |
| pitted and sliced | 1 tablespoon lemon juice |
| 2 cups plain non fat yogurt | 2 tablespoons sugar |
| 1 cup fresh orange juice | ¼ cup sherry |

Purée peaches in food processor until smooth. Add all remaining ingredients and blend well. Refrigerate to serve chilled. Yield: 10 servings.
*A light summer soup that would be great served with lunch.*

**Nutritional Information Per Serving:**

| Calories | Cholesterol (mg) | Fat (g) | % Calories from Fat |
|---|---|---|---|
| 91 | <1 | 0.2 | 1.8% |

# BROCCOLI AND CRAB BISQUE

1 bunch green onions,
    chopped
1 pound fresh mushrooms,
    sliced
2 cups fresh broccoli
    flowerets
3 cloves garlic, minced
3 tablespoons light
    margarine
½ cup flour

½ teaspoon dried thyme
⅛ teaspoon pepper
Salt to taste
1 bay leaf
2 cups skim milk
3 cups chicken broth
1½ cups grated Swiss cheese
1 pound crabmeat, picked for
    bones

In large pot, sauté green onions, mushrooms, broccoli flowerets, and garlic in margarine until tender. Blend in flour, thyme, salt and pepper, and bay leaf. Add milk and broth all at once. Cook and stir until thickened and bubbly. Add cheese stirring until melted. Gently fold in crabmeat and heat through. Yield: 8 servings.

**Nutritional Information Per Serving:**

| Calories | Cholesterol (mg) | Fat (g) | % Calories from Fat |
|---|---|---|---|
| 243 | 77 | 10 | 37.3% |

# ©Ⓕ STRAWBERRY RASPBERRY SOUP

1 quart fresh strawberries
3 cups fresh raspberries or
    1 (12-ounce) package
    frozen raspberries,
    drained
½ cup apple juice plus ⅔ cup
    apple juice

¼ cup sugar
2 tablespoons cornstarch
1 cup water
1 tablespoon lemon juice
½ cup non fat yogurt
1 teaspoon powdered sugar
½ teaspoon vanilla

Cut the strawberries in half. Place the strawberries, raspberries, ½ cup apple juice, and sugar in saucepan and let stand 15 minutes. Heat over low heat until boiling. Mix together the cornstarch and water, and stir into fruit mixture. Boil over low heat, stirring constantly, until fruits soften and soup is clear and thickened. Remove from heat and stir in the lemon juice. Chill. Before serving add ⅔ cup apple juice to make soup consistency, or more if needed. In small bowl, combine yogurt, powdered sugar, and vanilla. Serve soup in small bowls and top with tablespoon of yogurt mixture. Yield: 12 small servings.
*This is a rich soup that would be great served in a cup at a luncheon.*

**Nutritional Information Per Serving:**

| Calories | Cholesterol (mg) | Fat (g) | % Calories from Fat |
|---|---|---|---|
| 69 | <1 | 0.4 | 5.2% |

M. HANSBROUGH

SALADS

# ⓒ Ⓕ PASTA SALAD

2 cups snow peas
1 bunch broccoli, flowerets only
1 (12-ounce) package tri-colored pasta shells
1 (6-ounce) package tri-colored stuffed tortellini
½ pound fresh mushrooms, cut in half
1 cup cherry tomatoes, cut in half
1 red bell pepper, cut into strips
⅓ cup grated Romano cheese

Cook snow peas and broccoli in microwave until crisp tender. Drain and set aside. Cook pasta shells and tortellini according to directions on package omitting salt and oil. Drain and set aside. Combine all ingredients in large bowl. Toss with Dressing (see recipe below). Yield: 10 servings.

*An outstanding pasta salad!*

**Dressing**
1 bunch green onions, sliced
½ cup red wine vinegar
⅓ cup olive oil
2 tablespoons chopped parsley
3 cloves garlic, minced
2 teaspoons dried basil
1 teaspoon dried dill weed
½ teaspoon dried oregano
1 teaspoon salt
½ teaspoon pepper
½ teaspoon sugar
1½ teaspoons Dijon mustard

Combine all ingredients together, mixing well. Pour over pasta salad. Refrigerate.

**Nutritional Information Per Serving:**

| Calories | Cholesterol (mg) | Fat (g) | % Calories from Fat |
|----------|------------------|---------|---------------------|
| 324 | 3 | 9.4 | 26.2% |

## (F) TORTELLINI SHRIMP SALAD

2 (8-ounce) packages tri-
    colored tortellini stuffed
    with Parmesan cheese
1 pound cooked shrimp,
    peeled

⅓ cup grated Romano cheese
4 green onions, finely sliced
⅓ cup chopped red bell
    pepper
1 tablespoon dried basil

Cook tortellini according to directions on package omitting salt and oil. Drain well and cool slightly. In a large bowl, combine remaining ingredients and toss with Dressing (see recipe below). Serve or keep in refrigerator. Best when serve at room temperature. Yield: 8 servings.

**Dressing**
¼ cup red wine vinegar
2 tablespoons water
1 tablespoon canola oil

1 tablespoon dried basil
1 teaspoon Dijon mustard

Combine all ingredients together.

**Nutritional Information Per Serving:**

| Calories | Cholesterol (mg) | Fat (g) | % Calories from Fat |
|---|---|---|---|
| 190 | 160 | 5.9 | 27.8% |

## (F) SHRIMP PASTA SALAD

8 ounces tubular pasta
    (penne, ziti, etc.)
1 teaspoon garlic powder
2 pounds shrimp, cooked and
    peeled

1 (10-ounce) package frozen
    peas
1 red bell pepper, chopped
½ cup chopped red onion

Cook pasta according to directions on package omitting salt and oil; drain. Toss with garlic powder. Combine remaining ingredients in bowl and add pasta. Pour Basil Dressing (see recipe below) over salad and toss thoroughly. Yield: 8 to 10 servings.

**Basil Dressing**
1 tablespoon dried basil
3 cloves garlic, minced
⅓ cup olive oil

3 tablespoons fresh lemon
    juice

Combine all ingredients and pour over shrimp pasta mixture.

**Nutritional Information Per Serving:**

| Calories | Cholesterol (mg) | Fat (g) | % Calories from Fat |
|---|---|---|---|
| 320 | 217 | 10.0 | 28.1% |

# Ⓕ SHRIMP AND PASTA GARDEN SALAD

6 ounces small sea shell
 pasta
1 (6-ounce) package frozen
 snow pea pods
16 cherry tomatoes, halved
1 medium cucumber, peeled
 and sliced

½ cup shredded carrots
1 bunch green onions, thinly
 sliced
2 pounds shrimp, cooked and
 peeled

Cook sea shells according to directions on package omitting salt and oil; drain. Cook pea pods according to directions on package; drain. Combine all ingredients and toss with Dressing (see recipe below). Yield: 8 to 10 servings.

*This is great to use leftover shrimp.*

**Dressing**

½ cup non fat plain yogurt
½ cup fat free Italian
 dressing

3 cloves garlic, minced

Combine all ingredients, stirring well.

**Nutritional Information Per Serving:**

| Calories | Cholesterol (mg) | Fat (g) | % Calories from Fat |
|---|---|---|---|
| 166 | 109 | 1.6 | 8.9% |

# GREEK PASTA SALAD

½ pound small shrimp,
  cooked and peeled
1 pound bay scallops, cooked
1 (8-ounce) package tri-
  colored rotini

15 cherry tomatoes, halved
¼ cup thinly sliced black
  olives
3 ounces feta cheese,
  crumbled

Toss shrimp and scallops with ¼ cup Dressing (see recipe below). Refrigerate 4 hours or overnight. Refrigerate remaining dressing. Cook pasta according to directions on package omitting salt and oil. Drain well. In large bowl, toss pasta with marinated seafood and remaining ingredients. Add reserved dressing as needed. Yield: 4 servings.

**Dressing**
½ teaspoon dried dill weed
3 cloves garlic, minced
½ cup chopped red onion

3 tablespoons fresh lemon
  juice
½ cup olive oil
Salt and pepper to taste

Combine all ingredients in food processor until well combined. *For those really watching the fat content, use ⅓ cup olive oil.*

**Nutritional Information Per Serving:**

| Calories | Cholesterol (mg) | Fat (g) | % Calories from Fat |
|---|---|---|---|
| 681 | 139 | 36.5 | 48.3% |

# Ⓕ TURKEY AND BROCCOLI PASTA SALAD

12 ounces tri-colored pasta
2 tablespoons olive oil
1 (10-ounce) bag fresh
  spinach
1 bunch broccoli
3 cups cubed cooked turkey
  breast

1 bunch green onions,
  chopped
1 yellow bell pepper, seeded
  and chopped
2 tomatoes, peeled, seeded,
  and chopped
Salt and pepper to taste

Cook pasta according to directions on package omitting oil; drain. Toss pasta with olive oil and chill. Wash, stem, dry, and tear spinach into pieces. Cook broccoli in microwave, covered, in small amount of water for 4 minutes. Drain and cut into small pieces. Assemble salad in large shallow dish. Using half of each ingredient, alternate layers with salt and pepper to taste in the following order: spinach, pasta, turkey, broccoli, green onions, yellow pepper, and tomatoes. Repeat with remaining half of ingredients and top with Dressing (see recipe below). Refrigerate. Yield: 8 to 10 servings.

*A great way to use seasoned leftover turkey (or chicken).*

### Dressing

2 cups non fat plain yogurt
⅔ cup part skim ricotta
  cheese
3 tablespoons tarragon
  vinegar

1½ teaspoons minced garlic
1½ teaspoons dried basil
1 teaspoon sugar
Salt and pepper to taste

Mix all ingredients together.

### Nutritional Information Per Serving:

| Calories | Cholesterol (mg) | Fat (g) | % Calories from Fat |
|---|---|---|---|
| 298 | 65 | 7.4 | 22.5% |

## Ⓕ CHICKEN PASTA SALAD

8 ounces spiral pasta
2 cups cubed cooked chicken
breasts
1 (8-ounce) can sliced water
chestnuts, drained

⅓ cup thinly sliced green
onions
½ cup chopped celery
1 (10-ounce) box frozen snow
peas, thawed
Salt and pepper to taste

Cook pasta according to directions on package omitting oil; drain. Combine pasta with remaining ingredients and toss with Dressing (see recipe below). Refrigerate before serving. Yield: 6 servings.
*Great way to use leftover chicken. The sherry gives this salad a different flavor.*

**Dressing**
¼ cup non fat plain yogurt
3 tablespoons lite soy sauce

1 tablespoon sherry

Mix all ingredients together.

**Nutritional Information Per Serving:**

| Calories | Cholesterol (mg) | Fat (g) | % Calories from Fat |
|---|---|---|---|
| 269 | 73 | 3.7 | 12.5% |

## ⒸⒻ CARROT RAISIN CHICKEN SALAD

2 cups shredded, peeled
carrots (approximately 4)
½ cup golden raisins
1 tablespoon water
¼ teaspoon dried ginger
2 cups cubed cooked chicken
breasts

½ cup thin slices green bell
pepper
¼ cup light mayonnaise
2 tablespoons lemon juice
1 tablespoon sugar
Lettuce

Place carrots, raisins, water, and ginger in a 1½-quart casserole. Cover with lid. Microwave on high four minutes or until carrots are crisp tender. Add chicken and green pepper. Blend mayonnaise, lemon juice, and sugar together in small bowl. Pour over carrot mixture; toss to coat ingredients. Refrigerate for two hours. Arrange lettuce leaves on serving platter and mound chicken mixture in center. Yield: 4 servings.

**Nutritional Information Per Serving:**

| Calories | Cholesterol (mg) | Fat (g) | % Calories from Fat |
|---|---|---|---|
| 250 | 60 | 7.2 | 26.1% |

## Ⓒ MARINATED ITALIAN TUNA SALAD

2 ounces part-skim
   mozzarella cheese, cut
   into small cubes
2 (6½-ounce) cans tuna in
   water
1 cup quartered cherry
   tomatoes
1 small red onion, cut into
   thin rings

⅔ cup chopped celery
2 tablespoons olive oil
3 tablespoons red wine
   vinegar
1½ teaspoons dried basil
¼ teaspoon crushed red
   pepper flakes
⅛ teaspoon pepper

In large bowl, combine cheese, tuna, tomatoes, onion, and celery. In small bowl, mix together oil, vinegar, basil, red pepper flakes, and pepper. Pour dressing over tuna mixture and toss gently to coat. Cover and refrigerate for at least 1 hour. Yield: 4 to 6 servings.
*A super salad!*

**Nutritional Information Per Serving:**

| Calories | Cholesterol (mg) | Fat (g) | % Calories from Fat |
|---|---|---|---|
| 145 | 14 | 6.5 | 40.3% |

## Ⓒ Ⓕ TUNA SALAD

2 (7-ounce) cans white tuna,
   packed in water, drained
1 (11-ounce) can mandarin
   oranges, drained
¼ pound fresh mushrooms,
   sliced

1 (14-ounce) can artichoke
   hearts, drained and cut
   in half
1 cup sliced water chestnuts,
   drained

Carefully combine all ingredients in large bowl. Toss with Dressing (see recipe below). Serve immediately. Yield: 8 servings.

**Dressing**
¼ cup fat free mayonnaise
¼ cup non fat plain yogurt
1 tablespoon lemon juice

2 teaspoons sugar
1 bunch green onions, thinly
   sliced

Combine all ingredients together and fold into tuna mixture.

**Nutritional Information Per Serving:**

| Calories | Cholesterol (mg) | Fat (g) | % Calories from Fat |
|---|---|---|---|
| 104 | 8 | 0.4 | 3.9% |

# ⓒ SALADE NIÇOISE

3 or 4 red potatoes
1 tablespoon chopped green
   onions
½ pound fresh green beans
1 head Boston or romaine
   lettuce, rinsed and
   drained

2 (9¼-ounce) cans tuna fish
   packed in water, well
   drained
Salt and pepper to taste
1 cucumber, peeled and
   thinly sliced
2 ripe tomatoes, quartered

Place potatoes in medium saucepan; cover with salted water. Cook, uncovered, until tender when pierced with fork. Cool, peel, and slice. Combine with chopped green onions and salt and pepper; set aside. Snip ends off green beans. Place in small amount of salted water, cover, and cook 5 minutes. Drain, rinse, and slice julienne style. Line a large platter with lettuce. Arrange green beans over lettuce. Drizzle with ¼ cup Vinaigrette Dressing (see recipe below). Layer tuna fish over green beans. Sprinkle with salt and pepper. Drizzle with ¼ cup Vinaigrette Dressing. Around edges of tuna, arrange potato slices, cucumber, and tomato wedges. Pour remaining Vinaigrette Dressing over all. Cover with plastic wrap and refrigerate at least 1 hour. Yield: 6 to 8 servings. *An attractive as well as very good salad.*

**Vinaigrette Dressing**
1 clove garlic, minced
1 tablespoon chopped
   parsley
¼ cup chopped red onion
⅓ cup red wine vinegar

2 tablespoons lemon juice
1 teaspoon Dijon mustard
⅛ teaspoon sugar
¼ cup olive oil

Combine all ingredients together, mixing well.

**Nutritional Information Per Serving:**

| Calories | Cholesterol (mg) | Fat (g) | % Calories from Fat |
|---|---|---|---|
| 194 | 7 | 7.3 | 34.0% |

## ⓒ MARINATED VEGETABLE SALAD

⅔ cup olive oil
½ cup red wine vinegar
⅓ cup finely chopped fresh
   parsley
3 cloves garlic, finely minced
2 tablespoons Dijon mustard
2 tablespoons honey
1½ teaspoons dried basil
4 ounces crumbled bleu
   cheese
1 small head cauliflower, cut
   into flowerets

1 bunch broccoli, cut into
   flowerets
4 carrots, peeled and sliced
1 (14½-ounce) can quartered
   artichoke hearts, drained
3 green onions, finely sliced
¼ pound fresh mushrooms,
   sliced
6 cherry tomatoes, cut in half
1 cucumber, peeled and
   chopped

In a food processor, combine all dressing ingredients except bleu cheese. Blend until smooth. Add cheese and stir gently. Place vegetables in bowl and pour dressing over, tossing until mixed. Cover and refrigerate at least 2 hours. This salad can be made the day before. Yield: 8 servings.
*Any vegetable of your choice may be substituted or added such as green peppers, asparagus...*

**Nutritional Information Per Serving:**

| Calories | Cholesterol (mg) | Fat (g) | % Calories from Fat |
|----------|------------------|---------|---------------------|
| 283 | 11 | 22.8 | 72.5% |

## CRABMEAT SALAD

3 tablespoons cholesterol
   free mayonnaise
1 tablespoon lemon juice
½ teaspoon dry mustard
1 teaspoon Worcestershire
   sauce
½ teaspoon hot pepper sauce

⅛ teaspoon garlic salt
½ cup chopped celery
5 green onions, chopped
2 tablespoons chopped
   parsley
1 pound lump crabmeat,
   picked for shells

Combine all ingredients except for crabmeat, mixing well. Gently fold in crabmeat. Refrigerate until ready to serve. Yield: 6 servings.
*To lower fat content, substitute fat free mayonnaise.*

**Nutritional Information Per Serving:**

| Calories | Cholesterol (mg) | Fat (g) | % Calories from Fat |
|----------|------------------|---------|---------------------|
| 115 | 76 | 5.1 | 40.1% |

# ⓒ MARINATED CRABMEAT SALAD

¼ cup olive oil
3 tablespoons vinegar
Salt to taste
½ teaspoon pepper
¼ teaspoon dry mustard
⅛ teaspoon dried thyme
¼ teaspoon dried basil
2 tablespoons chopped fresh
    parsley

1 large red onion, chopped
2 tablespoons lime juice
1 pound lump or white
    crabmeat, picked for
    bones
1 head lettuce, washed and
    torn into bite-size pieces

Combine all ingredients except crabmeat and lettuce in bowl; mix well. Add crabmeat, tossing gently. Cover bowl with plastic wrap and refrigerate at least 4 hours. Stir occasionally. Before serving, gently toss crabmeat and marinade with lettuce. Serve immediately. Yield: 6 to 8 servings.

**Nutritional Information Per Serving:**

| Calories | Cholesterol (mg) | Fat (g) | % Calories from Fat |
|---|---|---|---|
| 131 | 57 | 8.0 | 55.0% |

# ⓒⒻ CORN SALAD

3 (11-ounce) cans white corn
    (shoe peg)
1 cucumber, peeled and
    chopped
1 bunch green onions,
    chopped

1 (2-ounce) jar diced
    pimientos
1 tomato, chopped
1 green bell pepper, chopped

Combine all ingredients in bowl and toss with Dressing (see recipe below). Refrigerate and serve. Yield: 10 to 12 servings.
*This colorful salad is absolutely delicious.*

**Dressing**
⅓ cup non fat plain yogurt
2 tablespoons fat free
    mayonnaise

1 tablespoon vinegar
½ teaspoon dry mustard

Combine all ingredients, mixing well. Pour over corn mixture.

**Nutritional Information Per Serving:**

| Calories | Cholesterol (mg) | Fat (g) | % Calories from Fat |
|---|---|---|---|
| 63 | <1 | 0.5 | 6.8% |

# ⓒⓕ BLACK BEAN AND CORN SALAD

1 (15-ounce) can black beans,
    drained and rinsed
1 (11-ounce) can golden
    sweet corn, drained
1 tomato, chopped

¼ cup fresh chopped cilantro
⅛ cup chopped red onion
3 tablespoons lemon juice
2 tablespoons olive oil
Salt and pepper to taste

Combine all ingredients in bowl. Refrigerate until ready to serve. Yield: 6 servings.

*A quick salad that adds to any plate and is delicious.*

**Nutritional Information Per Serving:**

| Calories | Cholesterol (mg) | Fat (g) | % Calories from Fat |
|----------|------------------|---------|---------------------|
| 172 | 0 | 5.2 | 27.1% |

# ⓒⓕ BLACK-EYED PEA AND RICE SALAD

1 (6-ounce) box long grain
    and wild rice
2 cups cooked rice
½ cup chopped red onions
¼ cup finely sliced green
    onions
1 red bell pepper, seeded and
    finely chopped

1 green bell pepper, seeded
    and finely chopped
¼ cup chopped fresh parsley
1 clove garlic, minced
2 (15-ounce) cans black-eyed
    peas, rinsed and drained

Cook wild rice according to directions on package omitting margarine. Cool. Combine with remaining ingredients in large bowl. Pour Dressing (see recipe below) over, tossing thoroughly to mix. Refrigerate until serving. Yield: 14 to 16 servings.

*Not only is this salad wonderful, it is colorful too.*

**Dressing**

¼ cup olive oil
⅓ cup red wine vinegar
1 tablespoon Dijon mustard

2 jalapeño peppers, seeded
    and finely chopped
Salt and pepper to taste

Combine all ingredients in small bowl.

**Nutritional Information Per Serving:**

| Calories | Cholesterol (mg) | Fat (g) | % Calories from Fat |
|----------|------------------|---------|---------------------|
| 138 | 0 | 3.8 | 24.5% |

# ⓒ ITALIAN POTATO SALAD

14 small red potatoes (about 1½ pounds)
1 medium red onion, thinly sliced
3 large cloves garlic, minced
2 cucumbers, peeled and sliced in round slices
1 large green bell pepper, seeded and sliced
½ cup chopped parsley
½ teaspoon dried dill weed
½ teaspoon dry mustard
⅓ cup feta cheese, crumbled
¼ cup olive oil
⅓ cup tarragon vinegar
1 tablespoon Worcestershire sauce

Cook potatoes with skins on in pot of boiling water until potatoes are tender when pricked with fork. Cool and cut potatoes in half. Add sliced onion, garlic, sliced cucumber, and sliced green pepper. Sprinkle with parsley and other dry ingredients. Mix together olive oil, vinegar, and Worcestershire sauce and pour over potato mixture, mixing well. Refrigerate. Yield: 4 to 6 servings.
*A delicious alternative to the usual potato salad.*

**Nutritional Information Per Serving:**

| Calories | Cholesterol (mg) | Fat (g) | % Calories from Fat |
|----------|------------------|---------|---------------------|
| 242 | 12 | 12.2 | 45.4% |

# ⓒ ITALIAN POTATOES

2½ pounds red potatoes
¼ cup chopped parsley
¼ cup chopped green onions
3 cloves garlic, minced
¼ teaspoon dry mustard
1 teaspoon sugar
1 teaspoon Worcestershire sauce
⅓ cup olive oil
¼ cup tarragon vinegar
Salt and pepper to taste

Boil potatoes in water to cover in saucepan until done. Peel and cut into chunks. Transfer to a bowl, and sprinkle parsley and green onions over potatoes. In small bowl combine remaining ingredients, mixing well. Pour over potatoes, tossing gently. Let stand at least 4 hours to marinate, stirring every hour. Serve at room temperature. Yield: 8 servings.

**Nutritional Information Per Serving:**

| Calories | Cholesterol (mg) | Fat (g) | % Calories from Fat |
|----------|------------------|---------|---------------------|
| 179 | 0 | 9.1 | 45.9% |

# ©Ⓕ CUCUMBER ONION SALAD

8 to 10 cucumbers, peeled
   and sliced
2 red onions, cut in thin
   rings and torn apart
1 cup non fat plain yogurt

¼ cup vinegar
1 teaspoon salt
1 teaspoon pepper
1 tablespoon dried dill weed

Combine cucumber and onion together in large bowl. In small bowl, mix remaining ingredients. Pour over cucumber onion mixture, mixing well. Refrigerate at least for several hours. Yield: 10 servings.
*A great summer salad with home grown cucumbers.*

**Nutritional Information Per Serving:**

| Calories | Cholesterol (mg) | Fat (g) | % Calories from Fat |
|---|---|---|---|
| 40 | 0.4 | 0.3 | 6.0% |

# © MARINATED SLAW

1 large head cabbage, thinly
   sliced
2 red onions, thinly sliced
1 green bell pepper, chopped
⅓ cup sugar
⅔ cup cider vinegar

½ cup canola oil
1 teaspoon celery seed
Salt and pepper, if desired
1 tablespoon dry mustard
2 tablespoons sugar

In large bowl, combine cabbage, onions, and green pepper. Sprinkle with ⅓ cup sugar and set aside. In small saucepan, combine remaining ingredients and bring to a boil. Pour over cabbage mixture. Mix, cover, and refrigerate until well chilled. Yield: 10 to 12 servings.

**Nutritional Information Per Serving:**

| Calories | Cholesterol (mg) | Fat (g) | % Calories from Fat |
|---|---|---|---|
| 149 | 0 | 9.6 | 58.0% |

# ©Ⓕ ORANGE MANDARIN SALAD

3 (3-ounce) packages orange-
   flavored gelatin
2 cups boiling water
1 pint orange sherbet

2 (11-ounce) cans mandarin
   oranges, use juice from
   one can only

Dissolve orange gelatin in boiling water in bowl. Stir until gelatin is dissolved; add orange sherbet, stirring until melted. Add oranges and juice from one can. Pour into mold and refrigerate. Yield: 10 servings.

**Nutritional Information Per Serving:**

| Calories | Cholesterol (mg) | Fat (g) | % Calories from Fat |
|---|---|---|---|
| 172 | 3 | 0.8 | 4.1% |

## © RASPBERRY SPINACH SALAD

3 tablespoons raspberry
  vinegar
3 tablespoons raspberry jam
¼ cup canola oil
8 cups fresh spinach, rinsed,
  stemmed and torn into
  pieces

¼ cup coarsely chopped
  macadamia nuts
1 cup fresh raspberries
3 kiwis, peeled and sliced

Combine vinegar and jam in food processor or blender. Add oil in a thin stream, blending well; set aside. Carefully toss spinach, nuts, raspberries, and kiwis with dressing. Serve immediately. Yield: 8 servings.
*Not only is this a pretty salad, it is light and delicious.*

**Nutritional Information Per Serving:**

| Calories | Cholesterol (mg) | Fat (g) | % Calories from Fat |
|---|---|---|---|
| 150 | 0 | 10.3 | 62.6% |

## © CAESAR SALAD

2 tablespoons grated
  Parmesan cheese
2 tablespoons water
2 tablespoons red wine
  vinegar
1 teaspoon Worcestershire
  sauce

1 tablespoon olive oil
1 clove garlic
¼ teaspoon dry mustard
1 large bunch romaine
  lettuce, cleaned and torn
  into pieces
⅓ cup croutons, optional

Combine all ingredients together except lettuce in food processor and blend until smooth. Pour over lettuce, tossing well. Top with croutons, if desired. Yield: 4 servings.
*You will not miss the "real thing" with this duplication.*

**Nutritional Information Per Serving:**

| Calories | Cholesterol (mg) | Fat (g) | % Calories from Fat |
|---|---|---|---|
| 71 | 2 | 4.7 | 60.0% |

## ⓒ ORANGE ALMOND SALAD

¼ cup canola oil
¼ cup red wine vinegar
1 tablespoon lemon juice
2 tablespoons sugar
½ teaspoon salt
½ teaspoon dry mustard

1 (11-ounce) can mandarin
    oranges, drained
¼ cup slivered almonds,
    toasted
1 head red leaf or butter
    lettuce

Combine all dressing ingredients together in jar with lid. Shake and refrigerate until ready to use. Toss mandarin oranges and almonds with cleaned torn lettuce. Before serving pour dressing over salad, tossing gently. Yield: 4 servings.

**Nutritional Information Per Serving:**

| Calories | Cholesterol (mg) | Fat (g) | % Calories from Fat |
|---|---|---|---|
| 223 | 0 | 18.5 | 74.3% |

## ⓒⒻ PRETZEL STRAWBERRY GELATIN

4 tablespoons light
    margarine, melted
2 tablespoons light brown
    sugar
2 cups crushed pretzels
1 (6-ounce) package
    strawberry gelatin
2 cups boiling water

3 cups sliced fresh
    strawberries
4 ounces light cream cheese
½ cup sugar
1 envelope dry whipped
    topping mix
½ cup skim milk

Combine margarine, brown sugar and pretzels and press into a 13x9x2-inch baking pan. Bake at 350 degrees for 10 minutes; cool. Meanwhile dissolve strawberry gelatin in boiling water, stirring until dissolved. Add sliced strawberries. Cool in refrigerator until gelatin begins to set. In mixer, beat cream cheese with sugar. Prepare whipped topping according to directions on package substituting skim milk. Fold into cream cheese mixture. Spread over cooled crust. Pour semi-firm gelatin mixture over cream cheese layer. Refrigerate until congealed. Yield: 16 servings.
*This is so delicious that you can even serve it for dessert!*

**Nutritional Information Per Serving:**

| Calories | Cholesterol (mg) | Fat (g) | % Calories from Fat |
|---|---|---|---|
| 145 | 4 | 4.1 | 25.3% |

# ⓒⒻ BLUEBERRY AND LEMON MOLD

1 (3-ounce) package
   raspberry gelatin
1 cup boiling water
1 (16½-ounce) can
   blueberries
1 (3-ounce) package lemon
   gelatin

1 cup boiling water
1 cup plain non fat yogurt
1 (20-ounce) can crushed
   pineapple, in its own
   juice

To raspberry gelatin, add 1 cup boiling water. Stir and add juice drained from blueberries. Let cool and add blueberries. Pour mixture into mold. Refrigerate until firm. Dissolve lemon gelatin in 1 cup boiling water. Cool and add yogurt. Mix and refrigerate until almost set. Drain pineapple and add to lemon gelatin mixture. Pour into mold on top of raspberry layer. Yield: 8 servings.
*Not only is this mold colorful, it is wonderful too.*

**Nutritional Information Per Serving:**

| Calories | Cholesterol (mg) | Fat (g) | % Calories from Fat |
|---|---|---|---|
| 189 | 0.5 | 0.3 | 1.4% |

# ⓒ CRANBERRY MOLD

1 (16-ounce) package fresh
   cranberries
1 whole orange
½ cup chopped pecans

1 cup crushed pineapple, in
   its own juices, drained
1 (3-ounce) package
   raspberry gelatin
1 cup boiling water

Combine cranberries, orange, and pecans in food processor and mix until mixture is chopped finely. Add crushed pineapple. Dissolve gelatin in boiling water, stirring, until dissolved. Combine with cranberry mixture, mixing well. Pour into a 5-cup mold. Refrigerate until firm. Yield: 10 servings.
*A great holiday mold! For even lower fat content, leave out pecans.*

**Nutritional Information Per Serving:**

| Calories | Cholesterol (mg) | Fat (g) | % Calories from Fat |
|---|---|---|---|
| 111 | 0 | 3.8 | 30.8% |

## ©Ⓕ MANGO SALAD

3 (3-ounce) packages lemon
  gelatin
3 cups boiling water

1 (32-ounce) jar mangos with
  juice
1 (8-ounce) package light
  cream cheese

Dissolve gelatin in boiling water. Place mangos with juice in food processor. Gradually add cream cheese and blend well. Stir in gelatin mixture. Pour into a 2-quart mold coated with no stick cooking spray. Refrigerate until set. Serve with Sauce (see recipe below). Yield: 12 servings.

**Sauce**
1 egg, slightly beaten
⅔ cup sugar

Juice of lemon
Juice of orange

Place all ingredients in small saucepan and bring to boil; boil 5 to 7 minutes. Remove from heat and cool. Store sauce in refrigerator and take out 30 minutes before serving to soften.
*The sauce keeps in refrigerator a long time. If have extra, serve over frozen yogurt.*

**Nutritional Information Per Serving:**

| Calories | Cholesterol (mg) | Fat (g) | % Calories from Fat |
|---|---|---|---|
| 218 | 28 | 3.9 | 16.3% |

## ©Ⓕ CHERRY RASPBERRY MOLD

1 (10-ounce) package frozen
  raspberries in syrup
½ cup currant jelly
2 cups water
2 (3-ounce) packages
  raspberry gelatin

½ cup sherry
¼ cup lemon juice
1 (16-ounce) can pitted dark
  cherries, drained

Drain raspberries, reserving syrup. In saucepan, combine jelly and ½ cup water. Heat, stirring, until jelly melts. Add remaining 1½ cups water and gelatin. Heat only until gelatin is dissolved. Remove from heat. Add sherry, lemon juice, and reserved raspberry juice. Chill until partially set and fold in raspberries and cherries. Pour into mold and refrigerate until firm. Yield: 8 servings.

**Nutritional Information Per Serving:**

| Calories | Cholesterol (mg) | Fat (g) | % Calories from Fat |
|---|---|---|---|
| 238 | 0 | 0.2 | 0.6% |

PASTA

OLIV
OIL

M.HANSBROUGH

# ©Ⓕ GARDEN LINGUINE

1 (14½-ounce) can chicken
broth with reduced fat
⅔ cup white wine
1 bunch broccoli, flowerets
only
2 carrots, peeled and sliced
1 pound fresh asparagus,
trimmed and sliced
1 tablespoon olive oil
1 bunch green onions, thinly
sliced
3 cloves garlic, minced

½ pound mushrooms, sliced
1 red bell pepper, julienne
sliced
1¼ cups skim milk
1 teaspoon dried basil
½ teaspoon dried oregano
¼ cup chopped parsley
Salt and pepper to taste
1 (12-ounce) package
linguine
⅓ cup grated Parmesan
cheese

In small saucepan, combine broth and wine. Boil until reduced to half. Cook broccoli, carrots, and asparagus in microwave until crisp tender. In large skillet, heat olive oil and sauté green onion, garlic, mushrooms, red pepper, broccoli, carrots and asparagus until soft. Add reduced broth, milk, basil, oregano, parsley, and salt and pepper to taste. Simmer for 10 minutes. Cook pasta according to directions on package omitting salt and oil. Drain well. Combine with vegetables, tossing gently. Sprinkle with Parmesan cheese and serve. Yield: 6 servings. *Great and tasty!*

**Nutritional Information Per Serving:**

| Calories | Cholesterol (mg) | Fat (g) | % Calories from Fat |
|---|---|---|---|
| 343 | 53 | 7.0 | 18.3% |

# ©Ⓕ VERMICELLI WITH FRESH TOMATOES

2 pounds tomatoes, peeled
and chopped
1 onion, chopped
2 cloves garlic, minced
1 tablespoon dried basil
⅓ cup olive oil

Salt and pepper to taste
1 (16-ounce) package
vermicelli
1 cup shredded reduced fat
Cheddar cheese

Mix tomatoes, onion, garlic, basil, olive oil, salt and pepper together in bowl. Let stand at room temperature for one hour. Cook vermicelli according to directions on package omitting salt and oil. Drain and toss with sauce. Sprinkle with cheese and serve. Yield: 8 servings. *An outstanding recipe to use with fresh tomatoes.*

**Nutritional Information Per Serving:**

| Calories | Cholesterol (mg) | Fat (g) | % Calories from Fat |
|---|---|---|---|
| 369 | 3 | 11.4 | 27.8% |

# ©Ⓕ FETTUCCINE WITH HERBS

1 (8-ounce) package
   fettuccine
2 tablespoons olive oil
3 cloves garlic, minced
½ cup chopped parsley
1 teaspoon dried basil

2 tomatoes, cored and
   chopped or 2 tablespoons
   sun dried tomatoes
   (rehydrated)
Pepper to taste

Cook fettuccine according to directions on package omitting salt. Drain; set aside. In large pan, heat olive oil and sauté garlic. Add pasta, herbs, and chopped tomato. Season to taste with pepper. Yield: 4 to 6 servings. *In the summer, use fresh tomatoes and fresh basil and you have a real hit.*

**Nutritional Information Per Serving:**

| Calories | Cholesterol (mg) | Fat (g) | % Calories from Fat |
|----------|------------------|---------|---------------------|
| 183      | 32               | 6.1     | 30.0%               |

# ©Ⓕ GARDEN PASTA MEDLEY

1 small zucchini, cut into
   julienne strips
1 bunch broccoli, flowerets
   only
1 pound fresh mushrooms,
   cut in half
1 pint cherry tomatoes, cut
   in half

2 cloves garlic, minced
1 teaspoon dried basil
1 teaspoon dried oregano
¼ cup chopped parsley
Salt and pepper to taste
½ cup plain non fat yogurt
2 tablespoons olive oil
6 ounces corkscrew pasta

Combine all ingredients except pasta in large bowl, tossing well. Cover and let stand at room temperature one hour. Cook pasta according to directions on package omitting salt and oil. In large skillet, combine pasta and vegetable mixture. Cook over medium heat, stirring, about 5 to 10 minutes or until thoroughly heated. Serve immediately. Yield: 12 servings.
*Great!*

**Nutritional Information Per Serving:**

| Calories | Cholesterol (mg) | Fat (g) | % Calories from Fat |
|----------|------------------|---------|---------------------|
| 108      | 0                | 2.9     | 24.5%               |

## ⓒⒻ TRI-COLORED ROTINI
## WITH RED SAUCE

1 (12-ounce) package tri-
   colored rotini
1 teaspoon olive oil
½ cup chopped onion
2 cloves garlic, minced
2 (14½-ounce) cans Italian-
   style whole tomatoes,
   chopped

¼ cup chopped parsley
2 teaspoons dried basil
4 ounces part-skim
   mozzarella cheese,
   shredded
Pepper to taste

Cook pasta according to directions on package omitting salt; drain. Meanwhile, coat a large pan with no stick cooking spray and heat olive oil. Sauté onion and garlic just until tender. Add tomatoes, parsley, and basil; simmer 15 minutes. Combine drained pasta with tomato sauce and cheese, tossing until cheese is melted. Sprinkle with pepper and serve. Yield: 4 to 6 servings.
*Delicious and easy.*

### Nutritional Information Per Serving:

| Calories | Cholesterol (mg) | Fat (g) | % Calories from Fat |
|---|---|---|---|
| 302 | 10 | 5.2 | 15.6% |

## ⓒⒻ FETTUCCINE WITH SUN DRIED
## TOMATOES

½ pound fettuccine
¼ cup grated Parmesan
   cheese
¼ cup shredded part-skim
   mozzarella cheese
1 tablespoon olive oil

2 cloves garlic, minced
2 tablespoons chopped sun
   dried tomatoes,
   rehydrated according to
   package directions
¼ teaspoon pepper

Prepare fettuccine according to directions on package omitting salt and oil. Drain and toss with all ingredients. Yield: 4 servings.

### Nutritional Information Per Serving:

| Calories | Cholesterol (mg) | Fat (g) | % Calories from Fat |
|---|---|---|---|
| 269 | 56 | 8.1 | 27.0% |

## ⓒⒻ PERFECT PASTA

12 ounces angel hair pasta
3 tablespoons olive oil
2 cloves garlic, minced

1 tablespoon finely chopped
parsley

Cook pasta according to directions on package, omitting salt and oil. Drain and set aside. In a small pan, combine all remaining ingredients and sauté for a few minutes. Pour over cooked pasta and toss. Serve immediately. Yield: 6 to 8 servings.
*Wonderful served with Italian Shrimp!*

**Nutritional Information Per Serving:**

| Calories | Cholesterol (mg) | Fat (g) | % Calories from Fat |
|---|---|---|---|
| 215 | 0 | 5.9 | 24.6% |

## ⓒⒻ OVERNIGHT BROCCOLI LASAGNE

1 green bell pepper, seeded
   and chopped
1 onion, chopped
2 cloves garlic, chopped
2 tablespoons flour
1 teaspoon dried oregano
½ teaspoon dried basil
Salt and pepper to taste
¾ cup skim milk
2 (10-ounce) packages frozen
   chopped broccoli, thawed
   and drained

1½ cups low-fat cottage
   cheese
1 egg white
1 tablespoon skim milk
5 lasagne noodles
1 cup shredded part-skim
   mozzarella cheese
2 tablespoons grated
   Parmesan cheese

Coat a large skillet with no stick cooking spray. Heat and add green pepper, onion, and garlic. Sauté until tender. Add flour, oregano, basil, and salt and pepper to taste. Cook 1 minute, stirring constantly. Gradually add ¾ cup milk, stirring constantly. Cook, stirring, until mixture is thickened. Stir in broccoli; set aside. Combine cottage cheese, egg white, and 1 tablespoon milk in food processor until smooth. Coat a 9-inch square baking pan with no stick cooking spray. Spoon ⅓ broccoli mixture into dish. Break noodles in half crosswise. Place 4 noodle halves over broccoli mixture. Spread half of cottage cheese mixture over noodles; top with mozzarella cheese. Repeat layers, ending with broccoli mixture. Cover and refrigerate at least 8 hours. Sprinkle with Parmesan cheese. Bake, uncovered, at 375 degrees for 40 minutes or until bubbly. Let stand 10 minutes before cutting. Yield: 6 to 8 servings.

**Nutritional Information Per Serving:**

| Calories | Cholesterol (mg) | Fat (g) | % Calories from Fat |
|---|---|---|---|
| 187 | 27 | 4.3 | 20.9% |

## Ⓒ Ⓕ VEGETABLE LASAGNE

1 onion, chopped
3 cloves garlic, minced
1 green bell pepper, chopped
1 (6-ounce) can tomato paste
1 (10-ounce) can diced
   tomatoes and green
   chilies
1 (10-ounce) can stewed
   tomatoes
1 (11.5-ounce) can tomato
   juice
1 teaspoon dried basil
1 teaspoon dried oregano

1 teaspoon dried thyme
1½ tablespoons red wine
   vinegar
1 bay leaf
½ pound fresh mushrooms,
   sliced
½ cup shredded peeled
   carrots
1 bunch broccoli flowerets
½ pound lasagne noodles
1½ cups shredded part-skim
   mozzarella cheese

Coat a large skillet with no stick cooking spray and add onion, garlic, and green pepper. Sauté until tender. Add tomato paste, diced tomatoes and green chilies, stewed tomatoes, and tomato juice bringing to a boil. Add remaining ingredients (except lasagne noodles and cheese), lower heat, and simmer at least 30 minutes or until vegetables are tender and sauce has slightly thickened. Discard bay leaf. Cook lasagne noodles according to directions on package omitting salt and oil; drain. In a 13x9x2-inch baking dish, spoon vegetable sauce along bottom. Layer one-third each of lasagne noodles, Cheese Mixture (see recipe below), vegetable sauce, and mozzarella cheese. Repeat layers. Bake at 350 degrees, covered, for 30 minutes. Let stand 10 minutes before cutting. Yield: 12 servings.
*Serve with a Caesar Salad to complete your meal.*

**Cheese Mixture**
2 cups low fat cottage cheese
1 egg white
2 tablespoons chopped
   parsley

¼ cup grated Parmesan
   cheese

Combine all ingredients in food processor blending well.

**Nutritional Information Per Serving:**

| Calories | Cholesterol (mg) | Fat (g) | % Calories from Fat |
|----------|------------------|---------|---------------------|
| 179 | 29 | 4.4 | 22.0% |

## ♡ FETTUCCINE AND BROCCOLI

1 large bunch broccoli
⅛ cup olive oil
1½ tablespoons minced
   garlic
½ cup chicken broth
2 tablespoons light
   margarine

1 teaspoon dried basil
½ teaspoon dried oregano
Salt and pepper to taste
12 ounces fettuccine
⅓ cup grated Parmesan
   cheese

Cut stems off broccoli. Steam flowerets in ½ cup boiling water, covered, in microwave or on top of stove for 5 minutes, until crisp tender. Drain. When cool, cut into ½-inch pieces. In saucepan, heat oil and sauté garlic until golden. Add chicken broth and margarine. Stir in basil, oregano, salt and pepper. Add broccoli. Cook fettuccine according to directions on package omitting oil and salt; drain. Stir broccoli with sauce into cooked pasta. Add Parmesan cheese, tossing to mix well. Yield: 6 to 8 servings. *This makes a wonderful pasta dish.*

**Nutritional Information Per Serving:**

| Calories | Cholesterol (mg) | Fat (g) | % Calories from Fat |
|---|---|---|---|
| 216 | 39 | 7.5 | 31.4% |

## ♡♡ BROCCOLI STUFFED SHELLS

1 (16-ounce) package frozen
   chopped broccoli
1 (15-ounce) container part-
   skim ricotta cheese
1 egg white
¼ cup grated Parmesan
   cheese
¼ teaspoon pepper

¼ teaspoon nutmeg
½ teaspoon dried oregano
1 (12-ounce) package jumbo
   shells
3 cups tomato sauce
1 cup shredded part-skim
   mozzarella cheese

Cook broccoli according to directions on package; cool. Combine broccoli, with ricotta, egg white, Parmesan cheese, pepper, nutmeg, and oregano, stirring until well combined. Cook shells according to directions on package omitting salt and oil. Stuff each cooked shell with 1 heaping tablespoon of the broccoli mixture. Place stuffed shells in oblong dish. Spoon sauce over shells. Sprinkle with mozzarella cheese. Bake at 375 degrees for 30 minutes. Yield: 8 servings.
*These shells freeze well.*

**Nutritional Information Per Serving:**

| Calories | Cholesterol (mg) | Fat (g) | % Calories from Fat |
|---|---|---|---|
| 317 | 24 | 7.7 | 22.0% |

## Ⓕ ANGEL HAIR WITH CRABMEAT

1 (8-ounce) package angel
   hair pasta
2 tablespoons olive oil
½ cup chopped onion
3 cloves garlic, minced
½ pound mushrooms, sliced

2 tablespoons chopped
   parsley
1 teaspoon dried basil
1 teaspoon dried oregano
1 teaspoon lemon juice
1 pound white crabmeat
Salt and pepper to taste

Cook pasta according to directions on package omitting oil. Drain and set aside. Meanwhile, coat a large skillet with no stick cooking spray and heat oil. Sauté onion and garlic until tender. Add mushrooms, seasonings, and lemon juice, cooking until mushrooms are tender. Add crabmeat, stirring gently. Add pasta tossing to mix well. Season to taste. Yield: 4 to 6 servings.

**Nutritional Information Per Serving:**

| Calories | Cholesterol (mg) | Fat (g) | % Calories from Fat |
|---|---|---|---|
| 279 | 76 | 6.9 | 22.2% |

## Ⓕ SHRIMP AND ANGEL HAIR

5 ounces Canadian bacon,
   diced
1 green bell pepper, chopped
2 onions, chopped
3 stalks celery, chopped
5 cloves garlic, minced
2 teaspoons dried basil
2 teaspoons dried oregano
1 bay leaf

¼ cup flour
1 (10-ounce) can chopped
   green chilies and
   tomatoes
2 pounds shrimp, peeled
1 (16-ounce) package angel
   hair pasta
1 large bunch green onions,
   thinly sliced

In large pot coated with no stick cooking spray, cook Canadian bacon until begins to brown. Add green pepper, onions, celery, garlic, basil, oregano, and bay leaf sautéing until tender. Gradually add flour and green chilies and tomatoes, stirring. Add shrimp, cooking until pink and done, still stirring. Meanwhile, cook angel hair according to directions on package omitting oil; drain. Toss with shrimp mixture and add green onions. Yield: 8 to 10 servings.
*One you will not want to miss!*

**Nutritional Information Per Serving:**

| Calories | Cholesterol (mg) | Fat (g) | % Calories from Fat |
|---|---|---|---|
| 291 | 151 | 4.1 | 12.6% |

# ♡Ⓕ SHRIMP SCAMPI PASTA

¼ cup light margarine
2 tablespoons garlic, finely
   chopped
1 bunch green onions,
   chopped
1 green bell pepper, chopped
1 red bell pepper, chopped
1 teaspoon dried basil

2 teaspoons dried oregano
1 pound medium shrimp,
   peeled
1 lemon, juiced
½ cup dry white wine
1 (8-ounce) package
   fettuccine

In large pan, melt margarine on medium heat. Sauté garlic, green onions, and peppers until tender. Add basil, oregano, and shrimp. Cook 5 minutes, stirring occasionally. Add lemon juice and wine. Simmer until shrimp are done. Cook fettuccine according to directions on package omitting oil; drain. Toss shrimp mixture with pasta. Yield: 4 to 6 servings.

*This pasta dish is a real winner and takes little time to make.*

**Nutritional Information Per Serving:**

| Calories | Cholesterol (mg) | Fat (g) | % Calories from Fat |
|---|---|---|---|
| 251 | 117 | 6.2 | 22.2% |

# ♡Ⓕ SHRIMP PRIMAVERA

1 (16-ounce) package angel
   hair pasta
1 large carrot, peeled and
   sliced in short strips
1 bunch broccoli, flowerets
   only
3 cloves garlic, minced
3 tablespoons finely chopped
   parsley
1 bunch green onions, finely
   chopped

2 pounds shrimp, peeled and
   deveined
3 tablespoons olive oil
¼ teaspoon hot sauce
Salt and pepper to taste
⅔ cup cherry tomatoes,
   quartered
½ cup grated Parmesan
   cheese

Cook pasta according to directions on package. Drain and set aside. In large pan, sauté carrots, broccoli, garlic, parsley, green onions, and shrimp in olive oil. Cook until shrimp are pink and vegetables are tender. Add seasonings. Toss with tomatoes, cheese, and cooked pasta. Yield: 6 to 8 servings.

*Easy, colorful, and excellent.*

**Nutritional Information Per Serving:**

| Calories | Cholesterol (mg) | Fat (g) | % Calories from Fat |
|---|---|---|---|
| 522 | 131 | 12.2 | 21.1% |

## Ⓕ SHRIMP FETTUCCINE

1 pound large shrimp, peeled
¼ cup white wine
1 bunch green onions, finely
    chopped
2 cloves garlic, minced
½ pound mushrooms, sliced
1 (6-ounce) package frozen
    snow peas

3 tablespoons light
    margarine
1 (8-ounce) package
    fettuccine
4 tablespoons finely chopped
    parsley
½ cup finely grated Romano
    cheese

Marinate shrimp in white wine for 1 hour. In large skillet, stir fry onions, garlic, mushrooms, and snow peas in margarine. When vegetables are crisp tender, add shrimp and sauté until shrimp are pink. Meanwhile, prepare fettuccine according to directions on package omitting oil. Drain. Add fettuccine to shrimp mixture with parsley and Romano cheese, tossing gently. Yield: 6 to 8 servings.
*Another great one-meal dish.*

**Nutritional Information Per Serving:**

| Calories | Cholesterol (mg) | Fat (g) | % Calories from Fat |
|---|---|---|---|
| 208 | 94 | 5.7 | 24.8% |

## Ⓕ SHRIMP AND VEGETABLE PASTA TOSS

1 pound uncooked shrimp,
    peeled
1 zucchini, thinly sliced
1 carrot, peeled and
    shredded
½ cup finely chopped green
    onions

⅛ teaspoon red pepper
8 ounces ziti pasta
½ cup evaporated skimmed
    milk
⅔ cup low fat 1% cottage
    cheese, puréed

Coat a skillet with no stick cooking spray, and add the shrimp, zucchini, carrots, green onions, and red pepper. Cook, stirring, until the shrimp are done, turning pink. Cook pasta according to directions on package omitting oil; drain. Stir cooked pasta into vegetable mixture, tossing until well mixed. Remove from skillet and transfer to dish. In same skillet, add milk and cottage cheese; bring to a boil. Cook, stirring, until the sauce thickens. Return shrimp pasta mixture to skillet cooking until thoroughly heated. Yield: 4 to 6 servings.
*This dish will be repeated many times because it is quick and is quite a presentation.*

**Nutritional Information Per Serving:**

| Calories | Cholesterol (mg) | Fat (g) | % Calories from Fat |
|---|---|---|---|
| 258 | 106 | 2.1 | 7.5% |

# SHRIMP AND FETA WITH PASTA

1½ pounds shrimp, cooked
   and peeled
½ pound feta cheese,
   crumbled
1 bunch green onions,
   chopped

2 teaspoons dried oregano
4 tomatoes, peeled, cored,
   and chopped
6 black olives, sliced thinly
Salt and pepper to taste
10 ounces fettuccine

In large bowl, combine the shrimp, cheese, onions, oregano, tomatoes, olives and salt and pepper to taste. Let stand at room temperature for at least 1 hour. Cook pasta according to directions on package omitting oil. Drain. Add pasta to shrimp mixture, tossing. Serve immediately. Yield: 6 to 8 servings.

**Nutritional Information Per Serving:**

| Calories | Cholesterol (mg) | Fat (g) | % Calories from Fat |
|---|---|---|---|
| 259 | 115 | 8.9 | 30.8% |

# SEAFOOD PASTA CASSEROLE

1 (16-ounce) package spiral
   pasta
1 (8-ounce) package light
   cream cheese
1 cup non fat plain yogurt
1 (15-ounce) container part
   skim ricotta cheese
½ cup chopped green onions
1½ teaspoons dried basil

¼ teaspoon garlic powder
1 (2-ounce) jar diced
   pimiento, undrained
1 pound cooked shrimp,
   peeled
1 pound lump crabmeat
1 cup shredded Monterey
   Jack cheese

Cook pasta according to directions on package omitting oil. Drain and set aside. Combine cream cheese and next six ingredients, stirring well. Coat a 2-quart baking dish with no stick cooking spray. Place half of pasta in baking dish. Sprinkle half of shrimp and crabmeat over pasta. Spoon half of cheese mixture over seafood. Repeat layers with remaining ingredients. Bake at 350 degrees for 30 minutes. Sprinkle with shredded Monterey Jack cheese and bake an additional 5 minutes or until cheese is melted. Let stand 10 minutes before cutting. Yield: 8 to 10 servings.

**Nutritional Information Per Serving:**

| Calories | Cholesterol (mg) | Fat (g) | % Calories from Fat |
|---|---|---|---|
| 416 | 193 | 14.2 | 30.7% |

# Ⓕ SEAFOOD LASAGNE

2 (14½-ounce) cans whole
    tomatoes, undrained
1 cup sliced fresh
    mushrooms
1 teaspoon dried oregano
1 clove garlic, minced
Salt and pepper to taste
1 pound cooked and peeled
    small shrimp
2 tablespoons light
    margarine

2 tablespoons flour
1¾ cups skim milk
1 cup shredded reduced fat
    Swiss cheese
1 pound white crabmeat
¼ cup dry white wine
8 lasagne noodles, cooked
    according to directions
    on package omitting oil
    and salt

In saucepan, combine tomatoes, mushrooms, oregano, garlic, and salt and pepper. Bring to a boil. Reduce heat and simmer, uncovered, about 20 minutes or until thickened. Stir in shrimp. Set aside. In another saucepan, melt margarine and stir in flour. Add milk and cook, stirring constantly, over medium heat until thickened and bubbly. Stir in Swiss cheese until melted. Add crabmeat and wine, stirring carefully. In a 13x9x2-inch pan coated with no stick cooking spray, layer half of the shrimp sauce, half of the noodles, and half of the cheese sauce. Repeat layering. Bake at 350 degrees for 25 minutes or until thoroughly heated. Let stand before serving. Yield: 8 servings.

*Yes, this recipe does use several pots, but it is one that you will want to try. Freeze it with success.*

**Nutritional Information Per Serving:**

| Calories | Cholesterol (mg) | Fat (g) | % Calories from Fat |
|---|---|---|---|
| 308 | 218 | 5.8 | 17.1% |

# ⓕ CRAWFISH FETTUCCINE

1 pound fettuccine
¼ cup margarine
1 large onion, chopped
2 green bell peppers,
  chopped
1 red bell pepper, chopped
3 cloves garlic, minced
¼ cup flour
1½ cups skim milk

½ pound light pasteurized
  processed cheese spread
2 pounds crawfish tails
2 tablespoons chopped
  parsley
1 tablespoon Worcestershire
  sauce
¼ teaspoon cayenne

Cook fettuccine according to directions on package omitting salt and oil. Drain; set aside. In large pot, melt margarine and sauté vegetables until tender. Add flour, stirring until mixed. Gradually add milk, stirring until smooth. Add cheese, stirring until melted. Rinse crawfish tails; drain well. Add crawfish and remaining seasoning. Toss with pasta. Transfer into a casserole dish and bake at 350 degrees for 20 minutes. Yield: 10 servings.
*With this delicious light dish, you will get requests for seconds!*

**Nutritional Information Per Serving:**

| Calories | Cholesterol (mg) | Fat (g) | % Calories from Fat |
|---|---|---|---|
| 382 | 209 | 9.3 | 21.9% |

# ⓕ CRAWFISH CAPELLINI

1 pound capellini pasta
2 onions, chopped
1 green bell pepper, chopped
4 cloves garlic, minced
3 tablespoons olive oil
2 cups chicken broth

1 pound crawfish tails,
  rinsed and drained
2 tablespoons finely chopped
  parsley
4 green onions, chopped

Cook capellini according to directions on package omitting salt and oil. Drain well. In a large, deep skillet sauté onions, green pepper, and garlic in olive oil until tender. Add chicken broth and cook for 15 minutes. Add crawfish, parsley, and green onions cooking until thoroughly heated. Serve over pasta or toss together if desired. Yield: 6 to 8 servings.
*Crawfish lovers will want to try this one.*

**Nutritional Information Per Serving:**

| Calories | Cholesterol (mg) | Fat (g) | % Calories from Fat |
|---|---|---|---|
| 365 | 102 | 7.6 | 18.7% |

# ©Ⓕ CRAWFISH OVER ANGEL HAIR PASTA

¼ cup light margarine
1 bunch green onions,
    chopped
1 onion, chopped
1 green bell pepper, chopped
1 pound crawfish tails

1 fresh tomato, chopped
¾ cup evaporated skimmed
    milk
½ teaspoon dried thyme
¼ cup grated Romano cheese
½ pound angel hair pasta

In a large skillet, melt margarine and sauté green onion, onion, and green pepper until tender. Add crawfish tails and sauté until liquid begins to evaporate. Stir in chopped tomato and cook a few minutes longer. Add evaporated milk, thyme, and cheese, cooking until thick. Cook pasta according to directions on package omitting oil. Serve crawfish over cooked angel hair pasta. Yield: 4 to 6 servings.
*You'll be a real winner with this dish.*

**Nutritional Information Per Serving:**

| Calories | Cholesterol (mg) | Fat (g) | % Calories from Fat |
|---|---|---|---|
| 294 | 60 | 5.9 | 18.0% |

# Ⓕ SCALLOPS PROVENÇALE WITH PASTA

3 tablespoons olive oil
1 pound sea scallops,
    trimmed and quartered
1 bunch green onions,
    chopped
3 cloves garlic, minced
2 teaspoons dried basil
1 teaspoon dried tarragon
¼ teaspoon dried thyme

½ cup dry white wine
4 cups well drained, crushed
    canned tomatoes
½ cup evaporated skimmed
    milk
1 teaspoon sugar
Salt and pepper to taste
1 (16-ounce) package
    linguine

Heat olive oil in large skillet and sauté scallops until barely firm, about two minutes. Using slotted spoon, transfer to bowl. Add green onions and sauté until tender. Stir in garlic and herbs; cook one minute. Add wine and cook until heated. Stir in tomatoes and bring to a boil, lower heat cooking until thickens. Stir in milk and sugar. Season to taste with salt and pepper. Return scallops to pan, mixing gently. Meanwhile, cook pasta according to directions on package omitting oil. Drain and toss with scallop mixture. Yield: 6 servings.
*The scallop part can be prepared one day ahead. Reheat slowly before tossing with hot pasta.*

**Nutritional Information Per Serving:**

| Calories | Cholesterol (mg) | Fat (g) | % Calories from Fat |
|---|---|---|---|
| 518 | 102 | 12.1 | 20.9% |

# ⓒⓕ SCALLOP, PEPPER, AND PASTA TOSS

1 tablespoon olive oil
1 clove garlic, minced
½ cup chopped red onion
4 green onions, thinly sliced
1 red bell pepper, julienne
   sliced
1 green bell pepper, julienne
   sliced
8 ounces bay scallops

1 (8-ounce) package frozen
   corn
2 tablespoons lemon juice
1 teaspoon dried basil
2 tablespoons finely chopped
   parsley
Pepper to taste
1 (8-ounce) package
   fettuccine

Coat a large skillet with no stick cooking spray and heat olive oil. Sauté garlic, onions, and peppers until tender. Increase heat; add scallops and corn. Stir-fry until scallops are opaque. Stir in lemon juice, basil, parsley, and pepper. Cook fettuccine according to directions on package omitting salt and oil. Toss scallop mixture with pasta; serve. Yield: 4 to 6 servings.

**Nutritional Information Per Serving:**

| Calories | Cholesterol (mg) | Fat (g) | % Calories from Fat |
|---|---|---|---|
| 235 | 45 | 4.4 | 16.7% |

# ⓕ CHICKEN AND LINGUINE

2 tablespoons margarine
1 medium onion, thinly
   sliced in rings
2 cloves garlic, minced
1 teaspoon dried basil
¼ teaspoon crushed red
   pepper

1½ pounds chicken breasts,
   cut into pieces
8 ounces linguine
¼ cup freshly grated
   Parmesan cheese
Salt and pepper, if desired

Melt margarine in a 13x9x2-inch baking dish in a preheated 400 degree oven. Remove pan from oven and stir in onion, garlic, basil and red pepper. Roll chicken pieces in margarine mixture and leave in pan. Return pan to oven and bake chicken, uncovered, about 45 minutes. Approximately 10 minutes before chicken is done, cook linguine according to package directions without oil. Drain. When chicken is done, add pasta, cheese, salt, and pepper to dish, mixing well. Yield: 4 servings. *Very good and light.*

**Nutritional Information Per Serving:**

| Calories | Cholesterol (mg) | Fat (g) | % Calories from Fat |
|---|---|---|---|
| 468 | 151 | 11.4 | 21.9% |

# Ⓕ GREEK LEMON CHICKEN OVER PASTA

**Marinade**

1 cup white wine
2 tablespoons olive oil
¼ cup fresh lemon juice
½ teaspoon salt

1 teaspoon pepper
4 cloves garlic, minced
8 skinless, boneless chicken
  breasts

In bowl, combine all ingredients except chicken. Mix well. Pound chicken breasts slightly and place in shallow casserole. Pour marinade over to cover and refrigerate up to 12 hours. Prepare chicken (see recipe below).

**Chicken**

2 tablespoons olive oil
2 tablespoons light
  margarine
2 tablespoons flour
1 tablespoon prepared
  mustard
½ cup skim milk
1 tablespoon fresh lemon
  juice

1 teaspoon dried dill weed
¼ cup finely chopped parsley
1 cup non fat plain yogurt
½ cup crumbled feta cheese
1 pound angel hair pasta
½ cup shredded Muenster
  cheese

Discard marinade. Coat a skillet with no stick cooking spray and heat oil. Sauté chicken until tender. Slice and set aside. In saucepan, melt 2 tablespoons margarine; blend in flour. Add mustard and slowly add milk, stirring constantly until thick and smooth. Remove from heat and add lemon juice, dill weed, and parsley. Stir in yogurt, mixing well. Cook pasta according to directions on package omitting salt and oil. Gently toss pasta with sauce and feta cheese. Place in 13x9x2-inch baking dish, and top with sliced chicken breasts and Muenster cheese. Broil until cheese is golden. Yield: 8 servings.
*Excellent choice!*

**Nutritional Information Per Serving:**

| Calories | Cholesterol (mg) | Fat (g) | % Calories from Fat |
|---|---|---|---|
| 504 | 89 | 14.6 | 26.1% |

# Ⓕ CHICKEN ROTINI

2½ pounds boneless, skinless
    chicken breasts
1 stalk celery
1 onion, quartered
¼ teaspoon cumin
Salt and pepper, if desired
1 (16-ounce) package rotini
    pasta
3 tablespoons olive oil
3 cloves garlic, minced
2 onions, chopped
2 stalks celery, chopped
1 large green pepper,
    chopped
½ pound fresh mushrooms,
    sliced
3 tablespoons flour
1 (12-ounce) can evaporated
    skimmed milk
2 cups chicken broth,
    reserved from boiling
    chicken
1 (8-ounce) can sliced water
    chestnuts, drained
1 tablespoon Worcestershire
    sauce
1 teaspoon white pepper
2 tablespoons sherry
1 (8-ounce) package reduced
    fat sharp Cheddar
    cheese, shredded

Place chicken in large pot and cover with water. Add 1 stalk celery, 1 quartered onion, cumin, and salt and pepper. Bring to a boil, reduce heat and cook until chicken is tender. Reserve broth and discard vegetables. Cook rotini according to directions on package omitting salt if desired. In a large, heavy pot, add olive oil and sauté garlic, onion, celery, green pepper, and mushrooms until tender. Add flour, stirring for one minute. Gradually add milk and chicken broth stirring until mixture comes to boil and thickens slightly. Add water chestnuts, seasonings, and sherry. Add chicken that has been cut into small pieces and drained pasta. Toss gently but thoroughly. Divide chicken mixture into two large shallow casseroles. Top with shredded cheese. Bake at 350 degrees for 30 minutes. Yield: 12 servings.
*This dish freezes well. It is also a great dish for a crowd.*

**Nutritional Information Per Serving:**

| Calories | Cholesterol (mg) | Fat (g) | % Calories from Fat |
|---|---|---|---|
| 394 | 61 | 7.6 | 17.3% |

# ⓒ ⓕ CHICKEN PRIMAVERA

1 (12-ounce) package
   linguine
1½ pounds skinless, boneless
   chicken pieces
¼ cup olive oil
3 cloves garlic, minced
½ pound mushrooms, sliced
1 onion, chopped

1 red bell pepper, chopped
½ teaspoon dried oregano
½ teaspoon dried basil
½ teaspoon dried thyme
Salt and pepper to taste
1 cup frozen peas
¼ cup grated Parmesan
   cheese

Cook linguine according to directions on package; drain. In large frying pan, cook chicken pieces in olive oil and garlic until lightly brown and done. Watch carefully, tossing to keep from sticking. Add mushrooms, onions, red pepper, and seasonings, sautéing until tender. Add peas, tossing until heated. When pasta is ready, add to vegetable mixture, combining well. Add Parmesan cheese and serve. Yield: 6 to 8 servings.

**Nutritional Information Per Serving:**

| Calories | Cholesterol (mg) | Fat (g) | % Calories from Fat |
|----------|------------------|---------|---------------------|
| 365 | 51 | 9.7 | 23.8% |

# ⓕ CHICKEN FETTUCCINE

1 pound skinless, boneless
   chicken breasts, cut into
   bite-size pieces
½ cup chopped onion
½ teaspoon dried basil
Salt and pepper as desired

2 large cloves garlic, minced
2 cups thinly sliced zucchini
4 cups cooked fettuccine
1 (5⅓-ounce) can evaporated
   skimmed milk

Coat a large pot with no stick cooking spray and sauté chicken, onion, basil, salt and pepper, and garlic until chicken is almost done. Add zucchini, sauté until tender. Cook fettuccine according to directions on package omitting oil; drain. Remove pan with chicken from heat and add fettuccine and milk, tossing gently. Yield: 4 servings.
*Easy to do with a wonderful result.*

**Nutritional Information Per Serving:**

| Calories | Cholesterol (mg) | Fat (g) | % Calories from Fat |
|----------|------------------|---------|---------------------|
| 391 | 120 | 4.0 | 9.2% |

# Ⓕ CHICKEN LASAGNE

1 (8-ounce) package lasagne
noodles
1½ pounds boneless, skinless
chicken breasts
Celery stalk
Small onion
1 bunch broccoli, flowerets
only
2 tablespoons light
margarine
6 tablespoons flour

2 cups chicken broth,
reserved from cooking
chicken
1 cup skim milk
Salt to taste
½ teaspoon white pepper
¼ teaspoon nutmeg
4 ounces sliced Canadian
bacon
½ pound sliced part skim
mozzarella cheese

Cook noodles according to directions on package omitting oil. Drain and cool. Boil chicken in simmering water seasoned with celery stalk, small onion, and salt and pepper until chicken is done. Remove chicken from broth; reserve broth. Cool chicken and cut into pieces. Cook broccoli until tender; set aside. Melt margarine in small saucepan; add flour stirring well. Gradually add chicken broth and milk, cooking until comes to a boil and thickens. Add seasonings. To assemble: layer lasagne noodles, layer chicken, broccoli, Canadian bacon, mozzarella cheese, and 1 cup sauce. Repeat layers. Pour remaining sauce over top. Bake at 350 degrees for 45 minutes. Yield: 8 servings.
*Fantastic and freezes well.*

**Nutritional Information Per Serving:**

| Calories | Cholesterol (mg) | Fat (g) | % Calories from Fat |
|----------|------------------|---------|---------------------|
| 371 | 97 | 11.8 | 28.6% |

# Ⓒ Ⓕ CHICKEN AND SPINACH CANNELLONI

3 cups skim milk, divided
1 onion, quartered
3 bay leaves
2 whole cloves
2 tablespoons cornstarch
¼ cup grated Parmesan
　cheese
¼ teaspoon white pepper
1 pound boneless, skinless
　chicken breasts, cooked
　and cut

1 cup finely chopped fresh
　mushrooms
½ cup finely chopped onion
2 cloves garlic, minced
1 (10-ounce) bag fresh
　spinach, coarsely
　chopped
⅛ teaspoon white pepper
1 (8-ounce) package
　cannelloni shells

Combine 2 cups milk, onion, bay leaves, and cloves in saucepan. Bring to a boil. Combine remaining 1 cup milk and cornstarch in small bowl; stir well. Gradually add cornstarch mixture to hot milk mixture, stirring constantly and cooking until thickened and bubbly. Remove onion, bay leaves and cloves. Add Parmesan cheese and ¼ teaspoon white pepper to milk mixture; set sauce aside. In food processor, chop chicken until finely chopped; set aside. In skillet coated with no stick cooking spray, sauté mushrooms, onion, and garlic until tender. Add spinach; cover and cook until spinach wilts, stirring occasionally. Cook, uncovered, 5 minutes or until liquid has evaporated. Remove from heat and add chicken and remaining ⅛ teaspoon white pepper; mix well and set aside. Meanwhile, cook shells according to directions on package omitting oil. Spoon ½ cup sauce over bottom of a 13x9x2-inch baking dish. Fill shells with chicken mixture and arrange in dish. Pour remaining sauce over shells. Cover and bake at 350 degrees for 30 minutes. Yield: 8 servings.

**Nutritional Information Per Serving:**

| Calories | Cholesterol (mg) | Fat (g) | % Calories from Fat |
|---|---|---|---|
| 213 | 56 | 3.6 | 15.3% |

 **LASAGNE**

**Sauce**

2 cups chopped onion
3 cloves garlic, crushed
1 (28-ounce) can salt-free
    crushed tomatoes
1 (16-ounce) can salt-free
    crushed tomatoes
1 (6-ounce) can salt-free
    tomato paste
⅓ cup minced fresh parsley

1 tablespoon light brown
    sugar
1 teaspoon dried basil
1 teaspoon dried oregano
¼ teaspoon dried thyme
1 bay leaf
1 whole stalk celery, cut in
    half
2 cups water

In a large heavy pot, combine all sauce ingredients. Simmer on a low heat for 2 hours, stirring occasionally. After cooking, remove bay leaf and celery stalk. Prepare lasagne (see recipe below).
Yield: 10 to 12 servings.
*An excellent lasagne recipe!*

**Lasagne**

1 (8-ounce) package lasagne
    noodles
1½ pounds ground sirloin

16 ounces low fat (1%)
    cottage cheese, mixed in
    food processor
¾ pound part-skim
    mozzarella cheese, sliced

Cook noodles according to directions on the package. Drain and set aside. In skillet, cook meat until done. Drain any grease and add cooked meat to prepared sauce. In a 13x9x2-inch baking dish, put a thin layer of the meat sauce, half the noodles, all the cottage cheese, and half of the mozzarella cheese. Repeat with half of the remaining meat sauce, all of the remaining noodles, then remainder of the meat sauce and remainder of mozzarella. Bake at 350 degrees for 30 minutes.

**Nutritional Information Per Serving:**

| Calories | Cholesterol (mg) | Fat (g) | % Calories from Fat |
|---|---|---|---|
| 289 | 49 | 8.4 | 26.3% |

## Ⓕ SHRIMP AND PASTA IN RED SAUCE

6 cloves garlic, minced
3 (14½-ounce) cans whole
    tomatoes, crushed
1 tablespoon sugar
2 teaspoons dried basil
Salt and pepper to taste

2 tablespoons olive oil
4 cloves garlic, minced
2 pounds shrimp, peeled
1 (12-ounce) package
    vermicelli

In pot coated with no stick cooking spray, sauté garlic until golden. Add tomatoes, sugar, basil, and salt and pepper to taste. Simmer on low heat while preparing remaining ingredients. In large skillet, heat olive oil and sauté garlic and shrimp until shrimp are pink and done. Cook vermicelli according to directions on package omitting salt and oil; drain. Add cooked shrimp with slotted spoon to tomato sauce. Toss with vermicelli. Yield: 6 servings.
*This is a very light tomato sauce.*

**Nutritional Information Per Serving:**

| Calories | Cholesterol (mg) | Fat (g) | % Calories from Fat |
|---|---|---|---|
| 430 | 169 | 7.8 | 16.4% |

## Ⓕ MEATY CHEESY SPAGHETTI

1½ pounds ground turkey
1½ pounds ground sirloin
Salt and pepper to taste
3 cloves garlic, minced
1 tablespoon dried oregano
1 tablespoon dried basil
4 (11⅛-ounce) cans Italian
    tomato soup

1 (15-ounce) can tomato
    sauce
24 ounces spaghetti
8 ounces part skim
    mozzarella cheese,
    shredded

In large pan, sauté turkey and sirloin until done. Drain any excess fat. Stir in remaining ingredients except spaghetti and cheese. Cook, stirring occasionally, 15 minutes or until heated. Stir in cheese cooking until cheese is melted, stirring. Cook spaghetti according to directions on package omitting salt and oil; drain. Toss spaghetti with sauce. Serve. Yield: 14 servings.
*My kids really loved this recipe. It freezes well, therefore, serve it one night and freeze the other portion for another time.*

**Nutritional Information Per Serving:**

| Calories | Cholesterol (mg) | Fat (g) | % Calories from Fat |
|---|---|---|---|
| 421 | 61 | 10.5 | 22.4% |

# Ⓕ MANICOTTI

2 pounds lean ground sirloin
1 onion, chopped
1 small green bell pepper, chopped
3 cloves garlic, minced
1 tablespoon chopped parsley
1 (15-ounce) can tomato sauce
1 (6-ounce) can tomato paste
6 ounces water
1 tablespoon dried basil

½ teaspoon dried oregano
1 teaspoon sugar
Salt and pepper to taste
1 (8-ounce) package manicotti shells
1 (16-ounce) carton part skim ricotta cheese
1 cup shredded part skim mozzarella cheese
¼ cup grated Parmesan cheese

In skillet, brown sirloin with onion, green pepper, garlic, and parsley. Drain any grease. Add tomato sauce, tomato paste, water, basil, oregano, sugar, and salt and pepper to taste. Mix well and simmer for 25 minutes, stirring occasionally. Meanwhile, cook manicotti shells according to directions on package omitting oil. Drain and set aside. Place ½ cup sauce in a 13x9x2-inch baking dish. Combine ricotta and mozzarella cheese. Stuff the cooked shells with cheese mixture and place on top of sauce in dish. Pour remaining sauce over shells and sprinkle with Parmesan cheese. Bake at 350 degrees for 30 minutes. Yield: 8 servings.
*A definite winner!*

**Nutritional Information Per Serving:**

| Calories | Cholesterol (mg) | Fat (g) | % Calories from Fat |
|---|---|---|---|
| 402 | 92 | 13.4 | 30.0% |

# Ⓕ JUMBO STUFFED SHELLS

1 (12-ounce) package jumbo
   shells
1½ pounds ground sirloin
2 egg whites
¼ cup grated Parmesan
   cheese
¼ cup breadcrumbs

1 tablespoon chopped
   parsley
1 teaspoon dried basil
½ teaspoon dried oregano
Salt and pepper to taste
1 (8-ounce) package part-
   skim mozzarella cheese,
   shredded

Cook pasta shells according to directions on package omitting oil; drain and set aside. In skillet, cook sirloin until done. Drain any excess fat. Combine with remaining ingredients except cheese. Stuff shells with filling. Pour half the Tomato Sauce (see recipe below) in a 2-quart baking dish. Arrange stuffed shells on top and cover with remaining sauce. Bake at 350 degrees for 20 minutes. Sprinkle with mozzarella cheese and continue baking for 10 minutes longer. Yield: 6 to 8 servings.

*This recipe the kids will enjoy.*

**Tomato Sauce**
1 tablespoon olive oil
1 medium onion, chopped
2 cloves garlic, minced
3 cups tomato juice

1 (6-ounce) can tomato paste
½ teaspoon sugar
Salt and pepper to taste

In skillet, sauté onion in olive oil until tender. Add remaining ingredients; simmer 10 minutes

**Nutritional Information Per Serving:**

| Calories | Cholesterol (mg) | Fat (g) | % Calories from Fat |
|----------|------------------|---------|---------------------|
| 425 | 66 | 12.0 | 25.4% |

M. HANSBROUGH

VEGETABLES

# ⓒ ALMOND ASPARAGUS

1½ pounds fresh asparagus
   spears
1 tablespoon light margarine
2 tablespoons lemon juice

¼ cup slivered almonds,
   toasted
Salt and pepper to taste

Trim off tough ends of asparagus. Coat a large skillet with no stick cooking spray; add margarine. When margarine is melted, add asparagus stems and sauté several minutes. Add lemon juice; cover, and simmer until crisp tender. Add almonds and season to taste, tossing gently. Yield: 6 servings.

**Nutritional Information Per Serving:**

| Calories | Cholesterol (mg) | Fat (g) | % Calories from Fat |
|---|---|---|---|
| 58 | 0 | 4.2 | 65.6% |

#  ⓒⒻ BAKED BEANS

2 ounces Canadian bacon,
   chopped in ½-inch pieces
½ pound ground sirloin
1 onion, chopped
⅓ cup light brown sugar
¼ cup sugar
½ cup tomato sauce
1 tablespoon molasses
1 tablespoon cider vinegar

1 tablespoon Worcestershire
   sauce
1 teaspoon onion powder
1 (15-ounce) can butter
   beans, very well drained
1 (15-ounce) can red kidney
   beans, very well drained
2 (19-ounce) cans small white
   beans, very well drained
Salt and pepper to taste

In large skillet, sauté bacon until slightly brown. Add sirloin and onion and cook until sirloin is done. Drain any excess fat. Combine with all remaining ingredients and pour into a 2 or 3-quart baking dish. Bake at 350 degrees for 1 hour. Yield: 12 servings.
*Outstanding — no one will believe you just opened cans!*

**Nutritional Information Per Serving:**

| Calories | Cholesterol (mg) | Fat (g) | % Calories from Fat |
|---|---|---|---|
| 196 | 13 | 1.6 | 7.3% |

## ⟨C⟩⟨F⟩ RED BEANS AND RICE

1 pound dried red kidney
   beans
1 pound turkey sausage,
   thinly sliced
1 large onion, chopped
½ cup chopped celery
¼ cup chopped green onion
½ cup chopped parsley

2 cloves garlic, minced
8 cups water
2 bay leaves
1 tablespoon Worcestershire
   sauce
Dash hot pepper sauce
Salt and pepper to taste

In large bowl, soak red beans in hot water to cover for at least 1 hour. Drain; set aside. In large pot, cook turkey sausage until done and sauté onion, celery, green onion, parsley, and garlic until tender. Add beans, 8 cups water, and remaining ingredients. Bring to boil, reduce heat, and cover for 30 minutes. Remove cover and cook on low heat for 1½ hours or until beans are tender. Serve over cooked brown rice. Yield: 6 to 8 servings.
*An excellent choice for a true Louisiana dish.*

**Nutritional Information Per Serving:**

| Calories | Cholesterol (mg) | Fat (g) | % Calories from Fat |
|---|---|---|---|
| 387 | 36 | 6.2 | 14.3% |

## ⟨C⟩⟨F⟩ WHITE BEANS

1 pound navy or pea beans
½ green pepper, chopped
3 stalks celery, chopped
1 onion, chopped
4 cloves garlic, minced
1 tablespoon olive oil
½ cup diced prosciutto
3 bay leaves

Salt and pepper to taste
2 tablespoons garlic powder
1 tablespoon Worcestershire
   sauce
2 tablespoons light brown
   sugar, optional
Salt and pepper to taste

Soak beans overnight in water. Rinse and drain. In pot coated with no stick cooking spray, sauté green pepper, celery, onion, and garlic in olive oil until tender. Add water to cover. Add remaining ingredients. Bring to a boil, lower heat, and simmer, covered, for 2 hours or until beans are tender. Yield: 6 servings.

**Nutritional Information Per Serving:**

| Calories | Cholesterol (mg) | Fat (g) | % Calories from Fat |
|---|---|---|---|
| 338 | 8 | 4.3 | 11.4% |

# ♡ Ⓒ BROCCOLI ELEGANTE

2 bunches fresh broccoli
1 tablespoon light margarine
3 tablespoons flour
¾ cup chicken broth
½ cup skim milk
¼ teaspoon garlic powder
Dash pepper
⅓ cup light mayonnaise

1 tablespoon freshly
   squeezed lemon juice
½ cup shredded reduced fat
   Cheddar cheese
¼ cup sliced almonds,
   toasted (bake at 350
   degrees until light brown,
   8 to 10 minutes)

Cut broccoli into flowerets and steam in a little water until crisp tender; drain. Place in casserole dish; set aside. Melt margarine in saucepan. Gradually add flour and stir for 1 minute; do not brown. Add chicken broth and milk, stirring constantly with whisk, until mixture comes to a boil. Add seasonings, continuing to cook 1 minute more. Remove from heat and stir in mayonnaise, lemon juice, and shredded cheese. Pour over broccoli and sprinkle with toasted almonds. Bake at 350 degrees for 10 minutes or until thoroughly heated. Yield: 6 to 8 servings.

**Nutritional Information Per Serving:**

| Calories | Cholesterol (mg) | Fat (g) | % Calories from Fat |
|---|---|---|---|
| 133 | 6 | 7.4 | 50.3% |

# ♡ Ⓒ BROCCOLI WITH MUSTARD VINAIGRETTE

¼ cup finely chopped green
   onions
2 cloves garlic, minced
½ teaspoon dried tarragon
½ teaspoon dry mustard
¼ cup olive oil
2 tablespoons red wine
   vinegar

1 teaspoon Dijon mustard
⅛ teaspoon salt
¼ teaspoon freshly ground
   pepper
1 bunch fresh broccoli,
   trimmed and cut into
   spears, steamed

Combine green onions, garlic, tarragon, and dry mustard in bowl; set aside. Heat oil in microwave until very hot. Pour oil over green onion mixture, stirring to combine. Whisk in vinegar, Dijon mustard, and salt and pepper. Pour warm vinaigrette over broccoli, tossing to coat. Serve hot, or at room temperature. Yield: 8 servings.
*This low calorie-low cholesterol recipe replaces a cheese sauce.*

**Nutritional Information Per Serving:**

| Calories | Cholesterol (mg) | Fat (g) | % Calories from Fat |
|---|---|---|---|
| 76 | 0 | 6.9 | 81.5% |

# ⓒ CARROTS WITH FLAIR

8 carrots (medium size)
⅓ cup chopped onion
½ cup light mayonnaise
2 tablespoons horseradish
⅛ teaspoon pepper

1 slice whole wheat bread
½ tablespoon light
    margarine
Paprika

Peel and slice carrots into julienne (slender short strips) strips. Place in microwave dish and add 1 cup water. Cover and cook in microwave approximately 5 minutes or until tender. Drain, reserving ¼ cup liquid. Place carrots in a shallow 1½-quart casserole coated with no stick cooking spray. Combine reserved carrot liquid, onion, mayonnaise, horseradish, and pepper. Spoon over top of carrots. Place bread in food processor until turns into crumbs. Stir in margarine and sprinkle over top of carrots. Sprinkle with paprika. Bake, uncovered, 15 to 20 minutes. Yield: 6 servings.

**Nutritional Information Per Serving:**

| Calories | Cholesterol (mg) | Fat (g) | % Calories from Fat |
|---|---|---|---|
| 110 | 8 | 7.2 | 59.3% |

# ⓒⒻ ORANGE GLAZED CARROTS

2 pounds baby carrots or
    carrots cut into 2-inch
    pieces
2 tablespoons light
    margarine

¼ cup chicken broth
1 cup orange marmalade
Salt and pepper to taste
2 tablespoons chopped
    parsley

Peel carrots. In saucepan, bring the margarine and broth to boil. Add the carrots and cook, covered, over medium heat for 10 to 20 minutes, until crisp tender. Uncover and stir in marmalade. Cook, stirring, over low heat until liquid has reduced to a glaze. Season to taste. Garnish with parsley before serving. Yield: 8 to 10 servings.
*This tasty carrot recipe will fill that extra spot on the plate.*

**Nutritional Information Per Serving:**

| Calories | Cholesterol (mg) | Fat (g) | % Calories from Fat |
|---|---|---|---|
| 133 | <1 | 1.4 | 9.4% |

VEGETABLES

## ©Ⓕ HONEY CARROTS

¾ cup boiling water
2 tablespoons light
  margarine
¼ teaspoon nutmeg
⅛ teaspoon pepper

2 tablespoons honey
5 cups sliced, peeled carrots,
  about ¼-inch thick
1 tablespoon lemon juice
¼ cup chopped parsley

In saucepan, combine water, margarine, nutmeg, pepper, and honey with carrots. Simmer, covered, for 10 minutes or until carrots are crisp tender. Stir in lemon juice and parsley before serving. Yield: 6 servings. *When looking for a vegetable to complete your menu, try this one.*

**Nutritional Information Per Serving:**

| Calories | Cholesterol (mg) | Fat (g) | % Calories from Fat |
|---|---|---|---|
| 84 | 0 | 2.1 | 22.8% |

## ©Ⓕ DIJON GLAZED CARROTS

1 pound carrots, peeled and
  sliced
1 tablespoon light margarine
1 tablespoon Dijon mustard

2 tablespoons honey
¼ teaspoon white pepper
¼ teaspoon ginger

Steam carrots in water until crisp tender. Drain cooking liquid. In a small saucepan, combine remaining ingredients over low heat, stirring just until combined. Pour sauce over carrots and toss gently to coat. Yield: 4 servings.

**Nutritional Information Per Serving:**

| Calories | Cholesterol (mg) | Fat (g) | % Calories from Fat |
|---|---|---|---|
| 76 | 0 | 1.7 | 20.4% |

## ⓒⒻ CAULIFLOWER SUPREME

1 head cauliflower, cut into
  flowerets
½ cup plain non fat yogurt
½ cup shredded reduced fat
  sharp Cheddar cheese
½ teaspoon dry mustard
½ teaspoon cayenne
Salt and pepper to taste

Cook cauliflower in ⅓ cup water, covered, in microwave for 8 minutes or until crisp tender. Drain and transfer to a baking dish coated with no stick cooking spray. Combine remaining ingredients and spread over cauliflower. Bake, uncovered, at 400 degrees for 8 to 10 minutes or until lightly browned. Yield: 4 servings.

**Nutritional Information Per Serving:**

| Calories | Cholesterol (mg) | Fat (g) | % Calories from Fat |
|---|---|---|---|
| 69 | 4 | 1.2 | 15.5% |

## ⓒ EGGPLANT PARMESAN

2 medium eggplants, peeled
  and cut in ½-inch slices
  (12 slices)
2 onions, sliced into rings
1 (28-ounce) can whole
  peeled tomatoes
1 teaspoon dried oregano
½ teaspoon dried basil
Salt and pepper to taste
1 (8-ounce) package part
  skim mozzarella cheese,
  shredded

Broil eggplant slices 5 inches from heat, about 5 minutes or until brown on one side. Arrange slices, brown side down, in a 2-quart long casserole dish coated with no stick cooking spray. Top with onions. In food processor, combine tomatoes with juice, and seasonings, chopping into small pieces. Pour over eggplant. Bake at 350 degrees for 45 minutes. Top with mozzarella cheese and bake an additional 15 minutes. Yield: 4 to 6 servings.

**Nutritional Information Per Serving:**

| Calories | Cholesterol (mg) | Fat (g) | % Calories from Fat |
|---|---|---|---|
| 168 | 22 | 6.7 | 35.8% |

VEGETABLES

## ⓒⒻ GREEN BEAN CASSEROLE

2 (9-ounce) packages French
   style green beans
1 onion, chopped
2 tablespoons light
   margarine
2 tablespoons flour

Salt and pepper to taste
½ cup skim milk
1 cup non fat plain yogurt
1 cup shredded reduced fat
   sharp Cheddar cheese

Cook green beans according to directions on package; drain well. Sauté onion in margarine until tender. Blend in flour, salt, and pepper. Gradually add milk, stirring, and cooking until thickened and bubbly. Stir in yogurt and green beans; heat thoroughly. Transfer to 1½-quart casserole. Sprinkle with cheese and broil in oven until cheese melts. Yield: 8 servings.

*Everyone loves a green bean casserole. You can substitute 1 (28-ounce) can cut green beans, if desired.*

**Nutritional Information Per Serving:**

| Calories | Cholesterol (mg) | Fat (g) | % Calories from Fat |
|---|---|---|---|
| 99 | 4 | 2.6 | 23.6% |

## ⓒ GREEN BEAN MARINATE

1 (16-ounce) package frozen
   French style green beans
1 onion, sliced into rings and
   separated
2 ounces Canadian bacon,
   cut into 1-inch pieces

¼ cup slivered almonds
⅛ cup sugar
¼ cup vinegar
2 tablespoons canola oil
¼ teaspoon liquid smoke

Thaw green beans and drain well. In a 1½-quart casserole, layer green beans, onion slices, Canadian bacon, and almonds. In a small bowl, combine sugar, vinegar, oil, and liquid smoke; mix with wire whisk until sugar is dissolved. Pour over layers in casserole and marinate overnight. Bake at 350 degrees for 45 minutes. Remove from oven and stir before serving. Yield: 8 servings.

*This is a sweet-sour green bean recipe — leftovers taste great cold the next day.*

**Nutritional Information Per Serving:**

| Calories | Cholesterol (mg) | Fat (g) | % Calories from Fat |
|---|---|---|---|
| 104 | 4 | 6.4 | 55.6% |

## ©Ⓕ HONEY BAKED ONIONS

3 large red onions (about 3
    pounds)
⅓ cup honey
¼ cup water

3 tablespoons light
    margarine, melted
1 teaspoon paprika
⅛ teaspoon red pepper

Peel and cut onions in half crosswise. Place cut side down in shallow baking dish large enough to hold all onion halves in one layer. Sprinkle with water; cover with foil. Bake at 350 degrees for 30 minutes. Turn onions cut side up. Combine remaining ingredients. Spoon half of mixture over onions. Return to oven and bake, uncovered, 15 minutes. Baste with remaining honey mixture; continue baking 15 minutes or until tender. Yield: 6 servings.
*This will add an extra to any plate.*

**Nutritional Information Per Serving:**

| Calories | Cholesterol (mg) | Fat (g) | % Calories from Fat |
|---|---|---|---|
| 160 | 0 | 3.2 | 17.9% |

## © STEWED OKRA AND TOMATOES

2 tablespoons safflower oil
1 large onion, chopped
2 pounds fresh okra
1 (14½-ounce) can tomatoes

1 (10-ounce) can chopped
    tomatoes and green
    chilies
Salt and pepper to taste

In pot, heat oil and sauté onion until tender. Cut ends off okra and slice. Add okra and cook until okra is not stringy, stirring occasionally. Add tomatoes, cover, and continue cooking over low heat until okra is tender. Season to taste. Yield: 8 servings.

**Nutritional Information Per Serving:**

| Calories | Cholesterol (mg) | Fat (g) | % Calories from Fat |
|---|---|---|---|
| 90 | 0 | 3.7 | 36.9% |

## ©Ⓕ SPICY BLACK EYED PEAS

¼ pound Canadian bacon
1 onion, chopped
1 green bell pepper, chopped
2 cloves garlic, minced
1 (14½-ounce) can whole
   tomatoes, undrained and
   chopped
½ cup water

1 (16-ounce) package black-
   eyed peas, soaked
   overnight in water
½ teaspoon cumin
1 teaspoon dry mustard
½ teaspoon chili powder
Salt and pepper to taste

Coat a pot with no stick cooking spray and sauté Canadian bacon. Add onion, green pepper, and garlic sautéing until tender. Add tomatoes, water, and drained peas, bringing to a boil. Add remaining seasonings. Reduce heat, cover, and cook slowly for 1 to 1½ hours, stirring occasionally. Yield: 6 servings.
*This is a different twist to a traditional dish.*

**Nutritional Information Per Serving:**

| Calories | Cholesterol (mg) | Fat (g) | % Calories from Fat |
|----------|------------------|---------|---------------------|
| 315 | 9 | 3.2 | 9.1% |

## ©Ⓕ ONE STEP MACARONI AND CHEESE

2 tablespoons light
   margarine
1 (12-ounce) package small
   sea shell pasta
Salt and pepper to taste

1 (8-ounce) package reduced
   fat Cheddar cheese,
   shredded
5 cups skim milk
½ cup water

Melt margarine in 2-quart casserole dish. Add dry sea shells, stirring to coat. Salt and pepper to taste. Sprinkle with cheese and pour milk and water over all. Mix well. Bake at 350 degrees for 1 hour to 1 hour 30 minutes or until all liquid is absorbed. Yield: 10 servings.
*With this recipe, you can make macaroni and cheese from scratch easier than from the box. If desired, you can add ¼ cup sugar for a sweeter taste.*

**Nutritional Information Per Serving:**

| Calories | Cholesterol (mg) | Fat (g) | % Calories from Fat |
|----------|------------------|---------|---------------------|
| 239 | 7 | 3.4 | 12.6% |

## Ⓒ Ⓕ PINEAPPLE NOODLE KUGEL

1 pound wide noodles
4 tablespoons light
   margarine, melted
1 (16-ounce) container low fat
   cottage cheese
1 pint container non fat plain
   yogurt

⅔ cup sugar
1 (20-ounce) can crushed
   pineapple, in own juice,
   drained
2 teaspoons vanilla
4 egg whites

Cook noodles according to directions on package omitting oil; drain. Combine with remaining ingredients except egg whites. In mixer, beat egg whites until stiff. Fold into noodle mixture. Pour into a 13x9x2-inch baking pan coated with no stick cooking spray. Bake, uncovered, at 350 degrees for 1 hour and 15 minutes. Yield: 24 servings.

### Nutritional Information Per Serving:

| Calories | Cholesterol (mg) | Fat (g) | % Calories from Fat |
|---|---|---|---|
| 142 | 18 | 2.1 | 13.3% |

## Ⓒ NOODLE KUGEL

1 (8-ounce) package wide
   noodles
¼ cup margarine, melted
½ cup sugar
1 cup low fat cottage cheese

1 (8-ounce) container non fat
   plain yogurt
4 ounces light cream cheese
3 egg whites
½ teaspoon vanilla

Boil noodles according to directions on package omitting oil. Rinse, drain, and combine with margarine, tossing evenly. Place noodles in a glass 13x9x2-inch baking pan coated with no stick cooking spray. In food processor or mixer, combine remaining ingredients beating until smooth. Combine with noodles, mixing well. Bake at 350 degrees for 45 minutes to 1 hour. Yield: 15 servings.
*This dish goes great when serving meat.*

### Nutritional Information Per Serving:

| Calories | Cholesterol (mg) | Fat (g) | % Calories from Fat |
|---|---|---|---|
| 147 | 18 | 5.1 | 31.6% |

# ©Ⓕ GARDEN VEGETABLE CASSEROLE

3 large red potatoes, peeled
   and sliced
4 large carrots, peeled and
   sliced
¾ pound green beans,
   snapped

4 yellow squash, sliced
2½ cups shredded reduced
   fat Monterey Jack cheese
2½ cups skim milk
½ cup flour
Paprika

Steam all vegetables in microwave or on stove until tender. Coat a 3-quart casserole with no stick cooking spray and layer potatoes on the bottom. Sprinkle with all the shredded cheese but ½ cup. Top cheese with carrots, green beans, and squash. In a small saucepan, combine milk and flour with whisk and cook over low heat until thickened to make a white sauce. Season to taste. Pour over top of layered vegetables. Top with remaining ½ cup shredded cheese. Sprinkle with paprika. Bake at 350 degrees for 25 to 30 minutes or until heated through. Yield: 8 servings.

*Vegetable lovers can use this dish as a meal.*

## Nutritional Information Per Serving:

| Calories | Cholesterol (mg) | Fat (g) | % Calories from Fat |
|---|---|---|---|
| 268 | 9 | 3.1 | 10.3% |

# ©Ⓕ SOUFFLÉED BAKED POTATOES

4 small baking potatoes
   (about 1¼ pounds)
½ cup plain non fat yogurt
¼ cup chives
Salt and pepper to taste

2 egg whites
⅓ cup shredded reduced fat
   Cheddar cheese
⅛ teaspoon paprika

Wash potatoes and bake at 400 degrees for 1 hour or until tender. Let potatoes cool completely. Cut in half lengthwise; carefully scoop out pulp, leaving ⅛-inch thick shells. Combine potato pulp, yogurt, chives, salt and pepper in bowl, beating until smooth. Set aside. Beat egg whites in mixer at high speed until stiff peaks form; fold into potato mixture. Spoon potato mixture into shells; place on an ungreased baking pan. Sprinkle 1 tablespoon shredded Cheddar cheese over each serving. Sprinkle paprika evenly on top. Bake at 375 degrees for 15 minutes or until thoroughly heated. Yield: 8 servings.

## Nutritional Information Per Serving:

| Calories | Cholesterol (mg) | Fat (g) | % Calories from Fat |
|---|---|---|---|
| 79 | 1 | 0.4 | 4.8% |

# ⓒ SOUTHWESTERN STUFFED POTATOES

3 medium potatoes
3 tablespoons light
   margarine
⅛ cup skim milk
½ cup non fat plain yogurt
1 (17-ounce) can whole
   kernel corn, drained

1 (4-ounce) can diced green
   chilies
4 green onions, chopped
1 cup shredded Cheddar
   cheese
Paprika

Wash potatoes well, and dry thoroughly. With fork, prick skins over entire surface. Place potatoes directly on oven rack, and bake at 400 degrees for approximately 1 hour or until soft when squeezed. When done, cut each potato in half lengthwise. Scoop out inside, leaving a thin shell. In mixer, mash potatoes until no lumps remain. Add margarine, skim milk, and yogurt, mixing well. Stir in corn, green chilies, green onions, and cheese, combining well. Spoon mixture into shells. Top with paprika. Bake at 350 degrees for approximately 20 minutes or until cheese is melted and potatoes are hot. Yield: 6 servings.

**Nutritional Information Per Serving:**

| Calories | Cholesterol (mg) | Fat (g) | % Calories from Fat |
|---|---|---|---|
| 244 | 20 | 9.8 | 36.0% |

# ⓒⒻ FANNED BAKED POTATOES

4 medium potatoes
3 tablespoons liquid
   margarine
2 tablespoons chopped
   parsley
2 green onion stems only,
   chopped

½ teaspoon dried thyme
1 tablespoon grated
   Parmesan cheese
2 tablespoons shredded
   Cheddar cheese

Scrub and rinse potatoes. Lay potato on cutting board and cut thin slices in a roll all the way across the potato but not cutting all the way through to bottom. Repeat with all potatoes. Put potatoes in baking dish and pull slices slightly apart to get fan effect. Drizzle with margarine. Sprinkle with herbs. Bake at 425 degrees for 50 minutes. Remove from oven and sprinkle with cheeses. Bake potatoes for another 10 to 15 minutes until cheeses are melted and potatoes are soft inside. Yield: 4 servings.

*An attractive alternative way to prepare potatoes.*

**Nutritional Information Per Serving:**

| Calories | Cholesterol (mg) | Fat (g) | % Calories from Fat |
|---|---|---|---|
| 199 | 5 | 5.8 | 26.3% |

# ⓒⒻ MEXICAN STUFFED POTATOES

4 baking potatoes
 (approximately 1½
 pounds)
1 (8-ounce) container non fat
 yogurt
¼ cup skim milk
⅛ teaspoon black pepper
2 large green onion stems,
 thinly sliced

1 (4-ounce) can diced green
 chilies, drained
1 (2-ounce) jar diced
 pimiento, drained
¼ cup shredded reduced fat
 Monterey Jack cheese
½ cup shredded reduced fat
 Cheddar cheese, divided

Wash potatoes well and dry thoroughly. With fork, prick skins over entire surface. Place potatoes directly on oven rack, and bake at 400 degrees for 1 hour or until soft when squeezed. Let cool to touch. Cut potatoes in half lengthwise; carefully scoop out pulp, leaving a thin shell. Set aside. In mixing bowl, combine potato pulp, yogurt, milk, and pepper, mixing until light and fluffy. Stir in green onion stems, chilies, pimiento, and ¼ cup each cheese into potato mixture. Fill potato shells with mashed potato mixture. Sprinkle with remaining ¼ cup shredded Cheddar cheese. Bake at 350 degrees for approximately 20 minutes or until cheese is melted and potatoes are hot. Yield: 8 servings.
*Make extra and freeze by wrapping individually. This stuffed potato recipe will be a winner.*

**Nutritional Information Per Serving:**

| Calories | Cholesterol (mg) | Fat (g) | % Calories from Fat |
|---|---|---|---|
| 123 | 3 | 0.9 | 6.7% |

# ⓒ POTATO BAKE

2 pounds potatoes, unpeeled
 and sliced
1 bunch green onions,
 chopped
1 red bell pepper, chopped
1 green bell pepper, chopped
1 teaspoon paprika

2 tablespoons dried basil
6 cloves garlic, minced
Salt and pepper to taste
3 tablespoons olive oil
1 (14½-ounce) can reduced
 salt chicken broth

Combine all ingredients, tossing to coat well. Place potato mixture in a 13x9x2-inch baking dish. Bake at 325 degrees for 1 hour and 15 minutes or until potatoes are tender and liquid is absorbed. Yield: 6 servings.
*A tasty colorful dish.*

**Nutritional Information Per Serving:**

| Calories | Cholesterol (mg) | Fat (g) | % Calories from Fat |
|---|---|---|---|
| 206 | 0 | 7.5 | 32.7% |

# ⓒ ROASTED SWEET AND WHITE POTATOES

**3 tablespoons canola oil**
**1 pound sweet potatoes,**
    **unpeeled, cut into 2-inch**
    **chunks**
**1 pound baking potatoes,**
    **unpeeled, cut into 2-inch**
    **chunks**

**2 cloves garlic, skins on**
**¼ cup chopped parsley**
**1 teaspoon dried thyme**
**½ teaspoon black pepper**

Pour oil into large roasting pan and heat for 5 minutes in 450 degree oven. Add potatoes and whole cloves of garlic, tossing to coat. Bake, shaking pan every 10 minutes, until potatoes are browned and crisp and garlic is soft, about 45 minutes to 1 hour. Remove garlic and press softened cloves and slip from skins. Mash garlic with remaining ingredients. Place potatoes in serving piece and sprinkle with garlic/parsley mixture. Yield: 8 servings.
*A colorful tasty dish that goes well with pork.*

**Nutritional Information Per Serving:**

| Calories | Cholesterol (mg) | Fat (g) | % Calories from Fat |
|---|---|---|---|
| 150 | 0 | 5.4 | 32.1% |

# ⓒⒻ GLAZED SWEET POTATOES

**5 sweet potatoes (about 3**
    **pounds)**
**¼ cup light brown sugar**
**¼ cup honey**
**1 tablespoon cornstarch**
**½ teaspoon cinnamon**

**2 tablespoons light**
    **margarine**
**½ cup apricot nectar**
**¼ cup finely chopped pecans,**
    **optional**

Boil sweet potatoes in water to cover until fork tender, about 25 minutes. Cool, peel, and cut into ½-inch slices. Arrange slices in a 2-quart casserole dish coated with no stick cooking spray; set aside. In saucepan, combine remaining ingredients except pecans. Cook until mixture begins to boil. Boil for 1 minute, stirring constantly, until mixture is thickened and bubbly. Pour over sweet potatoes; sprinkle with chopped pecans, if desired. Bake at 350 degrees for 30 minutes or until thoroughly heated. Yield: 8 to 10 servings.
*You will want to include this recipe on those holiday dinners.*

**Nutritional Information Per Serving:**

| Calories | Cholesterol (mg) | Fat (g) | % Calories from Fat |
|---|---|---|---|
| 244 | 0 | 3.2 | 11.7% |

## ©Ⓕ SOUTHWESTERN RICE

| | |
|---|---|
| 1 onion, chopped | Salt and pepper to taste |
| 2 tablespoons light margarine | 2 (4-ounce) cans diced green chilies |
| 5 cups cooked rice | 6 ounces reduced fat sharp Cheddar cheese, shredded |
| 2 cups non fat plain yogurt | |
| 1 cup low fat cottage cheese | |

Sauté onion in margarine until tender. Combine with all ingredients except cheese. Place into a 2-quart casserole dish. Cover with shredded cheese. Bake at 350 degrees for 20 minutes. Yield: 10 servings.
*A sure hit!*

**Nutritional Information Per Serving:**

| Calories | Cholesterol (mg) | Fat (g) | % Calories from Fat |
|---|---|---|---|
| 218 | 5 | 2.8 | 11.4% |

## ©Ⓕ WILD RICE AND PEPPERS

| | |
|---|---|
| 1 (6-ounce) box long grain and wild rice | 1 green bell pepper, sliced in long thin slices |
| ½ cup cooked rice | ½ pound mushrooms, sliced |
| ⅛ cup olive oil | 1 bunch green onions, chopped |
| 1 red bell pepper, sliced in long thin slices | |

Cook wild rice according to directions on package. In casserole dish combine wild rice and cooked rice. In skillet, heat olive oil and sauté peppers, mushrooms, and green onions until tender. Fold into rice mixture. Yield: 8 servings.
*This fantastic rice dish will add to any plate.*

**Nutritional Information Per Serving:**

| Calories | Cholesterol (mg) | Fat (g) | % Calories from Fat |
|---|---|---|---|
| 126 | 0 | 3.6 | 26.1% |

## ⓒⒻ RICE AND NOODLES

1 cup raw rice
1 tablespoon light margarine
1 cup medium noodles

2¾ cups chicken broth
Salt and pepper to taste

In heavy saucepan coated with no stick cooking spray, brown rice in margarine. Add remaining ingredients. Bring mixture to boil, lower heat and simmer, covered, for 20 minutes. Yield: 6 servings.
*When you do not know what to serve with a main dish, this recipe will solve your problems. It is quick and done in one pan.*

### Nutritional Information Per Serving:

| Calories | Cholesterol (mg) | Fat (g) | % Calories from Fat |
|---|---|---|---|
| 181 | 7 | 2.6 | 13.0% |

## ⓒⒻ GARDEN RICE CASSEROLE

1 tablespoon light margarine, melted
1½ cups raw brown rice
1 large onion, chopped
3 cups chicken broth
½ teaspoon dried thyme
1 tablespoon olive oil
2 cloves garlic, minced
1 bunch broccoli, flowerets only

1 head cauliflower, flowerets only
2 cups carrot julienne strips (thin strips)
⅔ cup shredded reduced fat Monterey Jack cheese
⅔ cup shredded reduced fat Cheddar cheese

In large 2-quart casserole, mix margarine, rice, onion, and chicken broth. Cover and bake at 350 degrees for 20 minutes or until rice is done. Remove from oven and stir in thyme. Heat olive oil in skillet coated with no stick cooking spray and sauté remaining vegetables until crisp tender. Pour over rice mixture. Cover and continue baking for 15 minutes. Combine cheeses and sprinkle over the casserole. Return to oven and bake another 5 minutes or until cheese is melted. Yield: 6 servings.
*Delicious and colorful!*

### Nutritional Information Per Serving:

| Calories | Cholesterol (mg) | Fat (g) | % Calories from Fat |
|---|---|---|---|
| 363 | 7 | 7.6 | 18.7% |

## ⓒⓕ RICE PRIMAVERA

1 tablespoon olive oil
1 clove garlic, minced
1 bunch broccoli, flowerets
    only
2 zucchini, sliced
1 medium tomato, seeded
    and chopped

⅓ cup light mayonnaise
½ cup skim milk
¼ cup grated Parmesan
    cheese
3 cups cooked rice

In large skillet, heat oil and sauté garlic. Add broccoli and zucchini cooking until tender crisp. Add tomatoes and cook one minute longer. Remove vegetables and set aside. In same skillet, add mayonnaise and stir in milk and cheese. Cook over medium heat until smooth. Add rice, tossing to coat. Stir in reserved vegetables and heat thoroughly. Serve immediately. Yield: 6 servings.
*Delicious!*

**Nutritional Information Per Serving:**

| Calories | Cholesterol (mg) | Fat (g) | % Calories from Fat |
|----------|------------------|---------|---------------------|
| 214      | 10               | 5.6     | 23.6%               |


## ⓒⓕ RICE PILAF DELUXE

1 tablespoon liquid
    margarine
1½ cups long grain rice
½ pound sliced mushrooms
1 bunch green onions,
    chopped
1 teaspoon dried oregano
½ teaspoon dried thyme

½ teaspoon dried marjoram
Salt and pepper to taste
3 cups chicken broth
1 (14-ounce) can artichoke
    hearts, drained and
    halved
⅓ cup slivered almonds

In skillet, melt margarine and add rice, mushrooms, and green onions. Sauté until tender. Add seasonings. Transfer mixture to a 2-quart casserole dish and stir in broth, artichokes and almonds. Bake at 325 degrees, covered, for one hour. Yield: 6 to 8 servings.
*Rice with a flair!*

**Nutritional Information Per Serving:**

| Calories | Cholesterol (mg) | Fat (g) | % Calories from Fat |
|----------|------------------|---------|---------------------|
| 215      | <1               | 5.2     | 21.6%               |

## ©Ⓕ WILD RICE AND BARLEY PILAF

1 (6-ounce) package long
    grain and wild rice
½ cup pearl barley
3 cups chicken broth

1 tablespoon light margarine
⅓ cup sliced almonds,
    toasted

In saucepan, combine rice, seasoning packet, barley, chicken broth, and margarine. Bring to a boil. Reduce heat, cover, and simmer for 10 minutes. Spoon into a 1½-quart casserole dish. Bake, covered, at 325 degrees for 1 hour or until rice and barley are tender and liquid is absorbed. Fluff rice mixture with a fork; stir in almonds. Yield: 6 to 8 servings.

*This is a nice alternative to the usual rice dishes.*

**Nutritional Information Per Serving:**

| Calories | Cholesterol (mg) | Fat (g) | % Calories from Fat |
|----------|------------------|---------|---------------------|
| 182      | <1               | 5.2     | 25.8%               |


## © DIRTY RICE

1 pound extra lean ground
    beef
2 cloves garlic, minced
2 stalks celery, chopped
1 onion, chopped
1 tablespoon chopped
    parsley
1 green bell pepper, seeded
    and chopped

1 red bell pepper, seeded and
    chopped
1 tablespoon Worcestershire
    sauce
¼ teaspoon red pepper
¼ teaspoon pepper
1 cup raw rice
1 (14½-ounce) can beef broth
1 cup water

In large skillet, add beef and all vegetables cooking until beef is done and vegetables are tender. Add seasonings, stirring well. Add rice, broth, and water, mixing well. Bring to a boil and reduce heat, cover, and cook for 25 to 30 minutes or until rice is done. Yield: 4 to 6 servings.

**Nutritional Information Per Serving:**

| Calories | Cholesterol (mg) | Fat (g) | % Calories from Fat |
|----------|------------------|---------|---------------------|
| 313      | 52               | 13.4    | 38.4%               |

## ⓒⒻ HERBED SQUASH

8 small yellow squash
1 tablespoon liquid
  margarine
¼ teaspoon dried thyme
¼ teaspoon dried rosemary

¼ teaspoon dried marjoram
2 tablespoons chopped green
  onion
¼ cup dry white wine
Salt and pepper to taste

Slice squash thinly. Heat margarine in pan and sauté squash until tender, but not mushy. Add remaining ingredients. Stir until blended. Yield: 4 servings.
*When you have fresh squash, this is quick and wonderful.*

**Nutritional Information Per Serving:**

| Calories | Cholesterol (mg) | Fat (g) | % Calories from Fat |
|----------|------------------|---------|---------------------|
| 99 | 0 | 2.4 | 21.7% |

## ⓒⒻ SQUASH ROCKEFELLER

6 yellow squash
2 (10-ounce) packages frozen
  chopped spinach
1 bunch green onions,
  chopped
½ cup finely chopped parsley

3 stalks celery, chopped
2 cloves garlic, minced
¼ cup light margarine
½ cup Italian breadcrumbs
Hot pepper sauce to taste
Salt and pepper to taste

Cut squash in half lengthwise. Steam in ½ inch water, covered, on stove or in microwave until almost tender. Cool, and scoop out pulp, being careful not to break shell. Cook spinach according to directions on package; drain well. In pan, sauté green onion, parsley, celery, and garlic in margarine until tender. Combine with spinach and remaining ingredients, mixing well. Stuff squash shells with mixture. Bake at 350 degrees for 20 minutes. Yield: 12 stuffed squash.
*This tasty dish will be an attraction to any plate.*

**Nutritional Information Per Serving:**

| Calories | Cholesterol (mg) | Fat (g) | % Calories from Fat |
|----------|------------------|---------|---------------------|
| 81 | <1 | 2.7 | 30.3% |

## ⓒ STUFFED MEXICAN SQUASH

3 medium-size yellow squash
  (approximately 1¼
  pounds)
2 cloves garlic, minced
¼ cup chopped onion
¼ cup chopped green bell
  pepper
1 tablespoon olive oil
1 teaspoon chili powder

Salt and pepper, if desired
½ cup shredded reduced fat
  Monterey Jack cheese
2 tablespoons non fat plain
  yogurt
2 tablespoons picante sauce
2 tablespoons shredded
  reduced fat Cheddar
  cheese

Cook squash in boiling water to cover 7 minutes or until tender, but still firm. Drain and cool slightly. Cut each squash in half lengthwise; scoop out pulp, leaving a ¼-inch shell. Reserve the pulp. Sauté garlic, onion, and green pepper in olive oil until tender. Stir in squash pulp; cook, stirring often, until liquid has been absorbed. Add chili powder and salt and pepper if desired. Remove from heat. Add Monterey Jack cheese and yogurt, stirring well. Place squash shells in a 12x8x2-inch baking dish coated with no stick cooking spray. Spoon squash mixture evenly into shells. Bake at 350 for 20 minutes. Divide picante sauce and Cheddar cheese evenly over squash; bake an additional 5 minutes. Yield: 6 servings.

**Nutritional Information Per Serving:**

| Calories | Cholesterol (mg) | Fat (g) | % Calories from Fat |
|---|---|---|---|
| 80 | 3 | 3.4 | 38.7% |

## ⓒⒻ SQUASH CASSEROLE

2 pounds fresh squash, sliced
2 green bell peppers,
  chopped
1 large onion, chopped
2 tablespoons canola oil

1 (17-ounce) can cream style
  corn
1 tablespoon sugar
¼ cup cornmeal
Salt and pepper to taste

Steam fresh squash until tender; drain. Mash or purée squash in food processor. In skillet, sauté green peppers and onion in oil until tender. Combine puréed squash, onion mixture, corn, sugar, and cornmeal. Add salt and pepper as desired. Place mixture into a 2-quart casserole dish. Bake at 350 degrees for 30 minutes. Yield: 6 to 8 servings.
*This family favorite now can be enjoyed!*

**Nutritional Information Per Serving:**

| Calories | Cholesterol (mg) | Fat (g) | % Calories from Fat |
|---|---|---|---|
| 129 | 0 | 4.1 | 28.4% |

## Ⓒ CHEESY SPICY SPINACH

3 (10-ounce) boxes frozen
    chopped spinach
½ cup spinach liquid,
    reserved from cooking
    spinach
1 tablespoon margarine
1 onion, chopped

3 tablespoons flour
1 cup skim milk
1 (6-ounce) roll hot pepper
    cheese, cubed
1 tablespoon Worcestershire
    sauce
½ teaspoon garlic powder

Cook spinach according to directions on package. Drain well reserving ½ cup spinach liquid; set aside. In pan coated with no stick cooking spray, melt margarine and sauté onion until tender. Add flour; stir. Gradually add milk and spinach liquid to make sauce. Cook until mixture thickens. Add cheese and seasonings, cooking until cheese is melted. Add spinach to pan, combining well. Yield: 10 servings.
*A favorite of spinach lovers.*

**Nutritional Information Per Serving:**

| Calories | Cholesterol (mg) | Fat (g) | % Calories from Fat |
|---|---|---|---|
| 107 | 16 | 6.1 | 51.5% |

## Ⓒ Ⓕ CHEESY SPINACH CASSEROLE

2 (10-ounce) packages frozen
    chopped spinach
½ pound fresh mushrooms,
    sliced
3 slices light American
    cheese, diced

1 (5-ounce) can evaporated
    skimmed milk
¼ teaspoon garlic powder
Salt and pepper if desired

Cook spinach according to directions on package; drain well. Coat a pan with no stick cooking spray and sauté mushrooms until tender; set aside. Melt cheese in milk in heavy saucepan over low heat. Turn spinach into a shallow baking dish. Sprinkle with garlic powder. Add cheese mixture and stir until thoroughly mixed. Salt and pepper if desired. Top with sautéed mushrooms and drippings. Bake, uncovered, at 350 degrees for 20 minutes. Yield: 6 servings.

**Nutritional Information Per Serving:**

| Calories | Cholesterol (mg) | Fat (g) | % Calories from Fat |
|---|---|---|---|
| 68 | 4 | 1.4 | 19.1% |

# Ⓒ Ⓕ SPINACH WITH HEARTS OF PALM

2 (14-ounce) cans hearts of
  palm, drained and
  coarsely chopped
4 (10-ounce) boxes frozen
  chopped spinach, thawed
  and well drained
4 tablespoons light
  margarine, divided

2 tablespoons flour
1 cup non fat plain yogurt
½ cup skim milk
3 cloves garlic, minced
Salt and pepper to taste
1 pound fresh mushrooms,
  sliced

In a 2-quart glass baking dish coated with no stick cooking spray, place chopped hearts of palm along the bottom. Squeeze all liquid from spinach. In skillet, melt 2 tablespoons margarine. Add spinach; heat, and add flour, yogurt, milk, garlic, and salt and pepper. Mix well and spread over hearts of palm. In remaining 2 tablespoons margarine, sauté mushrooms. Salt and pepper to taste. Spread mushrooms over spinach mixture (may be prepared day before to this point). Cover with Topping (see recipe below). Yield: 10 to 12 servings.
*Can substitute 2 cans artichoke hearts, if desired, for heart of palm.*
*This is a delicious spinach dish.*

**Topping**
⅔ cup non fat plain yogurt
⅔ cup fat free mayonnaise

¼ cup lemon juice
Paprika

Mix yogurt, mayonnaise, and lemon juice together. When ready to cook casserole, pour yogurt topping over mixture in pan. Bake at 350 degrees for 30 minutes. Sprinkle with paprika before serving.

**Nutritional Information Per Serving:**

| Calories | Cholesterol (mg) | Fat (g) | % Calories from Fat |
|---|---|---|---|
| 132 | <1 | 2.4 | 16.4% |

## ⓒ GARDEN STUFFED TOMATOES

6 medium tomatoes
2 tablespoons light
   margarine
1 medium zucchini,
   quartered and thinly
   sliced
1 yellow squash, quartered
   and thinly sliced

¼ pound mushrooms, thinly
   sliced
⅓ cup chopped onions
3 cloves garlic, minced
1 teaspoon dried basil
¼ cup Italian breadcrumbs
1 tablespoon grated
   Parmesan cheese

Cut a 1-inch slice from the top of each tomato, discarding top. Scoop out tomato reserving pulp and juice, discarding the core. Place tomatoes upside down on a paper towel to drain. In a skillet, melt margarine. Add remaining ingredients except breadcrumbs and cheese. Cook over a high heat, stirring frequently, until most of liquid has evaporated and vegetables are tender. If needed, add breadcrumbs to thicken. Spoon mixture into tomato shells and sprinkle with cheese. Place tomatoes in a shallow baking dish. Bake at 350 degrees for 15 to 20 minutes. Yield: 6 servings.
*Avoid overcooking; tomatoes can fall apart if cooked too long. This great summer vegetable dish will add color to your plate.*

**Nutritional Information Per Serving:**

| Calories | Cholesterol (mg) | Fat (g) | % Calories from Fat |
|---|---|---|---|
| 83 | <1 | 2.9 | 31.1% |

## ⓒⓕ SPICY CORN CASSEROLE

1 large onion, chopped
1 tablespoon light margarine
1 (10-ounce) can diced
   tomatoes and green
   chilies

1 (16-ounce) can whole
   kernel yellow corn
1 (16-ounce) can shoe peg
   white corn
1 (16-ounce) can cream style
   yellow corn

In saucepan, sauté onion in margarine until tender. Add remaining ingredients, mixing well. Transfer to a glass baking dish and refrigerate at least 8 hours or overnight. Put in cold oven and bake at 325 degrees for 2 hours. Yield: 8 servings.
*Great because it can be made ahead of time.*

**Nutritional Information Per Serving:**

| Calories | Cholesterol (mg) | Fat (g) | % Calories from Fat |
|---|---|---|---|
| 129 | 0 | 1.5 | 10.6% |

# MEATS

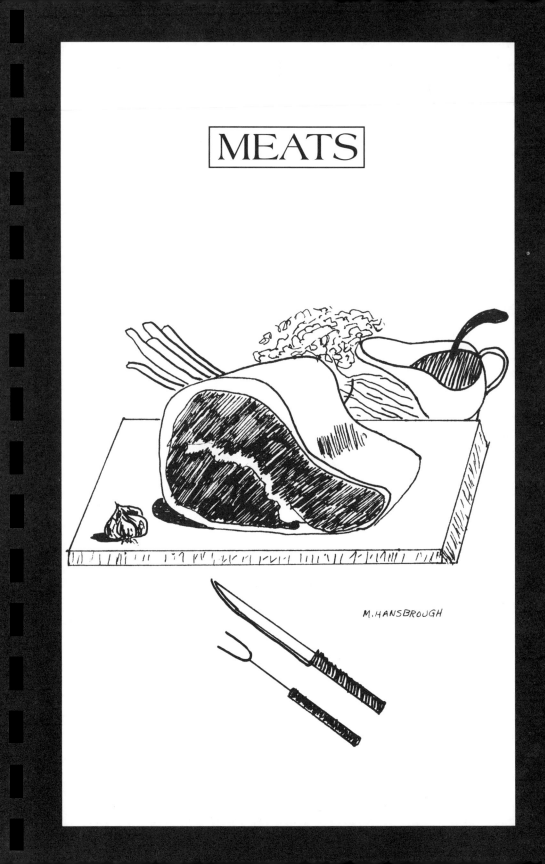

M.HANSBROUGH

# EASY BRISKET

5 to 6 pound very lean
   brisket
Garlic powder
1 cup light brown sugar

1 cup water
1 envelope dry onion soup
   mix
1 cup ketchup

Season brisket heavily with garlic powder. Combine remaining ingredients in small bowl. Pour over brisket in baking pan or roaster. Cover and bake at 350 degrees for 4 hours or until tender. Yield: 12 servings. *This light barbecue taste everyone will enjoy.*

**Nutritional Information Per Serving:**

| Calories | Cholesterol (mg) | Fat (g) | % Calories from Fat |
|---|---|---|---|
| 386 | 123 | 13.2 | 30.7% |

# MUSTARD BRISKET

1 (3-pound) lean beef brisket
2 cups water
⅓ cup Dijon mustard
2 teaspoons dried thyme
½ teaspoon pepper

½ teaspoon salt
4 cloves garlic, minced
2 cups sliced carrots
1 large onion, quartered

Trim all fat from brisket. In a baking pot, add water. In a small bowl, combine mustard, thyme, pepper, salt, and garlic into a paste. Cover brisket with mixture and place in pot. Add carrots and onions around meat. Cover and cook at 325 degrees for 4 hours or until brisket is tender. Slice against grain. Yield: 6 servings.
*A brisket is great because you can put it in the oven and forget about it.*

**Nutritional Information Per Serving:**

| Calories | Cholesterol (mg) | Fat (g) | % Calories from Fat |
|---|---|---|---|
| 390 | 134 | 15.1 | 34.8% |

# MARINATED EYE OF ROUND ROAST

2 tablespoons olive oil
½ cup red wine
4 cloves garlic, minced
⅓ cup red wine vinegar
1 tablespoon lemon-pepper
  seasoning

⅓ cup lemon juice
⅓ cup Worcestershire sauce
1 (4-pound) lean eye of round
  roast

Combine all marinade ingredients together. Cover meat with marinade and keep covered in refrigerator for a day or two, turning several times. Let meat stand at room temperature for an hour before cooking. Roast, uncovered, with marinade, in oven at 325 degrees for two hours. Yield: 10 to 12 servings.

**Nutritional Information Per Serving:**

| Calories | Cholesterol (mg) | Fat (g) | % Calories from Fat |
|----------|------------------|---------|---------------------|
| 238      | 82               | 8.9     | 33.5%               |

# Ⓕ SIRLOIN WITH HERBED WINE SAUCE

2 pounds lean boneless beef
  sirloin steak (¾-inch
  thick)
¼ pound fresh mushrooms,
  sliced
½ cup chopped green onions
¾ cup dry red wine

¾ cup water
2 tablespoons tomato paste
1 teaspoon dried tarragon
1 beef-flavored bouillon cube
2 tablespoons chopped fresh
  parsley

Coat a large skillet with no stick cooking spray and brown steak. Add sliced mushrooms and green onions, sautéing until tender. Add wine, water, tomato paste, tarragon, and bouillon cube. Bring to a boil; reduce heat, and cook 10 minutes or until meat is tender and liquid is reduced by half. Stir in chopped parsley and serve. Yield: 6 to 8 servings.
*To complete your meal, serve with carrots and potatoes.*

**Nutritional Information Per Serving:**

| Calories | Cholesterol (mg) | Fat (g) | % Calories from Fat |
|----------|------------------|---------|---------------------|
| 174      | 69               | 5.1     | 26.6%               |

# SIRLOIN AND SAUCE

1 (1-pound) lean boneless
   sirloin steak
¼ teaspoon dried rosemary
¼ teaspoon pepper
1 tablespoon light margarine
1 tablespoon plain non fat
   yogurt

1 tablespoon Dijon mustard
1 tablespoon Worcestershire
   sauce
1 tablespoon chopped
   parsley

Trim any fat from steak. Sprinkle rosemary and pepper on both sides of steak. Heat a large skillet with no stick cooking spray and melt margarine. Cook steak to desired doneness on both sides. In small saucepan or microwave, combine remaining ingredients except parsley (do not boil); heat. To serve: spoon sauce over warm steak; sprinkle with parsley. Yield: 4 servings.

*This recipe takes little time to prepare with great results!*

**Nutritional Information Per Serving:**

| Calories | Cholesterol (mg) | Fat (g) | % Calories from Fat |
|---|---|---|---|
| 161 | 65 | 6.6 | 37.0% |

## Ⓕ BEEF STROGANOFF

2 pounds lean boneless
   sirloin steak or top round
1 tablespoon light margarine
1 onion, chopped
½ pound fresh mushrooms,
   sliced
2 cloves garlic, minced

2 cups beef broth
2 tablespoons flour
1 teaspoon Worcestershire
   sauce
Dash nutmeg
1 cup non fat plain yogurt
¼ cup white wine

Cut beef into thin strips 1-inch long and ¼-inch wide. In pan, melt margarine and add onions, mushrooms, and garlic, cooking over low heat until tender. Add meat and continue cooking for 10 minutes. Add beef broth and simmer 45 minutes to 1 hour or until meat is tender. Mix flour with Worcestershire sauce, nutmeg and yogurt. Gradually add to meat mixture. Cook slowly until thick; do not boil. Stir in white wine; heat. Yield: 6 servings.

*Great served over noodles.*

**Nutritional Information Per Serving:**

| Calories | Cholesterol (mg) | Fat (g) | % Calories from Fat |
|---|---|---|---|
| 262 | 87 | 6.4 | 22.0% |

# MEATBALLS AND SAUCE

2 pounds ground sirloin
½ teaspoon garlic powder
2 tablespoons chopped
   parsley
1 onion, finely chopped

1 teaspoon dried basil
½ teaspoon dried oregano
1 egg white
Salt and pepper to taste

Combine all ingredients together and shape into balls. Broil in oven on baking sheet approximately 10 minutes, turn, and broil on other side until done. Drain any grease. Add meatballs to Sauce (see recipe below). Yield: 6 to 8 servings.
*This easy, quick version will become a family favorite.*

**Sauce**

1 (26 to 28-ounce) jar
   traditional spaghetti
   sauce

1 (14½-ounce) can whole
   tomatoes, chopped
1 teaspoon dried oregano
1 teaspoon dried basil

Combine all ingredients in large pan and heat.

**Nutritional Information Per Serving:**

| Calories | Cholesterol (mg) | Fat (g) | % Calories from Fat |
|---|---|---|---|
| 227 | 69 | 6.7 | 26.6% |

# MEAT SAUCE

2 pounds ground sirloin
2 cups chopped onion
4 cloves garlic, minced
2 (28-ounce) cans whole
   tomatoes, chopped
1 (6-ounce) can salt-free
   tomato paste

⅔ cup dry red wine
1 tablespoon dried oregano
1 tablespoon dried basil
1 teaspoon dried thyme
1 bay leaf
Salt and pepper to taste
⅓ cup chopped parsley

Brown ground sirloin, onion, and garlic in pan coated with no stick cooking spray. Add remaining ingredients. Bring to boil; reduce heat, and simmer for 1 hour, stirring occasionally. Serve over pasta. Yield: 8 to 10 servings.
*This is the best ever meat sauce! You can double and freeze this recipe so you will have it on hand.*

**Nutritional Information Per Serving:**

| Calories | Cholesterol (mg) | Fat (g) | % Calories from Fat |
|---|---|---|---|
| 193 | 55 | 4.7 | 21.8% |

# Ⓕ CHILI

2 onions, chopped
1 green bell pepper, chopped
4 cloves garlic, minced
2 stalks celery, chopped
2½ pounds ground sirloin
1 (14½-ounce) can natural-no
    salt stewed tomatoes

1 (8-ounce) can tomato sauce
1 (14½-ounce) can beef broth
1 tablespoon flour
5 tablespoons chili powder
1 teaspoon cumin
⅛ teaspoon red pepper
Salt and pepper as desired

Coat a large pot with no stick cooking spray and sauté onion, green pepper, garlic, and celery until tender. Add ground sirloin and cook until done. Skim off any fat. Add remaining ingredients bringing mixture to a boil. Lower heat, and simmer for 1 hour, stirring occasionally. Yield: 6 to 8 servings.
*For a real treat, serve with light shredded Cheddar cheese and light fritos.*

**Nutritional Information Per Serving:**

| Calories | Cholesterol (mg) | Fat (g) | % Calories from Fat |
|---|---|---|---|
| 197 | 65 | 6.2 | 28.4% |

# Ⓒ Ⓕ GRECO

4 onions, chopped
2 green bell peppers,
    chopped
1 red bell pepper, chopped
1 pound fresh mushrooms,
    sliced
2 pounds diet lean ground
    beef
2 cups shell macaroni

2 (15-ounce) cans tomato
    sauce
1 (6-ounce) can tomato paste
1 tablespoon chili powder
1 (17-ounce) can corn,
    drained
Salt and pepper as desired
½ pound shredded reduced
    fat Cheddar cheese

In large pot coated with no stick cooking spray, sauté onion, green and red pepper, and mushrooms until tender. Add meat and cook until done. Drain any grease. Cook macaroni according to directions on package omitting salt and oil. Drain; add to meat mixture. Add remaining ingredients except cheese, mixing well. Place in a large casserole and top with shredded cheese. Bake at 300 degrees for 1 hour. Yield: 12 servings.
*This dish freezes well and feeds a crowd.*

**Nutritional Information Per Serving:**

| Calories | Cholesterol (mg) | Fat (g) | % Calories from Fat |
|---|---|---|---|
| 366 | 50 | 12.0 | 29.4% |

# ⓒ SOUTHWESTERN GRILLED FAJITAS

1 (10-ounce) can light beer
¼ cup chopped cilantro
2 cloves garlic, minced
¼ cup fresh lime juice
2 tablespoons red wine
  vinegar

1 tablespoon Worcestershire
  sauce
1 tablespoon grated lime
  rind
1 teaspoon cumin
1 tablespoon chili powder
2 pounds flank steak

Combine all ingredients except meat; mix well. Pour into a zip-top plastic bag. Add meat, seal bag, and refrigerate overnight. Drain well and grill or broil until done. Yield: 6 to 8 servings.
*Chicken can be used too. Serve with tortillas and condiments.*

**Nutritional Information Per Serving:**

| Calories | Cholesterol (mg) | Fat (g) | % Calories from Fat |
|---|---|---|---|
| 185 | 59 | 9.0 | 43.6% |


# Ⓕ STUFFED GREEN PEPPERS

8 medium green bell peppers
2 onions, chopped
2 stalks celery, chopped
4 green onions, chopped
4 cloves garlic, minced
2 pounds ground sirloin
2 cups cooked rice
Salt and pepper to taste

1 teaspoon dried oregano
½ teaspoon dried basil
2 tablespoons Worcestershire
  sauce
¼ teaspoon cayenne
3 tablespoons tomato paste
½ cup shredded reduced fat
  Cheddar cheese

In large pot, bring water to boil. Meanwhile, cut top off each green pepper and scoop out seeds. Place in boiling water for 5 to 10 minutes or until pepper is tender. Remove from water and place in 3-quart baking dish. In large skillet coated with no stick cooking spray, sauté onions, celery, green onions, and garlic until tender. Add ground sirloin cooking until done. Drain any excess grease. In large bowl, combine cooked rice with ground meat mixture. Add remaining ingredients except cheese, mixing well. Stuff each pepper with meat mixture and divide cheese on top. Bake at 350 degrees for 20 to 25 minutes or until cheese is melted and peppers are heated. Yield: 8 servings.

**Nutritional Information Per Serving:**

| Calories | Cholesterol (mg) | Fat (g) | % Calories from Fat |
|---|---|---|---|
| 259 | 66 | 5.8 | 20.2% |

## ©Ⓕ MEXICAN LASAGNE

1 pound lean ground sirloin
½ cup chopped celery
½ cup chopped onion
2 cloves garlic, minced
¼ cup chopped green bell
    pepper
1 (14½-ounce) can tomatoes,
    crushed

1 (14-ounce) can enchilada
    sauce, divided
Salt and pepper to taste
4 slices light (⅓ less fat)
    American cheese
1 cup low fat cottage cheese
1 egg white, beaten
6 medium flour tortillas, cut
    into thirds

Combine ground sirloin with first four ingredients in pan, cooking over medium heat. Drain any fat. Add tomatoes, ⅔ of the can of enchilada sauce, and salt and pepper to taste. Bring to boil; reduce heat and simmer for 10 minutes. Meanwhile, combine both cheeses and egg white in food processor until blended and American cheese is in pieces; set aside. In frying pan coated with no stick cooking spray, heat remaining enchilada sauce a little at a time and fry flour tortillas until soft. Remove, continuing to add sauce and fry tortillas until all have been done. Spoon one-third meat mixture into a 12x8x2-inch baking dish. Spoon half cheese mixture over meat. Top with half of tortillas. Repeat layers ending with meat. Bake at 350 degrees for 25 minutes. Let stand for 5 minutes before cutting. Yield: 8 servings.

*A great way to serve a Mexican dish to a crowd and it's so good!*

**Nutritional Information Per Serving:**

| Calories | Cholesterol (mg) | Fat (g) | % Calories from Fat |
|---|---|---|---|
| 217 | 37 | 6.9 | 28.7% |

# ITALIAN MEAT LOAF

2 pounds ground sirloin
1 egg white
¾ cup tomato juice
Salt and pepper to taste
2 cloves garlic, minced
1 teaspoon dried oregano
1 teaspoon dried thyme
1 tablespoon dried basil

1 tablespoon olive oil
1 onion, chopped
2 ounces sun-dried tomatoes,
  rehydrated, drained, and
  finely chopped
3 ounces sliced part skim
  mozzarella cheese

In large bowl, combine ground sirloin, egg white, tomato juice, and seasonings. In small skillet coated with no stick cooking spray, heat oil and sauté onions until tender. Add cooked onions and sun-dried tomatoes to meat mixture, mixing well. Put half of meat mixture into a 9x5x3-inch loaf pan, top with mozzarella cheese, and cover with remaining meat mixture. Bake at 350 degrees for 1 hour. Yield: 6 servings.

**Nutritional Information Per Serving:**

| Calories | Cholesterol (mg) | Fat (g) | % Calories from Fat |
|----------|------------------|---------|---------------------|
| 304 | 100 | 11.9 | 35.3% |

# STUFFED FLANK STEAK

1 green pepper, roasted (see
  recipe below)
1 red pepper, roasted (see
  recipe below)
1 yellow pepper, roasted (see
  recipe below)
1 (10-ounce) bag fresh
  spinach

3 cloves garlic
½ cup breadcrumbs
½ cup grated Parmesan
  cheese
1 tablespoon olive oil
3 pounds lean flank steak,
  butterflied

Combine all ingredients in food processor except flank steak and process until chopped in small pieces and well mixed. Place mixture on flank steak. Starting with long side, roll the steak up jelly-roll style. Season with salt and pepper. Secure with toothpick to keep together. Place in baking pan and bake at 350 degrees for 45 minutes. Slice into pinwheels. Yield: 4 to 6 servings.

*To roast peppers: Place peppers on pan and bake at 400 degrees for 30 minutes. Place in paper bag for 20 minutes. Remove skin easily and use in recipe.*

**Nutritional Information Per Serving:**

| Calories | Cholesterol (mg) | Fat (g) | % Calories from Fat |
|----------|------------------|---------|---------------------|
| 451 | 118 | 24.8 | 42.9% |

# GRILLED FLANK STEAK

2½ pounds flank steak
2 tablespoons dry red wine
1 tablespoon Worcestershire
  sauce
1 tablespoon red wine
  vinegar

1 tablespoon prepared
  horseradish
1 tablespoon ketchup
½ teaspoon pepper
1 teaspoon dried thyme
2 cloves garlic, minced

Trim any visible fat from steaks. Combine remaining ingredients together and pour over flank steak. Turn to coat all sides. Cover and marinate in refrigerator 8 hours or overnight, turning steaks occasionally. Grill, covered, over hot fire approximately 7 minutes on each side. Flank steak is served rare. To serve, cut steaks diagonally across the grain into thin slices. Yield: 6 servings.
*Flank steak is easy and very tasty.*

**Nutritional Information Per Serving:**

| Calories | Cholesterol (mg) | Fat (g) | % Calories from Fat |
|----------|------------------|---------|---------------------|
| 304      | 94               | 14.1    | 41.8%               |

# BARBECUED PORK ROAST

1 (3-pound) boneless rolled
  loin pork roast
3 large cloves garlic, sliced
1 teaspoon pepper
1 teaspoon dried thyme
1 onion, sliced
½ cup reduced salt chicken
  broth
1 (6-ounce) can no salt
  tomato paste

½ cup cider vinegar
¼ cup lemon juice
2 tablespoons Worcestershire
  sauce
2 tablespoons light brown
  sugar
1 tablespoon Dijon mustard
½ teaspoon paprika
⅛ teaspoon red pepper

Trim fat from pork roast. Cut deep slits in roast and insert garlic slices. Combine pepper and thyme; rub over surface of roast. In a saucepan coated with no stick cooking spray, sauté onions. Add remaining ingredients and stir until heated and mixed. Place roast in pot coated with no stick cooking spray and cover with barbecue sauce. Bake at 350 degrees for 1½ to 2 hours. Slice and serve. Yield: 6 to 8 servings.
*This sauce is very tasty and will win over barbecue lovers.*

**Nutritional Information Per Serving:**

| Calories | Cholesterol (mg) | Fat (g) | % Calories from Fat |
|----------|------------------|---------|---------------------|
| 262      | 81               | 10.7    | 36.7%               |

# Ⓕ PORK MEDALLIONS WITH BRANDY SAUCE

1 (2 to 2½-pound) boneless
   pork tenderloin
Black pepper
⅔ cup chicken broth
2 tablespoons chopped green
   onion
½ cup evaporated skimmed
   milk

2 tablespoons brandy
2 tablespoons light
   margarine
1 tablespoon lemon juice
Salt to taste
⅛ teaspoon white pepper

Rub tenderloin with pepper. Place on a rack in shallow baking pan; insert meat thermometer. Roast in a 325 degree oven until meat thermometer registers 160 degrees (about 30 minutes per pound). Meanwhile, in a saucepan combine chicken broth and green onions. Bring to boil; reduce heat. Cover and simmer 2 minutes. Add evaporated milk and brandy. Simmer, uncovered, over medium heat until sauce is reduced to ⅔ cup. Add margarine to sauce, one piece at a time, stirring constantly with a wire whisk. Stir in lemon juice, salt, and white pepper. To serve, slice meat across the grain into 18 slices. Top with sauce. Yield: 6 servings.
*This was a rich sauce reduced to one you can enjoy without much guilt.*

**Nutritional Information Per Serving:**

| Calories | Cholesterol (mg) | Fat (g) | % Calories from Fat |
|----------|------------------|---------|---------------------|
| 251 | 107 | 7.7 | 27.7% |

# Ⓕ GARLIC GRILLED PORK TENDERLOIN

3 tablespoons olive oil
1 tablespoon white wine
   vinegar
2 teaspoons chopped dried
   rosemary

¼ teaspoon salt, if desired
¼ teaspoon black pepper
2 cloves garlic, minced
2 (1 pound) lean pork
   tenderloins

Combine all ingredients except meat, stirring well. Place tenderloins in a 12x8x2-inch dish and brush with olive oil mixture over all sides. Cover and refrigerate for 3 hours. Grill tenderloins on barbecue or cook in oven at 350 degrees until meat thermometer registers 160 degrees. Slice and serve. Yield: 8 servings.

**Nutritional Information Per Serving:**

| Calories | Cholesterol (mg) | Fat (g) | % Calories from Fat |
|----------|------------------|---------|---------------------|
| 146 | 79 | 4.6 | 28.4% |

# GLAZED PORK TENDERLOINS

1½ tablespoons Dijon
   mustard
1 clove garlic, minced
¼ teaspoon dried rosemary

¼ teaspoon pepper
1 (1 pound) pork tenderloin
¼ cup orange marmalade

Combine first 4 ingredients; set aside. Trim fat from tenderloin. Slice tenderloin lengthwise, cutting almost to, but not through, outer edge. Spread mustard mixture in each pocket; press gently to close. Spread orange marmalade over tenderloin. Place tenderloin on rack coated with no stick cooking spray. Place rack in broiler pan; add water to pan. Bake at 325 degrees for 40 to 45 minutes or until meat thermometer inserted into thickest portion registers 160 degrees. Slice tenderloin. Yield: 4 servings.

**Nutritional Information Per Serving:**

| Calories | Cholesterol (mg) | Fat (g) | % Calories from Fat |
|---|---|---|---|
| 266 | 81 | 12.7 | 42.8% |

# Ⓕ PORK TENDERS

2 (¾ pound) pork tenderloins
2½ tablespoons Dijon
   mustard
1½ tablespoons honey

1 teaspoon dried rosemary
½ teaspoon dried thyme
¼ teaspoon pepper

Trim fat from tenderloins and place on a rack coated with no stick cooking spray in a shallow roasting pan. In a small bowl, combine remaining ingredients; brush over tenderloins. Insert a meat thermometer into thickest part of tenderloin. Bake at 325 degrees for 45 minutes or until meat thermometer registers 160 degrees, basting frequently with Dijon mustard mixture. Yield: 4 to 6 servings.

*Pork tenderloins are the leanest cut of pork, a crowd pleaser, and easy to prepare.*

**Nutritional Information Per Serving:**

| Calories | Cholesterol (mg) | Fat (g) | % Calories from Fat |
|---|---|---|---|
| 153 | 79 | 4.3 | 25.4% |

# HONEY MUSTARD LAMB CHOPS

8 (4-ounce) lean lamb loin
   chops (2 pounds)
2 large cloves garlic, minced
3 teaspoons dried rosemary

⅛ teaspoon pepper
3 tablespoons honey
2 tablespoons Dijon mustard

Trim any fat from chops. Rub both sides of chops with garlic. Press rosemary and pepper onto both sides also. Place on broiler pan covered with foil. Combine honey and mustard; set aside. Broil chops close to heat for four minutes. Turn chops and spread with honey mixture; broil 4 minutes longer or until done. Yield: 4 servings.
*Fantastic flavor with very little effort to make.*

**Nutritional Information Per Serving:**

| Calories | Cholesterol (mg) | Fat (g) | % Calories from Fat |
|---|---|---|---|
| 413 | 179 | 16.0 | 34.9% |

# VEAL, PEPPERS AND MUSHROOMS

1½ pounds veal round steak,
   about ½-inch thick
¼ cup flour
1 teaspoon paprika
½ teaspoon garlic powder
½ teaspoon dried basil
½ teaspoon dried oregano
2 tablespoons olive oil
½ cup dry white wine

½ cup chicken broth
1 large red bell pepper, cut
   in thin strips
1 large green bell pepper, cut
   in thin strips
¼ pound fresh mushrooms,
   sliced
1 tablespoon lemon juice
2 green onions, chopped

Cut veal into six serving pieces. Mix flour and seasonings together. Coat veal with flour mixture; pound until ¼-inch thick. In large skillet coated with no stick cooking spray, heat oil and brown veal, turning as needed. When done, remove from pan; set aside. Add wine, chicken broth, red and green pepper slices, and mushrooms. Scrape sides and bottom of pan. Add lemon juice and cook until vegetables are tender. Add green onions and sauté few minutes longer. Return veal to pan and serve. Yield: 6 servings.
*This is a great tasting dish.*

**Nutritional Information Per Serving:**

| Calories | Cholesterol (mg) | Fat (g) | % Calories from Fat |
|---|---|---|---|
| 238 | 89 | 8.5 | 32.3% |

# VEAL SALTIMBOCCA

10 small thin veal cutlets
  (approximately 2 pounds)
4 tablespoons flour
2 tablespoons olive oil
10 tablespoons shredded
  part-skim mozzarella
  cheese

10 slices prosciutto
  (approximately 2 ounces)
1½ cups chicken broth
½ cup white wine
Chopped parsley

Dust cutlets with flour and brown on both sides in olive oil in skillet. Remove cutlets from pan and top with cheese. Place prosciutto over cheese (it will adhere to cheese). Add chicken broth and wine to pan, scraping to get all pieces off pan. Reduce liquid by half, by boiling for about 10 minutes. Carefully place prepared veal in pan, cooking over low heat for 10 minutes. Garnish with chopped parsley. Yield: 4 to 6 servings.

*This dish will surely impress your family or guests.*

**Nutritional Information Per Serving:**

| Calories | Cholesterol (mg) | Fat (g) | % Calories from Fat |
|---|---|---|---|
| 387 | 138 | 21.5 | 50.0% |

## Ⓕ VEAL STROGANOFF

1½ pounds lean, trimmed
  veal cutlets (¼-inch thick)
2 cups sliced fresh
  mushrooms
1 cup chopped onion
2 cloves garlic, minced

1 cup beef broth
½ teaspoon pepper
¼ teaspoon dry mustard
¼ teaspoon paprika
¾ cup non fat plain yogurt
¼ cup chopped fresh parsley

Coat a skillet with no stick cooking spray and heat. Add veal; cook until browned. Remove from skillet; drain and wipe pan with paper towel. Add mushrooms, onion, and garlic to skillet; sauté until tender. Add veal, beef broth, pepper, dry mustard, and paprika. Cover, simmer 20 minutes or until veal is tender. Add yogurt, cooking over low heat only until heated. Sprinkle with parsley. Yield: 6 servings.

*With little effort, you will be a hit. Serve over cooked noodles.*

**Nutritional Information Per Serving:**

| Calories | Cholesterol (mg) | Fat (g) | % Calories from Fat |
|---|---|---|---|
| 169 | 91 | 4.1 | 21.9% |

# POULTRY

M. HANSBROUGH

# Ⓕ TURKEY PARMESAN

2 tablespoons flour
½ teaspoon paprika
¼ teaspoon pepper
1 egg white
1 tablespoon water
2 cups dry breadcrumbs

2 tablespoons grated
    Parmesan cheese
1½ pounds turkey cutlets,
    ¼-inch thick
2 tablespoons olive oil
4 ounces part skim
    mozzarella cheese, sliced

Combine flour, paprika, and pepper. Beat together egg white and water in small bowl. Combine breadcrumbs and Parmesan cheese in shallow dish. Dredge turkey in flour mixture. Dip in egg white, then in breadcrumb mixture. Place on plate, cover, and chill in refrigerator for one hour. Coat a skillet with no stick cooking spray and heat olive oil. Brown prepared cutlets on each side. Remove to shallow baking dish. Pour Tomato Sauce (see recipe below) over turkey and top each cutlet with slice of cheese. Bake at 350 degrees for 20 minutes. Yield: 6 servings.
*This easy dish will be a family favorite.*

Tomato Sauce
1 (6-ounce) can tomato paste
½ cup water

½ teaspoon dried basil

Combine all ingredients together.

**Nutritional Information Per Serving:**

| Calories | Cholesterol (mg) | Fat (g) | % Calories from Fat |
| --- | --- | --- | --- |
| 398 | 81 | 11.8 | 26.6% |

# Ⓕ ROASTED TURKEY BREAST

1 (3-pound) turkey breast
1 tablespoon minced garlic
½ teaspoon red pepper

½ teaspoon pepper
½ teaspoon salt

Remove skin from turkey breast. Rinse breast and pat dry. Place in shallow baking dish and add water to ¼-inch high. In small bowl combine seasonings. Rub all over turkey. Place in oven at 325 degrees for 1½ to 2 hours or until internal temperature is 170 degrees on meat thermometer. Yield: 8 servings.
*The turkey has a great flavor. Season the turkey overnight and cook the next day.*

**Nutritional Information Per Serving:**

| Calories | Cholesterol (mg) | Fat (g) | % Calories from Fat |
| --- | --- | --- | --- |
| 213 | 93 | 4.4 | 18.4% |

## Ⓕ TURKEY STEAKS WITH PROSCIUTTO

4 turkey breast steaks (about
   1½ pounds)
Salt and pepper to taste
¼ cup flour, for dredging
2 tablespoons olive oil
1 tablespoon light margarine

4 thin slices prosciutto
   (about 2 ounces)
½ cup chicken broth
1 clove garlic, minced
¼ cup Marsala wine
2 tablespoons chopped
   parsley

Place the turkey steaks between sheets of wax paper and pound them to about ¼-inch thick. Sprinkle with salt and pepper. Dredge lightly in flour and shake off excess. Heat oil and margarine in skillet and cook turkey steaks until golden brown, turn, and cook until done on the other side. Remove to dish. In same skillet, sauté prosciutto briefly, about 15 seconds. Add chicken broth and garlic. Return turkey to pan and top each steak with prosciutto. Pour in Marsala wine and cook for a few minutes reducing sauce. Sprinkle with parsley; serve. Yield: 4 servings.
*Absolutely delicious and will leave quite an impression.*

**Nutritional Information Per Serving:**

| Calories | Cholesterol (mg) | Fat (g) | % Calories from Fat |
|----------|------------------|---------|---------------------|
| 335 | 123 | 10.4 | 28.0% |

## ⒸⒻ TURKEY ENCHILADAS

1 pound ground turkey
½ cup chopped onion
1 clove garlic, minced
1 (4-ounce) can chopped
   green chilies

1 (10-ounce) can enchilada
   sauce
10 to 12 corn tortillas
1 cup shredded reduced fat
   Cheddar cheese

In skillet, cook turkey, onion, and garlic until turkey is done. Add green chilies and continue cooking 5 minutes. In small skillet, heat enchilada sauce and dip each tortilla in sauce to coat both sides. Spoon ¼ cup turkey mixture onto each tortilla. Roll up and place in oblong glass dish coated with no stick cooking spray. Pour remaining sauce over rolled tortillas. Sprinkle with shredded cheese. Bake at 350 degrees for 10 to 15 minutes or until heated through. Yield: 5 to 6 servings.
*This is a Mexican favorite for all.*

**Nutritional Information Per Serving:**

| Calories | Cholesterol (mg) | Fat (g) | % Calories from Fat |
|----------|------------------|---------|---------------------|
| 320 | 60 | 9.8 | 27.6% |

# ⓒ TURKEY VEGETABLE PIZZA

1 (4-ounce) can tomato sauce
1 (6-ounce) can tomato paste
2 tablespoons grated
   Parmesan cheese
1 teaspoon dried oregano
1 teaspoon dried basil
¼ teaspoon garlic powder
1 teaspoon sugar
Salt and pepper to taste
1 pound ground turkey meat

1 (4-ounce) can sliced
   mushrooms, drained
⅓ cup onion slices
1 green bell pepper, cut into
   strips
1 cup broccoli flowerets, cut
   in slices
2 cups shredded part skim
   mozzarella cheese

Combine first 8 ingredients in bowl; mix well. Let stand 1 hour. In skillet, cook ground turkey until done; drain any excess fat. Season to taste. Spread sauce over Pizza Crust (see recipe below). Crumble cooked turkey over sauce. Top with mushrooms, onion slices, green pepper, and broccoli. Bake at 425 degrees for 15 minutes. Top with cheese and bake 5 minutes longer or until cheese is melted. Yield: 10 servings.

*If you are in a pinch, buy a prepared crust and use this recipe for the topping.*

### Pizza Crust
1 package dry yeast
¼ cup warm water
1 cup whole wheat flour
1 cup flour

¼ teaspoon salt
1 tablespoon olive oil
⅔ cup warm water

Dissolve yeast in ¼ cup warm water in small bowl; let stand 5 minutes. Combine flours and salt in large bowl; stir in yeast mixture and oil. Add warm water to make a stiff dough; stir well. Cover and let stand 15 minutes. Turn dough onto a lightly floured surface and knead 8 times. Roll dough into a 16-inch circle; place on pizza pan coated with no stick cooking spray. Bake at 425 degrees for 5 minutes.

*Dough can be divided in half and made into 2 pizza crusts. Freeze extra crust for later date.*

### Nutritional Information Per Serving:

| Calories | Cholesterol (mg) | Fat (g) | % Calories from Fat |
|---|---|---|---|
| 252 | 40 | 9.5 | 33.9% |

# (F) TURKEY JAMBALAYA

1 pound turkey sausage
2 large onions, chopped
2 (6-ounce) packages long
    grain and wild rice mix
1 pound fresh mushrooms,
    sliced
2 tablespoons light
    margarine

1½ pounds (4 cups) cooked,
    diced turkey breasts or
    thighs
1 (2¼-ounce) can sliced black
    olives
1 (14½-ounce) can artichoke
    hearts, quartered
½ cup chopped green onions

In large pot, cut sausage into pieces and brown. Add onions cooking until tender. Drain off any excess grease. Add wild rice to sausage and cook according to directions on package omitting margarine. In another pan, sauté mushrooms in margarine and drain. Add mushrooms, turkey, black olives, and artichoke hearts to cooked rice, tossing gently. Top with chopped green onions. Bake at 350 degrees for 30 minutes or until thoroughly heated. Yield: 8 to 10 servings.
*This is a great way to use leftover turkey meat — you can be a hit twice.*

**Nutritional Information Per Serving:**

| Calories | Cholesterol (mg) | Fat (g) | % Calories from Fat |
|----------|------------------|---------|---------------------|
| 343 | 80 | 10.2 | 26.5% |

# (C)(F) LEMON HERB TURKEY CUTLETS

½ teaspoon dried basil
½ teaspoon dried tarragon
½ teaspoon dried thyme
½ teaspoon dried marjoram
¼ teaspoon pepper
¼ teaspoon salt
1¼ pounds turkey breast
    cutlets (¼-inch thick)

1 tablespoon olive oil
3 cloves garlic, minced
1 tablespoon flour
½ cup chicken broth
2 tablespoons fresh lemon
    juice

Combine first six ingredients; sprinkle over both sides of cutlets and set aside. Coat a large skillet with no stick cooking spray; add oil and heat. Add garlic, stirring, in pan. Add cutlets and cook until browned on each side. Remove to platter. Add flour to skillet, stirring all drippings. Gradually add chicken broth and lemon juice stirring until heated and thick. Return cutlets to sauce and serve. Yield: 4 to 6 servings.
*A quick and very tasty dish. Everyone wanted seconds.*

**Nutritional Information Per Serving:**

| Calories | Cholesterol (mg) | Fat (g) | % Calories from Fat |
|----------|------------------|---------|---------------------|
| 145 | 57 | 4.0 | 24.8% |

# Ⓕ OVEN FRIED PARMESAN CHICKEN

**Marinade**

¾ cup non fat plain yogurt
4 tablespoons lemon juice
1½ tablespoons Dijon
   mustard
3 cloves garlic, minced

½ teaspoon dried oregano
10 boneless, skinless chicken
   breasts
2 tablespoons light
   margarine, melted

Combine all ingredients except margarine. Pour over chicken, coating chicken. Marinate, covered, 2 hours or overnight in refrigerator. Drain chicken and coat with Breadcrumb Coating (see recipe below). Place on baking sheet coated with no stick cooking spray and chill for one hour (if time permitted). Drizzle chicken with margarine. Bake at 350 degrees for 45 minutes to 1 hour or until tender and golden brown. Yield: 10 servings.
*You will not miss fried chicken with this recipe.*

**Breadcrumb Coating**
2 cups dry breadcrumbs
        4½ tablespoons Parmesan
           cheese

Combine all coating ingredients in shallow bowl.

**Nutritional Information Per Serving:**

| Calories | Cholesterol (mg) | Fat (g) | % Calories from Fat |
|---|---|---|---|
| 247 | 71 | 5.3 | 19.5% |

# Ⓕ HONEY MUSTARD CHICKEN

1 tablespoon olive oil
⅓ cup Dijon mustard
3 tablespoons honey
½ teaspoon curry

½ teaspoon dried tarragon
8 skinless, boneless chicken
   breasts

Blend oil, mustard, honey, curry, and tarragon. Arrange chicken in 11x7x2-inch baking dish coated with no stick cooking spray. Pour sauce over chicken. Bake at 350 degrees for 35 minutes or until chicken is done. Yield: 8 servings.
*Quick, tasty, and spicy.*

**Nutritional Information Per Serving:**

| Calories | Cholesterol (mg) | Fat (g) | % Calories from Fat |
|---|---|---|---|
| 171 | 68 | 3.8 | 20.2% |

# Ⓕ COMPANY CHICKEN

8 boneless, skinless chicken
   breasts or thighs
Salt and pepper to taste
2 tablespoons olive oil
1 bunch green onions,
   chopped
2 cloves garlic, minced

½ pound fresh mushrooms,
   sliced
½ cup white wine
1 (28-ounce) can tomatoes,
   slightly chopped
½ cup chicken broth

Season chicken breasts with salt and pepper. In large skillet coated with no stick cooking spray, heat olive oil and brown chicken pieces. Remove from pan and set aside. Add green onions, garlic, and mushrooms, and sauté until tender. Add white wine, tomatoes, and broth. Bring to boil, adjust seasonings, and reduce to simmer. Add the chicken, cover, and continue to cook for about 30 to 40 minutes, or until chicken is tender. Yield: 8 servings.

*The ingredients for this recipe will usually be on hand for the unexpected guest.*

**Nutritional Information Per Serving:**

| Calories | Cholesterol (mg) | Fat (g) | % Calories from Fat |
|---|---|---|---|
| 206 | 69 | 5.4 | 23.5% |

# Ⓕ CHICKEN ELEGANTE

2 tablespoons light
   margarine
⅓ cup chopped mushrooms
1 green bell pepper, chopped
4 green onions, chopped
⅓ cup plus 1 tablespoon flour
⅛ teaspoon pepper

2 cups chicken broth
1 cup evaporated skimmed
   milk
2 cups diced cooked chicken
¼ teaspoon chopped
   pimiento

In large skillet, melt margarine and sauté mushrooms, green pepper and green onions until tender. Blend in flour and pepper and stir until vegetables are coated. Remove from heat and slowly stir in broth and evaporated skimmed milk. Return to heat and bring to a boil, stirring constantly. Boil for 1 minute. Add chicken and pimiento continuing to stir until chicken is heated through. Yield: 4 to 6 servings.

*Can be served over toast points or noodles.*

**Nutritional Information Per Serving:**

| Calories | Cholesterol (mg) | Fat (g) | % Calories from Fat |
|---|---|---|---|
| 195 | 42 | 5.1 | 23.5% |

# Ⓕ CHICKEN BREASTS DIANE

6 large skinless, boneless
chicken breasts
Salt and pepper to taste
1 tablespoon olive oil
1 bunch green onions,
chopped

Juice of 1 lemon
2 tablespoons chopped
parsley
1 tablespoon Dijon mustard
⅓ cup chicken broth

Place chicken breasts between sheets of waxed paper and pound slightly with mallet to flatten. Sprinkle with salt and pepper, if desired. In large skillet, heat olive oil. Cook chicken for several minutes on each side until done. Remove from skillet and set aside. Add green onions, lemon juice, parsley, and mustard to pan. Cook, stirring constantly, for 1 minute. Whisk in broth and stir until smooth. Pour sauce over chicken and serve immediately. Yield: 6 servings.
*This last minute dish is delicious!*

**Nutritional Information Per Serving:**

| Calories | Cholesterol (mg) | Fat (g) | % Calories from Fat |
|---|---|---|---|
| 163 | 69 | 4.0 | 22.3% |

# EASY CHICKEN

⅓ cup olive oil
⅓ cup sherry
1 tablespoon fresh lemon
juice
⅓ cup finely chopped onion

2 cloves garlic, minced
1 teaspoon dried rosemary
Pepper to taste
4 skinless, boneless chicken
breasts

In small bowl, whisk together olive oil, sherry, lemon juice, onion, garlic, rosemary, and pepper. Place chicken in a shallow glass dish and pour marinade over. Cover and refrigerate 2 to 4 hours. Broil or grill chicken until done, basting with marinade. Yield: 4 servings.
*A good marinade for other meats.*

**Nutritional Information Per Serving:**

| Calories | Cholesterol (mg) | Fat (g) | % Calories from Fat |
|---|---|---|---|
| 329 | 67 | 20.9 | 57.2% |

## Ⓕ CHICKEN CHERRY JUBILEE

15 to 20 skinless, boneless
   chicken breasts and
   thighs
Salt and pepper to taste
2 onions, thinly sliced
1 cup water

1 (12-ounce) bottle chili
   sauce
½ cup light brown sugar
1 cup sherry
1 (16-ounce) can pitted dark
   cherries, drained

Season chicken with salt and pepper. Place in large broiler pan and cover with sliced onions. Broil until chicken is brown. Meanwhile, combine water, chili sauce, brown sugar, sherry, and cherries over low heat and mix well. When chicken is brown, remove and discard onions and transfer chicken to a baking dish. Pour sauce over chicken. Bake, covered, at 325 degrees for 2 hours. Yield: 12 servings.
*This recipe had to be included because it's different and tasty.*

**Nutritional Information Per Serving:**

| Calories | Cholesterol (mg) | Fat (g) | % Calories from Fat |
|---|---|---|---|
| 282 | 86 | 2.0 | 6.3% |

## Ⓕ CHICKEN IN SHERRY

12 boneless, skinless chicken
   breasts
Paprika and pepper to
   season chicken
1 (10¾-ounce) can 99% fat
   free cream of mushroom
   soup

1 (3-ounce) can sliced
   mushrooms, drained
1 cup non fat plain yogurt
½ cup cooking sherry

Season chicken breasts with paprika and pepper on both sides. Place in large casserole dish. In bowl, combine remaining ingredients and pour over chicken. Bake at 350 degrees for 1¼ hours or until chicken is tender. Yield: 12 servings.
*Need a quick success, try this one.*

**Nutritional Information Per Serving:**

| Calories | Cholesterol (mg) | Fat (g) | % Calories from Fat |
|---|---|---|---|
| 171 | 69 | 2.5 | 13.0% |

# Ⓕ CHICKEN IN VINEGAR SAUCE

4 tablespoons olive oil
5 cloves garlic, minced
12 skinless, boneless chicken
    breasts
1 tablespoon dried rosemary

Salt and pepper to taste
Dash cayenne
½ cup red wine vinegar
½ cup dry white wine
¼ cup finely chopped parsley

Coat a large skillet with no stick cooking spray and heat olive oil and garlic. Add chicken and sprinkle with rosemary, salt and pepper, and cayenne. Turn chicken to brown on both sides and sprinkle other side with seasoning. Add vinegar and wine. Cook over low heat for 30 minutes. Remove chicken to serving platter. Bring vinegar sauce to boil, stirring, and cook until sauce thickens slightly. Pour sauce over chicken, and sprinkle with parsley. Yield: 6 servings.
*Do not skip this recipe because of the name as it will be one you will really enjoy.*

**Nutritional Information Per Serving:**

| Calories | Cholesterol (mg) | Fat (g) | % Calories from Fat |
|----------|------------------|---------|---------------------|
| 361      | 137              | 12.0    | 30.0%               |


# BASIL CHICKEN BREASTS

2 pounds boneless, skinless
    chicken breasts
1 tablespoon basil
2 teaspoons minced garlic

2 tablespoons olive oil
¼ teaspoon white pepper
Dash hot pepper sauce

Cut chicken breasts into half-inch chunks. Toss with basil and garlic. In pan heat oil and sauté chicken chunks until done, stirring to keep from sticking. Add seasonings. Yield: 4 to 6 servings.
*Great tossed with the pasta of your choice. For a variation, add chopped green onions.*

**Nutritional Information Per Serving:**

| Calories | Cholesterol (mg) | Fat (g) | % Calories from Fat |
|----------|------------------|---------|---------------------|
| 219      | 86               | 9.1     | 37.5%               |

# (F) TARRAGON CHICKEN

3 pounds boneless, skinless
  chicken breasts, cut in
  pieces
Flour
1¼ cups dry white wine
3 large cloves garlic, minced

1½ teaspoons dried tarragon
Salt and pepper to taste
¾ cup non fat plain yogurt
1½ tablespoons flour
1 tablespoon chopped
  parsley

Dust chicken pieces in flour. Coat a pan with no stick cooking spray and heat. Add chicken and toss in skillet until brown. Add wine, garlic, and seasonings. Cover and simmer for 20 to 30 minutes until chicken is done and wine reduced, spooning sauce over chicken. In small bowl, combine yogurt and flour. Add to wine sauce, blending well. Cook only until sauce is hot. Sprinkle with parsley and serve. Yield: 4 to 6 servings.
*Serve over rice or even as an hor d'oeuvre with toothpicks.*

**Nutritional Information Per Serving:**

| Calories | Cholesterol (mg) | Fat (g) | % Calories from Fat |
|---|---|---|---|
| 312 | 132 | 2.9 | 8.5% |

# (F) HERBED CHICKEN IN WINE

4 boneless, skinless chicken
  breasts
½ teaspoon dried basil
½ teaspoon dried oregano
¼ teaspoon white pepper
½ cup dry white wine
2 tablespoons flour

2 tablespoons water
1 tablespoon olive oil
2 carrots, julienne sliced
2 green onions, thinly sliced
½ pound mushrooms, sliced
Salt and pepper to taste

Place chicken breasts in an 8-inch square baking dish coated with no stick cooking spray. Sprinkle with herbs and pour in wine. Cover and bake at 350 degrees for 25 to 30 minutes or until chicken is done. Combine flour with water; set aside. In skillet, heat olive oil and sauté vegetables until tender. Pour pan juices from chicken into flour mixture and then pour into skillet. Salt and pepper to taste. Cook, stirring over medium heat until thickened. Serve sauce over chicken breasts. Yield: 4 servings.
*Wonderful!*

**Nutritional Information Per Serving:**

| Calories | Cholesterol (mg) | Fat (g) | % Calories from Fat |
|---|---|---|---|
| 226 | 68 | 5.2 | 20.8% |

## Ⓕ CHICKEN BREASTS WITH ARTICHOKES AND MUSHROOMS

2 pounds skinless, boneless chicken breasts
Onion powder and lots of paprika
Salt and pepper to taste
1 (14-ounce) can artichoke hearts, drained
½ pound fresh mushrooms, sliced

1 bunch green onions, chopped
2 cloves garlic, minced
2 tablespoons light margarine
2 tablespoons flour
⅔ cup chicken broth
3 tablespoons sherry

Season chicken heavily with onion powder, paprika, and salt and pepper. Place chicken in bottom of a 3-quart casserole. Cut artichoke hearts and place around chicken. In small skillet coated with no stick cooking spray, sauté mushrooms, green onions, and garlic until tender. Place mushroom mixture on top of chicken. In same skillet, melt margarine and add flour, stirring. Gradually add chicken broth and sherry, cooking until smooth. Pour sauce over all in casserole. Bake, covered, at 350 degrees for 1 hour. Remove cover, and continue baking for 15 minutes to brown chicken. Yield: 8 servings.
*This attractive chicken dish is very tasty. If desired, boneless, skinless thighs can be used.*

**Nutritional Information Per Serving:**

| Calories | Cholesterol (mg) | Fat (g) | % Calories from Fat |
|---|---|---|---|
| 179 | 66 | 3.2 | 16.1% |

## Ⓒ Ⓕ CHICKEN NUGGETS

⅓ cup honey
½ cup dry sherry
2 tablespoons lemon juice
1 teaspoon ginger

1 teaspoon cinnamon
2 cloves garlic, minced
1½ pounds boneless, skinless chicken breasts, cubed

Combine honey, sherry, lemon juice, ginger, cinnamon, and garlic in a zip-top plastic bag. Add chicken cubes, seal, and marinate overnight in pan coated with no stick cooking spray. Broil for 5 minutes or until done, basting with marinade. Serve with toothpicks.
*An unusual flavor makes this recipe special.*

**Nutritional Information Per Piece:**

| Calories | Cholesterol (mg) | Fat (g) | % Calories from Fat |
|---|---|---|---|
| 19 | 7 | 0.1 | 6.8% |

# COUNTRY CHICKEN

5 cloves garlic, minced
1 tablespoon lemon juice
4 chicken breasts, skin
   removed
1½ tablespoons light
   margarine
1½ tablespoons olive oil
1 cup sliced fresh
   mushrooms

½ cup dry white wine
1 bay leaf
1 teaspoon Dijon mustard
½ cup chicken broth
1 tablespoon chopped
   parsley
2 green onions, finely sliced

Combine garlic and lemon juice and rub over chicken. Let stand for 10 minutes. In large pan, melt margarine and olive oil over low heat. Add chicken pieces and sauté for 15 minutes, turning once. Add mushrooms, wine, and bay leaf. Cover and cook over a low heat for 10 minutes. Blend mustard with chicken broth. Pour over chicken and continue cooking, covered, until chicken is tender. Add parsley and green onions. Discard bay leaf. Cook only until sauce thickens (remove chicken and turn heat higher if needed). Yield: 4 servings.

*This chicken has a light flavorful sauce. It's good with rice.*

**Nutritional Information Per Serving:**

| Calories | Cholesterol (mg) | Fat (g) | % Calories from Fat |
|---|---|---|---|
| 238 | 69 | 9.2 | 34.7% |

## Ⓕ DILLED CHICKEN AND ARTICHOKES

3 tablespoons flour
½ teaspoon pepper
½ teaspoon grated lemon
   rind
1½ pounds skinless, boneless
   chicken breasts, cut in
   strips

2 tablespoons light
   margarine
1 (14½-ounce) can artichoke
   hearts, quartered and
   drained
¼ cup white wine
1 tablespoon lemon juice
1 teaspoon dried dill weed

Combine flour, pepper, and lemon rind; dredge chicken in flour mixture. Coat a skillet with no stick cooking spray; add margarine. Heat until hot and add chicken, cooking until chicken is browned on each side. Add artichokes, cooking and stirring until heated. Combine wine, lemon juice and dill weed; pour over chicken. Cover, reduce heat, and simmer 5 minutes; serve. Yield: 6 servings.

*Dill gives this dish a wonderful flavor.*

**Nutritional Information Per Serving:**

| Calories | Cholesterol (mg) | Fat (g) | % Calories from Fat |
|---|---|---|---|
| 181 | 66 | 3.5 | 17.6% |

# Ⓕ CHICKEN FULL OF FLAVOR

4 tablespoons flour
¼ teaspoon salt, if desired
¼ teaspoon pepper
8 boneless, skinless chicken
   breasts
1 tablespoon olive oil
1 bunch green onions, sliced

½ pound sliced mushrooms
1 cup reduced fat chicken
   broth
½ cup dry white wine
1 tablespoon lemon juice
1 tablespoon chopped
   parsley

Combine flour, salt and pepper together in small bowl. Dredge chicken breasts in the flour mixture. In a skillet coated with no stick cook spray, heat olive oil and cook chicken until golden brown and no longer pink inside. Remove to platter. Coat skillet again with no stick cooking spray, and add green onions and mushrooms, cooking and stirring until tender. Pour in chicken broth, wine and lemon juice; bring to a boil, stirring. Cook for 5 minutes or until slightly thickened. Reduce heat to low and stir in parsley. Return chicken to pan; cook over low heat until thoroughly heated. Yield: 8 servings.
*The name says it all with this dish.*

**Nutritional Information Per Serving:**

| Calories | Cholesterol (mg) | Fat (g) | % Calories from Fat |
|---|---|---|---|
| 192 | 69 | 3.9 | 17.2% |

# Ⓕ SKILLET CHICKEN STROGANOFF

1 (14½-ounce) can stewed
   tomatoes
1 pound boneless, skinless
   cubed chicken breasts
½ pound mushrooms,
   quartered

1 onion, chopped
1 teaspoon dried thyme
4 ounces rotini pasta,
   uncooked
½ cup non fat plain yogurt

Drain tomatoes reserving liquid. Add water to liquid, if needed, to measure ¾ cup. In large skillet coated with no stick cooking spray, cook chicken with mushrooms, onion, and thyme. If desired, salt and pepper to taste. Stir in pasta, reserved liquid, and tomatoes. Cover and cook over medium heat 10 minutes or until pasta is done, stirring occasionally. Remove from heat; stir in yogurt. Yield: 4 servings.
*In a pinch, open your cabinet for this dish.*

**Nutritional Information Per Serving:**

| Calories | Cholesterol (mg) | Fat (g) | % Calories from Fat |
|---|---|---|---|
| 301 | 93 | 3.1 | 9.3% |

## Ⓒ Ⓕ CHICKEN ETOUFFÉE

½ cup flour
1 onion, chopped
½ cup chopped celery
1 green bell pepper, chopped
4 cloves garlic, minced
1 (28-ounce) can tomatoes, chopped
1 (14½-ounce) can chicken broth
Salt and pepper to taste

½ teaspoon dried thyme
1 tablespoon Worcestershire sauce
3 boneless, skinless chicken breasts, cubed
¼ cup minced parsley
1 bunch green onions, chopped
1½ cups rice

Place flour on baking sheet and bake at 400 degrees for 20 minutes or until dark brown. Check and stir flour while baking. In large pot coated with no stick cooking spray, sauté onion, celery, green pepper, and garlic until tender. Add browned flour and mix well. Stir in tomatoes, chicken broth, and seasonings. Add cubed chicken. Heat to boiling, reduce heat, and simmer uncovered for about 15 minutes, stirring occasionally. Add parsley and green onions, cooking another 5 minutes. Cook rice according to directions on package. Serve étouffé over cooked rice. Yield: 6 servings.

**Nutritional Information Per Serving:**

| Calories | Cholesterol (mg) | Fat (g) | % Calories from Fat |
|----------|------------------|---------|---------------------|
| 331 | 35 | 2.1 | 5.8% |

## Ⓕ BARBECUED CHICKEN

½ cup finely chopped onion
2 tablespoons light brown sugar
2 tablespoons cider vinegar
2 tablespoons prepared mustard
1 tablespoon chili powder

1 teaspoon Worcestershire sauce
1 large clove garlic, minced
½ cup reduced-calorie ketchup
8 (6-ounce) skinless chicken breast halves (or thighs)

Combine first 8 ingredients in saucepan; stir well. Bring to a boil over medium heat. Cover, reduce heat, and simmer for 20 minutes. Place chicken on foil lined broiler pan and coat with barbecue sauce. Broil 15 minutes in oven, baste, turn over and broil another 15 minutes. Yield: 8 servings.
*Great for an indoor barbecue.*

**Nutritional Information Per Serving:**

| Calories | Cholesterol (mg) | Fat (g) | % Calories from Fat |
|----------|------------------|---------|---------------------|
| 239 | 97 | 5.5 | 20.9% |

## Ⓕ CHICKEN FRICASSEE

1 large onion, chopped
3 cloves garlic, minced
2 tablespoons canola oil
½ cup water
3 to 4 pounds skinless,
    boneless chicken breasts
    (or thighs)
½ cup flour dissolved in 1
    cup water

1½ cups chicken broth
1 bunch green onions,
    chopped
2 tablespoons chopped
    parsley
Dash cayenne
Salt and pepper to taste

In a large, heavy pot, sauté onion and garlic in oil until browned, stirring frequently. Add ½ cup water and continue cooking 5 minutes. Add chicken; bring to a boil. Cover and reduce heat, cooking approximately 30 minutes or until chicken is tender. Add water and flour mixture, stirring until smooth. Gradually add chicken broth cooking until chicken is done. If necessary, add water to make gravy right consistency. Stir in green onion, parsley, cayenne, and salt and pepper if desired. Yield: 8 to 10 servings.
*This dish is super served over rice as it makes a good white gravy.*

**Nutritional Information Per Serving:**

| Calories | Cholesterol (mg) | Fat (g) | % Calories from Fat |
|----------|------------------|---------|---------------------|
| 238      | 92               | 5.0     | 19.0%               |

## HERBED CHICKEN

2 tablespoons light
    margarine
2 tablespoons olive oil
½ cup finely chopped onion
¼ cup lemon juice
2 tablespoons Worcestershire
    sauce

1 teaspoon dried basil
¼ teaspoon marjoram
1 teaspoon dried oregano
2 large cloves garlic, minced
8 boneless, skinless, chicken
    breasts

Heat margarine and oil in a 13x9x2-inch rectangular pan in a 375 degree oven until margarine is melted. Stir in remaining ingredients except chicken. Place chicken in pan, turning to coat with herb mixture. Cook, uncovered, 20 minutes. Turn chicken, cooking about 30 minutes longer. Yield: 8 (one-piece) servings.
*Dark meat can be used for this easy tasty recipe.*

**Nutritional Information Per Serving:**

| Calories | Cholesterol (mg) | Fat (g) | % Calories from Fat |
|----------|------------------|---------|---------------------|
| 183      | 68               | 6.3     | 31.0%               |

# ♥ CHICKEN AND VEGETABLE STIR-FRY

**Marinade**

2 tablespoons lite soy sauce
2 tablespoons vinegar
1 tablespoon olive oil
4 cloves minced garlic
½ teaspoon sugar

¼ teaspoon black pepper
¼ teaspoon dry mustard
12 chicken breasts, cut into
  strips

Combine all ingredients together in glass dish. Toss and cover chicken pieces for at least three hours. Refrigerate. Remove chicken from marinade and Stir-Fry (see recipe below).

**Stir-Fry**

⅛ cup lite soy sauce
1 tablespoon olive oil
1 onion, coarsely chopped
1 green bell pepper, coarsely
  chopped
1 bunch broccoli flowerets
3 carrots, sliced diagonally
¼ pound fresh mushrooms,
  cut in half

1 (6-ounce) box frozen
  Chinese pea pods
1 (8-ounce) can sliced water
  chestnuts, drained
1 cup reduced fat chicken
  broth
1 teaspoon cornstarch
½ teaspoon sugar
⅛ teaspoon red pepper

Using a non-stick skillet, brown chicken strips in soy sauce. Stir fry several minutes until done; remove from skillet. Heat oil and add onions, green pepper, broccoli flowerets, carrots, and mushrooms to skillet, stirring until vegetables are crisp tender. Add pea pods and heat. Return chicken to skillet and stir in water chestnuts. In small bowl, combine chicken broth with cornstarch and sugar. Pour over chicken and vegetables. Add red pepper. Heat until thick. Serve over cooked rice. Yield: 6 to 8 servings.

**Nutritional Information Per Serving:**

| Calories | Cholesterol (mg) | Fat (g) | % Calories from Fat |
|----------|------------------|---------|---------------------|
| 269 | 103 | 4.6 | 15.6% |

# Ⓕ CHICKEN ROLL UPS

4 skinless, boneless chicken
　breasts
1 tablespoon Dijon mustard
⅓ pound fresh asparagus,
　trimmed
2 tablespoons flour
½ teaspoon dried thyme,
　divided

¼ teaspoon garlic powder
¼ teaspoon paprika
⅛ teaspoon white pepper
1 tomato, cored and sliced
1 red onion, thinly sliced
½ cup chicken broth
½ cup dry white wine

Pound chicken breasts ½-inch thick. Spread with mustard. Place 2 asparagus spears on each chicken breast and roll up, securing with toothpick. Combine flour with ¼ teaspoon thyme, garlic powder, paprika, and pepper. Roll chicken breasts in flour mixture. Place tomato and onion slices in an 11x7x2-inch baking dish coated with no stick cooking spray. Arrange chicken rolls on top. Combine chicken broth, wine, and remaining ¼ teaspoon thyme. Pour over chicken. Cover loosely with foil. Bake at 350 degrees for 20 minutes, basting occasionally. Uncover and bake 10 to 15 minutes longer or until chicken is done. Yield: 4 servings.
*Colorful and impressive.*

**Nutritional Information Per Serving:**

| Calories | Cholesterol (mg) | Fat (g) | % Calories from Fat |
|---|---|---|---|
| 194 | 69 | 2.3 | 10.8% |

# Ⓕ CHICKEN DIVAN

2 bunches fresh broccoli
3 cups chopped, cooked
   chicken breasts (about
   1½ pounds boneless,
   skinless breasts)
1 cup skim milk
1 (10¾-ounce) can one-third-
   less-salt cream of chicken
   soup
1 teaspoon lemon juice

⅛ teaspoon pepper
3 tablespoons flour
3 tablespoons water
½ cup finely crushed whole
   wheat breadcrumbs
1 tablespoon light margarine
1 cup reduced fat sharp
   Cheddar cheese,
   shredded

Cut stems of broccoli off leaving flowerets. Place in a 2-quart casserole with ⅓ cup water. Cover and cook on high in microwave for 8 minutes or until tender. Arrange broccoli in an oblong dish. Spoon chicken on top of broccoli. In a heavy saucepan, combine milk, chicken soup, lemon juice, and pepper. Stir well. In a small bowl, combine flour and water. Add to soup mixture. Bring to a boil over medium heat, stirring constantly with wire whisk, about 5 minutes. Mixture will get thick and bubbly. Pour evenly over chicken. Combine breadcrumbs and margarine in a small bowl. Sprinkle over soup mixture. Top with shredded cheese. Bake at 350 degrees for 20 minutes or until thoroughly heated. Yield: 6 servings.
*Always a hit!*

**Nutritional Information Per Serving:**

| Calories | Cholesterol (mg) | Fat (g) | % Calories from Fat |
|---|---|---|---|
| 310 | 95 | 9.1 | 26.4% |

# CHICKEN BREASTS FLORENTINE

8 boneless, skinless chicken
   breasts
Flour (approximately ⅓ cup)
2 tablespoons olive oil
2 tablespoons light
   margarine
1 (10-ounce) package frozen
   chopped spinach

8 thin square slices part skim
   mozzarella cheese (about
   6 ounces)
½ cup chicken broth
¼ cup white wine
¼ cup lemon juice

Dust chicken breasts with flour. In large skillet coated with no stick cooking spray, heat olive oil and margarine and sauté breasts about 4 minutes on each side until lightly browned. Remove to a 3-quart oblong dish. Cook spinach according to directions on package; squeeze and drain well. Top each chicken breast with cooked spinach and slice of mozzarella cheese. Add chicken broth to the same pan used to sauté breasts. Next, add wine and lemon juice, scraping to remove drippings and stirring until heated. Pour sauce over chicken. Bake at 325 degrees for 25 minutes. Cheese should be melted and breasts heated thoroughly. Yield: 8 servings.
*This impressive dish is absolutely delicious.*

**Nutritional Information Per Serving:**

| Calories | Cholesterol (mg) | Fat (g) | % Calories from Fat |
|---|---|---|---|
| 293 | 80 | 12.6 | 38.7% |

## ©Ⓕ HACIENDA CHICKEN

8 (3½-ounce) boneless,
   skinless chicken breasts
1 tablespoon cumin
2 tablespoons canola oil
2 cloves garlic, minced
1 large onion, thinly sliced
   and separated into rings

¾ cup picante sauce
½ cup non fat plain yogurt
1 tablespoon flour
1 tablespoon chopped
   parsley

Sprinkle chicken breasts evenly with cumin. Brown chicken in oil in skillet. Add garlic and arrange onion rings over all. Drizzle with picante sauce. Cover and cook over a low heat until chicken is cooked through, 25 to 30 minutes. Remove chicken onto a platter. Combine yogurt and flour and whisk into juices in skillet. Heat but do not boil. Pour over chicken and top with parsley. Yield: 8 servings.
*Chicken is great served over rice.*

**Nutritional Information Per Serving:**

| Calories | Cholesterol (mg) | Fat (g) | % Calories from Fat |
|---|---|---|---|
| 168 | 58 | 5.0 | 26.9% |

## ⓒⒻ CHICKEN FAJITA PIZZA

1 pound boneless, skinless chicken breasts, cut into strips
1 teaspoon chili powder
Salt and pepper as desired
½ teaspoon garlic powder
1 medium onion, thinly sliced
1 medium green bell pepper, thinly sliced into strips
1 (10-ounce) can prepared pizza crust
½ cup prepared picante sauce
1 cup shredded reduced fat Monterey Jack cheese

In large skillet coated with no stick cooking spray, sauté chicken over medium heat until done. Stir in seasoning. Add onion and green pepper, cooking until vegetables are partially done. Coat a pizza pan with no stick cooking spray and unroll dough and place in pan; starting at center, press out with hands. Bake at 425 degrees for 6 to 8 minutes or until light golden brown. Remove from oven and spoon chicken mixture over partially baked crust. Spoon picante sauce over chicken and sprinkle with cheese. Return to oven and bake for 10 to 12 minutes. Yield: 8 servings.

*Need a quick supper and something to please the kids — this one will please all.*

**Nutritional Information Per Serving:**

| Calories | Cholesterol (mg) | Fat (g) | % Calories from Fat |
|---|---|---|---|
| 194 | 35 | 5.5 | 25.5% |

# ©Ⓕ MEXICAN CHICKEN CASSEROLE

1½ cups chicken stock
1 cup skim milk
½ cup flour
½ cup non fat plain yogurt
1 (10-ounce) can diced
    tomatoes and green
    chilies, drained
1 (4-ounce) can diced green
    chilies, drained
¼ cup chopped parsley
1 tablespoon chili powder
1 teaspoon dried oregano
Salt and pepper to taste

1 onion, chopped
1 red bell pepper, seeded and
    chopped
1 green bell pepper, seeded
    and chopped
2 cloves garlic, minced
10 flour tortillas, cut in
    quarters
2 cups skinless, cooked
    chicken chunks
½ cup shredded reduced-fat
    sharp Cheddar cheese

In saucepan, bring chicken stock to a simmer. In small bowl, whisk milk into flour to make a smooth paste. Add to chicken stock and cook until thickened and smooth, stirring constantly. Remove from heat and stir in yogurt, tomatoes and green chilies, green chilies, parsley, chili powder, and oregano. Season with salt and pepper to taste; set aside. In skillet coated with no stick cooking spray, sauté onions, red and green peppers, and garlic until tender. Line bottom of a shallow 3-quart baking dish with half the tortillas. Sprinkle half of the chicken and half of the onion mixture over the tortillas. Spoon half of the sauce evenly on the top. Repeat layers ending with cheese. Bake at 350 degrees for 25 to 30 minutes or until bubbly. Yield: 8 servings.
*This will be a family favorite.*

**Nutritional Information Per Serving:**

| Calories | Cholesterol (mg) | Fat (g) | % Calories from Fat |
|----------|------------------|---------|---------------------|
| 208 | 31 | 4.8 | 20.7% |

# ©Ⓕ CHICKEN ENCHILADA CASSEROLE

1 (4-ounce) can chopped
   green chilies
2 onions, chopped
1 (28-ounce) can tomatoes,
   undrained and chopped
¼ teaspoon garlic powder
½ teaspoon dried oregano
½ cup water

1½ pounds cooked skinless,
   boneless chicken breasts,
   chopped
2 cups non fat plain yogurt
4 (12-inch) flour tortillas,
   torn into 1-inch strips
1 (8-ounce) package part
   skim mozzarella cheese,
   shredded

Coat a skillet with no stick cooking spray and sauté the green chilies and onion until tender. Stir in tomatoes, garlic powder, oregano, and water. Simmer, uncovered, about 30 minutes or until thick. Combine chicken and yogurt and place in a shallow 3-quart baking dish coated with no stick cooking spray. Add tortilla strips on top of chicken mixture; cover with tomato sauce. Top casserole with shredded mozzarella cheese. Bake at 350 degrees for 20 to 30 minutes or until thoroughly heated. Yield: 10 servings.

**Nutritional Information Per Serving:**

| Calories | Cholesterol (mg) | Fat (g) | % Calories from Fat |
|---|---|---|---|
| 304 | 53 | 9.2 | 27.3% |

# Ⓕ CHICKEN AND CHEESE ENCHILADAS

1½ pounds skinless, boneless
  chicken breasts
1 clove garlic, minced
1 bay leaf
2 green onions, thinly sliced
½ teaspoon dried oregano
Salt and pepper to taste
1 tablespoon olive oil
3 cloves garlic, minced

2 tablespoons chili powder
3 tablespoons flour
1 teaspoon cumin
2 cups chicken broth,
  reserved from boiling
  chicken
12 (6-inch) flour tortillas
½ cup shredded reduced fat
  sharp Cheddar cheese

In heavy pot, place chicken, 1 clove minced garlic, and bay leaf. Fill pot with water and bring to a boil. Reduce heat and simmer until chicken is done. Remove chicken and cut into strips. Set aside broth. In a bowl, combine chicken, green onions, oregano, and salt and pepper. In another saucepan, heat oil and add remaining garlic, chili powder, flour, and cumin, stirring constantly. Gradually add reserved 2 cups chicken broth. Cook until thick and smooth. Cool slightly. Coat a 13x9x2-inch pan with no stick cooking spray. Heat a medium skillet over high heat until hot. Add 1 tortilla and cook until heated, turning frequently. Using tongs, grasp tortilla and dip into sauce, coating both sides; place in prepared dish. Spoon 3 tablespoons chicken filling near one edge of tortilla. Starting at filled end, roll tortilla up jelly roll style. Turn seam side down. Repeat with remaining tortillas, sauce, and filling. Spoon any remaining sauce over enchiladas. Sprinkle with cheese. Bake at 425 degrees for 15 minutes or until hot and bubbly. Yield: 6 servings

**Nutritional Information Per Serving:**

| Calories | Cholesterol (mg) | Fat (g) | % Calories from Fat |
|---|---|---|---|
| 403 | 67 | 12.2 | 27.2% |

# ⓒⒻ CHICKEN AND BLACK BEAN ENCHILADAS

1 pound skinless, boneless
   chicken breasts
3 slices center cut bacon
2 cloves garlic, minced
1½ cups salsa
1 (15-ounce) can black beans,
   undrained
1 red bell pepper, seeded and
   chopped

1 teaspoon ground cumin
1 bunch green onions,
   chopped
Salt and pepper to taste
12 flour tortillas
6 ounces reduced fat
   Monterey Jack cheese,
   shredded

Cut chicken into cubes; set aside. In skillet, cook bacon until crisp. Remove bacon to paper towel to soak any excess grease and discard any grease in skillet. In same skillet, coat with no stick cooking spray, and sauté chicken and garlic until chicken is almost done. Stir in ½ cup salsa, beans, red pepper, cumin, and salt and pepper to taste. Simmer until thickened, about 7 minutes, stirring occasionally. Stir in green onions and reserved bacon. Divide chicken-bean mixture among 12 tortillas, placing down center of each tortilla. Top with 1 tablespoon shredded cheese. Roll up and place seam side down in 13x9x2-inch baking dish coated with no stick cooking spray. Spoon remaining 1 cup salsa evenly over enchiladas. Top with remaining cheese. Bake at 350 degrees for 15 minutes or until thoroughly heated and cheese is melted. Yield: 6 servings.

*Easy and will make quite an impression.*

### Nutritional Information Per Serving:

| Calories | Cholesterol (mg) | Fat (g) | % Calories from Fat |
|---|---|---|---|
| 467 | 52 | 9.8 | 18.8% |

POULTRY

## ⓕ CHICKEN AND SAUSAGE WITH RICE

9 boneless, skinless chicken
   breasts
2 tablespoons olive oil
1 green bell pepper, chopped
1 red bell pepper, chopped
1 bunch green onions, sliced
4 cloves garlic, minced
1 (16-ounce) can whole
   tomatoes, drained
2 to 3 cups reserved chicken
   broth

1 cup dry white wine
Salt and pepper to taste
1½ tablespoons paprika
1 teaspoon dried marjoram
1½ cups raw long grain rice
1 pound cooked turkey
   sausage, cut into 2-inch
   pieces
¼ cup chopped parsley

Boil chicken in seasoned water reserving broth when chicken is done. Cut chicken into small pieces. In large pot coated with no stick cooking spray, heat olive oil. Sauté peppers and onion until tender. Add garlic, tomatoes, 2 cups reserved chicken broth, wine, and seasonings, scraping up any browned bits in skillet. Bring to boil, add rice, and stir together. Add cooked chicken and sausage, mix, lower heat, and cover, cooking for 30 minutes or until done. Add more reserved broth, if necessary. Sprinkle with chopped parsley before serving. Yield: 8 servings.

*A great version of jambalaya.*

**Nutritional Information Per Serving:**

| Calories | Cholesterol (mg) | Fat (g) | % Calories from Fat |
|---|---|---|---|
| 469 | 114 | 13.9 | 26.6% |

## ⓕ LIME CHICKEN

4 (6-ounce) skinless, boned
   chicken breasts
1 tablespoon olive oil
1 teaspoon light margarine
1 tablespoon flour

½ cup chicken broth
2 tablespoons orange-
   flavored liqueur
1½ tablespoons lime juice
1 tablespoon tequila

Brown chicken on both sides in olive oil in large skillet coated with no stick cooking spray. Remove chicken from skillet; set aside and keep warm. Melt margarine in skillet and add flour, cooking for 1 minute. Gradually add chicken broth, stirring constantly. Bring to a boil and cook until thickened. Stir in orange-flavored liqueur and lime juice. Return chicken to pan. Heat tequila and add to one side of skillet. Ignite tequila with long match; let flames subside. Serve. Yield: 4 servings.

*Impress your guests with your cooking talent!*

**Nutritional Information Per Serving:**

| Calories | Cholesterol (mg) | Fat (g) | % Calories from Fat |
|---|---|---|---|
| 279 | 99 | 6.3 | 20.4% |

# ⓕ CHICKEN AND DUMPLINGS

3 pounds boneless, skinless
   chicken breasts and
   thighs
1 onion, sliced
3 stalks celery, chopped
Salt and pepper as desired
2 bay leaves
12 cups water

3 carrots, peeled and sliced
½ pound mushrooms,
   quartered
1 (6-ounce) package frozen
   snow peas
2 tablespoons flour plus ¼
   cup water, if needed

Place chicken, onion, celery, salt and pepper, bay leaves, and water in large pot. Heat to boiling. Reduce heat, cover, and simmer 1½ hours. Strain soup and cut chicken into pieces. Broth can be refrigerated at this point and skim fat off top next day. If broth has been refrigerated, heat again to boiling; add carrots and cook 10 minutes until carrots are tender. Add mushrooms. While soup is boiling, add Dumplings (see recipe below) on top of boiling broth. Cover, bring to boil, reduce heat, and simmer for 15 minutes. Do not lift cover. Add snow peas, stirring carefully. If soup needs thickening, combine flour and water to make smooth paste; quickly stir into broth. Serve in bowls. Yield: 8 servings.

**Dumplings**
1 cup flour
2 teaspoons baking powder
¼ teaspoon salt

½ cup skim milk
2 tablespoons canola oil

Combine flour, baking powder, and salt. Mix together milk and oil. Add to dry ingredients; stir only until moistened. Drop by tablespoon into boiling broth. If desire a thinner dumpling, roll dough on floured surface and cut into pieces.
*A wonderful dish always.*

**Nutritional Information Per Serving:**

| Calories | Cholesterol (mg) | Fat (g) | % Calories from Fat |
|---|---|---|---|
| 329 | 120 | 8.2 | 22.5% |

# ♡ Ⓕ PAELLA

1½ pounds shrimp
1½ pounds boneless, skinless
chicken breasts and
thighs
4 cloves garlic, minced
1 green bell pepper, chopped
1 red bell pepper, chopped
1 red onion, chopped
1½ pounds fresh green
beans, ends snapped
¾ cup wine
2 cups water
½ cup shrimp liquid,
reserved from boiling
shrimp

½ teaspoon dried basil
½ teaspoon crushed red
pepper
4 slices (3 ounces) broiled
Canadian bacon, cut into
pieces
1 large tomato, diced
1½ cups raw rice
1 (5-ounce) package saffron
yellow long grain rice
1 (14-ounce) can artichoke
heart quarters, drained
1 pound cooked fish, cut into
pieces (broil in oven)
Salt and pepper to taste

Boil shrimp in seasoned water. When shrimp are done, peel, and reserve ½ cup shrimp liquid for later use. Coat a large skillet with no stick cooking spray and sauté chicken pieces, stirring, until almost done. Add garlic, green and red peppers, and onion, sautéing until tender. Add green beans, wine, water, reserved shrimp liquid, basil, red pepper, bacon, and tomato. Bring to boil and add both kinds of rice. Lower heat, cover, and cook 25 minutes or until rice is done. Add cooked shrimp, cooked fish and artichoke hearts, tossing gently. Season to taste. Yield: 12 servings.
*This recipe is a winner and worth the effort!*

**Nutritional Information Per Serving:**

| Calories | Cholesterol (mg) | Fat (g) | % Calories from Fat |
|----------|------------------|---------|---------------------|
| 322      | 126              | 4.2     | 11.7%               |

# ⓒⒻ WHITE CHILI

1 tablespoon olive oil
2 pounds boneless, skinless
   chicken breasts, diced
1 onion, chopped
4 cloves garlic, minced
2 (14½-ounce) cans no-salt-
   added whole tomatoes,
   not drained and coarsely
   chopped
2 (14½-ounce) cans no-salt-
   added chicken broth

2 (4-ounce) cans chopped
   green chilies
1 teaspoon dried oregano
½ teaspoon ground cumin
2 (11-ounce) cans cannellini
   beans, drained
3 tablespoons fresh lime
   juice
¼ teaspoon pepper
½ cup shredded reduced fat
   Monterey Jack cheese

Coat a large pot with no stick cooking spray. Add olive oil and cook diced chicken breasts until done, stirring. Remove chicken from pan; set aside. Add onion and garlic to pan and sauté until tender. Stir in next five ingredients. Bring to boil, reduce heat, and simmer for 20 minutes. Add chicken and beans; cook until heated. Add lime juice and pepper. Serve into bowls and top with cheese. Yield: 8 to 10 servings.
*Serve with salsa on top of cheese, if desired.*

## Nutritional Information Per Serving:

| Calories | Cholesterol (mg) | Fat (g) | % Calories from Fat |
|----------|------------------|---------|---------------------|
| 230 | 55 | 4.2 | 16.3% |

# (F) CHICKEN JAMBALAYA

2 pounds skinless, boneless chicken breasts (and thighs)
Carrot, peeled and cut, stalk celery, and half onion
1 onion, chopped
1 green bell pepper, chopped
2 cloves garlic, minced
2 tablespoons olive oil

1 (14½-ounce) can stewed tomatoes
1 bay leaf
1 teaspoon Worcestershire sauce
3 cups chicken broth, reserved from boiling chicken
1½ cups raw rice

Combine chicken with carrot, celery, and half onion in pot filled with water. Boil until chicken is done, reserving broth. In a large pot, sauté onion, green pepper, and garlic in olive oil until tender. Add stewed tomatoes, bay leaf, Worcestershire sauce, 3 cups reserved chicken broth, rice and cooked chicken that has been cut into pieces. Bring to a boil, reduce heat, and cover for 20 to 30 minutes or until rice is done. Yield: 6 servings.

*A favorite in Louisiana.*

**Nutritional Information Per Serving:**

| Calories | Cholesterol (mg) | Fat (g) | % Calories from Fat |
|----------|------------------|---------|---------------------|
| 457 | 89 | 13.1 | 25.7% |

# SEAFOOD

M. HANSBROUGH

# PECAN TROUT WITH DIJON SAUCE

6 (4-ounce) trout fillets
1 tablespoon olive oil
½ cup fine dry breadcrumbs
¼ cup non fat plain yogurt

1 tablespoon Dijon mustard
1 tablespoon lemon juice
3 tablespoons chopped
 pecans, toasted

Brush fillets with olive oil. Dredge in breadcrumbs. Arrange fillets in single layer in rectangular baking dish coated with no stick cooking spray. Cook under broiler until fish flakes easily when tested with fork. Transfer to serving dish; keep warm. In small saucepan, combine yogurt, mustard, and lemon juice. Cook over low heat, stirring constantly, until thoroughly heated (do not boil). Spoon 1 tablespoon sauce and sprinkle pecans evenly over each fillet. Serve immediately. Yield: 6 servings.

*A quick way to prepare fish — one that will become a favorite.*

**Nutritional Information Per Serving:**

| Calories | Cholesterol (mg) | Fat (g) | % Calories from Fat |
|---|---|---|---|
| 218 | 65 | 8.9 | 36.9% |

## ♥Ⓕ TROUT SUPREME

2 pounds fresh fillets (or red
 snapper)
Salt and pepper to taste
1 tablespoon margarine
1 onion, chopped
2 green onions, chopped
2 cloves garlic, minced
1 tablespoon flour
½ cup dry white wine

2 tomatoes, peeled, seeded,
 and coarsely chopped
1 tablespoon chopped
 parsley
¼ teaspoon dried basil
½ teaspoon dried tarragon
¼ cup fine breadcrumbs
1 tablespoon grated
 Parmesan cheese

Place fish fillets in glass baking dish coated with no stick cooking spray. Season both sides with salt and pepper. In saucepan, melt margarine and sauté onion, green onions, and garlic until tender. Stir in flour, and gradually add wine. Bring to a boil stirring until thickens. Salt and pepper to taste. Add tomatoes, parsley, basil, and tarragon. Pour sauce over fish and sprinkle with breadcrumbs and cheese. Bake, uncovered, at 350 degrees for 30 minutes. Yield: 4 servings.

*An outstanding flavorful dish that can be made ahead and baked before serving. Great with fresh home-grown tomatoes*

**Nutritional Information Per Serving:**

| Calories | Cholesterol (mg) | Fat (g) | % Calories from Fat |
|---|---|---|---|
| 363 | 131 | 10.0 | 24.7% |

# ♡F BAKED TROUT WITH LEMON SAUCE

2 pounds trout fillets (or fish
    of your choice)
Salt and pepper to taste
4 green onions, chopped

1 tablespoon finely chopped
    parsley
Paprika

Place fillets on baking sheet lined with foil. Sprinkle with salt, pepper, green onions, and parsley. Then sprinkle with paprika. Cover with Lemon Sauce (see recipe below). Bake at 375 degrees for 25 minutes. Baste with Lemon Sauce during cooking. Yield: 6 servings.
*A great dish for fresh fish because the sauce is light yet tasty.*

**Lemon Sauce**
¼ cup light margarine,
    melted

2 tablespoons lemon juice
2 cloves garlic, minced

Combine all ingredients and pour over prepared fish.

**Nutritional Information Per Serving:**

| Calories | Cholesterol (mg) | Fat (g) | % Calories from Fat |
|----------|------------------|---------|---------------------|
| 159 | 76 | 5.0 | 28.5% |

# POACHED PAN TROUT

3 tablespoons light
    margarine
4 large cloves garlic, minced
Salt and pepper to taste
2 to 3 pounds trout fillets

½ cup white wine
3 tablespoons green onion,
    chopped
2 tablespoons finely chopped
    parsley

Melt margarine in large skillet coated with no stick cooking spray. Add garlic and sauté for several minutes. Season fillets with salt and pepper. Add fillets, cooking until almost done. Add white wine and turn fish. Sprinkle with green onions and parsley; continue cooking until fish is flaky. Yield: 6 servings.
*For a real treat, top with lump crabmeat.*

**Nutritional Information Per Serving:**

| Calories | Cholesterol (mg) | Fat (g) | % Calories from Fat |
|----------|------------------|---------|---------------------|
| 266 | 108 | 9.3 | 31.3% |

## Ⓒ TROUT WITH LEMON SAUCE

| | |
|---|---|
| 1 pound fish fillets | 1 tablespoon olive oil |
| Salt and pepper to taste | 1 tablespoon light margarine |
| Flour | |

Season trout fillets with salt and pepper and dust with flour. Coat a skillet with no stick cooking spray; add olive oil and margarine. When melted, sauté fish in pan until done. Remove fish and set aside while cooking Sauce (see recipe below).
*Substitute the fish of your choice.*

**Sauce**

| | |
|---|---|
| 1 tablespoon light margarine | 2 cloves garlic, minced |
| 4 tablespoons lemon juice | ½ cup chicken broth |
| 1 tablespoon chopped parsley | |

In saucepan, combine all sauce ingredients and heat until boiling. Reduce heat, and simmer until sauce is reduced. Serve immediately over prepared fish. Yield: 4 servings.

**Nutritional Information Per Serving:**

| Calories | Cholesterol (mg) | Fat (g) | % Calories from Fat |
|---|---|---|---|
| 188 | 63 | 10.1 | 48.3% |

## SPICY BAKED CATFISH

| | |
|---|---|
| 1 pound catfish fillets | ¼ teaspoon Worcestershire sauce |
| 2 tablespoons light mayonnaise | ¼ teaspoon onion powder |
| 1 teaspoon lemon juice | ¼ teaspoon garlic powder |
| ½ teaspoon prepared mustard | ⅛ teaspoon cayenne |
| ½ teaspoon sugar | Paprika |

Rinse catfish and pat dry. In small dish combine remaining ingredients except paprika, mixing well. Lay catfish in oblong baking dish coated with no stick cooking spray. Spread mayonnaise mixture over fillets. Marinate 30 minutes. Sprinkle with paprika. Bake at 500 degrees for 10 to 15 minutes or until fish flakes easily with fork. Yield: 4 servings.
*Substitute the type mayonnaise of your choice.*

**Nutritional Information Per Serving:**

| Calories | Cholesterol (mg) | Fat (g) | % Calories from Fat |
|---|---|---|---|
| 145 | 65 | 6.0 | 37.3% |

# Ⓕ SHRIMP, CRAB, AND RICE CASSEROLE

1 (14½-ounce) can stewed
   tomatoes (no salt)
2 cloves garlic, minced
1 green bell pepper, chopped
1 onion, chopped
1 (10¾-ounce) can cream of
   mushroom soup (with ⅓
   less salt)

1 bunch green onions,
   chopped
1 tablespoon Worcestershire
   sauce
1 pound cooked shrimp,
   peeled
1 pound lump or white
   crabmeat
3 cups cooked rice

In a large, heavy pot, pour stewed tomatoes. Add garlic, green pepper, and onion. Cook over low heat approximately 20 minutes or until vegetables are tender. Add cream of mushroom soup, green onions, and Worcestershire sauce, mixing well. Add shrimp, crabmeat, and rice, mixing thoroughly but gently. Yield: 8 servings.

*Shrimp may be boiled in seasoned water or sautéed in 2 tablespoons margarine and then seasoned to taste.*

**Nutritional Information Per Serving:**

| Calories | Cholesterol (mg) | Fat (g) | % Calories from Fat |
|---|---|---|---|
| 259 | 147 | 5.1 | 17.7% |

# Ⓕ SEAFOOD CASSEROLE

2 tablespoons light
   margarine
½ cup chopped onion
2 cloves garlic, minced
1 pound shrimp, peeled
¼ cup flour
¾ cup chicken broth
⅔ cup evaporated skimmed
   milk

1 teaspoon dried dill weed
1 (14-ounce) can quartered
   artichoke hearts
1 pound lump crabmeat
4 ounces reduced fat sharp
   Cheddar cheese,
   shredded

In saucepan, melt margarine and sauté onion, garlic, and shrimp until done. Stir in flour and gradually add chicken broth, stirring until smooth and comes to a boil. As sauce thickens, add milk, stirring until mixed. Add dill weed. Gently fold in artichoke hearts, crabmeat, and cheese heating until cheese is melted and thoroughly heated. Serve in individual dishes or casserole dish. Yield: 6 servings.

*This dish can be used as an appetizer or as a main course. Whichever way it is served, it will receive rave reviews.*

**Nutritional Information Per Serving:**

| Calories | Cholesterol (mg) | Fat (g) | % Calories from Fat |
|---|---|---|---|
| 266 | 165 | 6.2 | 20.8% |

# Ⓕ SEAFOOD AND WILD RICE CASSEROLE

1 pound cooked shrimp,
   peeled
1 pound white crabmeat
1 (10-ounce) package green
   peas (uncooked)
1 cup chopped celery
1 green bell pepper, chopped
1 onion, chopped
½ cup fat free mayonnaise

1 teaspoon Worcestershire
   sauce
Salt and pepper to taste
1 (6-ounce) package long
   grain and wild rice mix
   (cooked according to
   directions on package
   omitting oil)

Mix all ingredients together tossing carefully. Pour into a 2-quart casserole coated with no stick cooking spray. Bake at 350 degrees for 20 to 30 minutes. Yield: 6 to 8 servings.
*An excellent choice! It can be made ahead and reheated.*

**Nutritional Information Per Serving:**

| Calories | Cholesterol (mg) | Fat (g) | % Calories from Fat |
|---|---|---|---|
| 228 | 146 | 2.3 | 9.0% |

# EGGPLANT SHRIMP CASSEROLE

1 cup chopped onions
1 green bell pepper, chopped
4 cups peeled and diced
   eggplant (about 1 pound)
3 cloves garlic, minced
2 tablespoons light
   margarine
1 pound peeled raw shrimp

3 cups cooked rice
1 tablespoon Worcestershire
   sauce
½ teaspoon pepper
½ teaspoon dried thyme
¾ cup light mayonnaise
1 bunch green onions, sliced

In skillet, sauté onion, green pepper, eggplant, and garlic in margarine until tender. Stir occasionally. Add shrimp, cooking until shrimp are done (they will turn pink). Add remaining ingredients except green onions, mixing well. Turn mixture into a 2-quart casserole dish coated with no stick cooking spray. Top with sliced green onions. Bake at 350 degrees for 30 minutes. Yield: 6 to 8 servings.

**Nutritional Information Per Serving:**

| Calories | Cholesterol (mg) | Fat (g) | % Calories from Fat |
|---|---|---|---|
| 245 | 87 | 9.8 | 35.9% |

## ⓒ EGGPLANT STUFFED WITH CRABMEAT

2 (1-pound) eggplants
3 cloves garlic, minced
1 onion, chopped
1 green bell pepper, chopped
2 tablespoons chopped
    parsley

2 tablespoons olive oil
Salt and pepper to taste
1 cup white crabmeat
Paprika

Halve eggplants lengthwise. Place on large foil-lined baking dish, with cut side down. Cover pan with foil and bake at 375 degrees for 30 minutes, or until eggplant is tender. Scoop out pulp and chop. Reserve shells. In medium skillet, sauté garlic, onion, green pepper, and parsley in olive oil until tender. Add chopped eggplant and salt and pepper. Cook for 5 minutes, stirring occasionally. Add White Sauce (see recipe below) and gently fold in crabmeat. Pour into eggplant shells. Sprinkle lightly with paprika. Place on baking sheet and bake at 425 degrees for 10 to 20 minutes. Yield: 4 servings.

**White Sauce**

2 tablespoons light
    margarine
1½ tablespoons flour

¾ cup skim milk
¼ teaspoon salt
Dash hot pepper sauce

In small saucepan, melt margarine over low heat. Add the flour, stirring to keep mixture smooth. Gradually stir in milk, stirring constantly. Cook over low heat until mixture thickens. Remove from heat and stir in salt and hot pepper sauce. Yield: 1 cup.

**Nutritional Information Per Serving:**

| Calories | Cholesterol (mg) | Fat (g) | % Calories from Fat |
|----------|------------------|---------|---------------------|
| 217      | 32               | 10.9    | 45.0%               |

## Ⓕ CRABMEAT AU GRATIN

1 cup thinly sliced green
  onions
2 tablespoons finely chopped
  fresh parsley
6 tablespoons light
  margarine
3 tablespoons flour

Salt and pepper to taste
1½ cups skim milk
1 tablespoon sherry
1½ to 2 pounds lump
  crabmeat
1 cup shredded reduced fat
  sharp Cheddar cheese

In saucepan, sauté green onions and parsley in margarine until tender. Remove from heat and stir in flour. Salt and pepper to taste. Gradually add milk, stirring over low heat until mixture thickens. Remove pan from heat; add sherry. Gently fold in crabmeat. Place in casserole dish or individual ramekins. Sprinkle with cheese. Bake at 375 degrees for 10 to 15 minutes or until cheese is melted. Yield: 6 to 8 servings.

**Nutritional Information Per Serving:**

| Calories | Cholesterol (mg) | Fat (g) | % Calories from Fat |
|---|---|---|---|
| 184 | 103 | 5.1 | 25.1% |

## Ⓕ CRABMEAT IMPERIAL

½ cup chopped onion
⅓ cup chopped green bell
  pepper
3 tablespoons flour
½ teaspoon dry mustard
1 cup skim milk
2 tablespoons lemon juice
1 teaspoon Worcestershire
  sauce

Dash hot pepper sauce
Salt and pepper to taste
1 (2-ounce) jar diced
  pimiento, drained
3 tablespoons cholesterol
  free mayonnaise
1 pound lump crabmeat,
  picked for bones
2 tablespoons breadcrumbs

In a saucepan coated with no stick cooking spray, sauté onion and green pepper until tender. Combine flour and dry mustard together. Add to milk mixing until smooth. Pour milk mixture into saucepan, cooking until thickened. Remove from heat and add lemon juice, Worcestershire sauce, hot pepper sauce, and salt and pepper. Gently fold in pimiento, mayonnaise, and crabmeat. Sprinkle with breadcrumbs. Yield: 4 servings.

*If desired, serve as dip with melba rounds.*

**Nutritional Information Per Serving:**

| Calories | Cholesterol (mg) | Fat (g) | % Calories from Fat |
|---|---|---|---|
| 216 | 115 | 5.8 | 24.3% |

# ©Ⓕ CRABMEAT ENCHILADAS

**Crabmeat Filling**

1 pound white crabmeat
½ cup chopped onion
¾ cup shredded Monterey
  Jack cheese

1 (4-ounce) can chopped
  green chilies
16 to 20 flour tortillas (whole
  wheat if desired)

In mixing bowl, combine crabmeat, onion, cheese, and green chilies. Warm tortillas to make easier to roll. Place a heaping tablespoon filling on the edge of each tortilla, rolling up with filling in the center. Place filled tortillas in a 2-quart baking dish. Pour Sauce (see recipe below) over filled tortillas. Yield: 8 to 10 servings.

**Sauce**

2 tablespoons chopped onion
2 cloves garlic, minced
2 tablespoons light
  margarine
¼ cup flour

1 (14½-ounce) can chicken
  broth with ⅓ less fat
1 (4-ounce) can chopped
  green chilies
¼ teaspoon white pepper
2 cups non fat plain yogurt

In saucepan, sauté onion and garlic in margarine until tender. Add flour stirring for 1 minute. Gradually add chicken broth, green chilies, and white pepper. Bring to a boil, stirring, until mixture thickens; reduce heat. Stir in yogurt until smooth. Pour over filled enchiladas. Bake at 350 degrees for 30 minutes or until thoroughly heated.

**Nutritional Information Per Serving:**

| Calories | Cholesterol (mg) | Fat (g) | % Calories from Fat |
|---|---|---|---|
| 302 | 54 | 9.1 | 27.2% |

#  CRAB CAKES

| | |
|---|---|
| 1 pound lump crabmeat | ¼ teaspoon pepper |
| 1 (8-ounce) can water chestnuts, drained and finely chopped | Dash hot sauce |
| | 3 tablespoons fat free mayonnaise |
| ¼ cup soft breadcrumbs (bread in food processor) | 1 egg white, slightly beaten |
| 1 tablespoon finely chopped parsley | 2 green onions, chopped |

Combine all ingredients gently together. Shape into 8 patties. Coat a skillet with no stick cooking spray; heat until hot. Add crab patties and cook until lightly browned on both sides, turning once. Yield: 4 servings. *For an appetizer, make into smaller patties (approximately 16).*

**Nutritional Information Per Serving:**

| Calories | Cholesterol (mg) | Fat (g) | % Calories from Fat |
|---|---|---|---|
| 179 | 114 | 2.4 | 12.1% |

# ITALIAN SHRIMP

| | |
|---|---|
| 4 tablespoons light margarine | 1 teaspoon dried oregano |
| 5 tablespoons olive oil | 1 teaspoon dried rosemary |
| ½ cup fat free Italian dressing | 1 teaspoon dried thyme |
| | 1 teaspoon pepper |
| 6 cloves garlic, minced | 1 teaspoon salt, if desired only |
| 1 teaspoon hot pepper sauce | 2 pounds headless large shrimp (not peeled) |
| ¼ cup Worcestershire sauce | |
| 8 bay leaves | 2 ounces dry white wine |
| 2 teaspoons paprika | |

In a large heavy skillet, melt margarine, then add oil and mix well. Add all the other ingredients, except for shrimp and wine, and cook over medium heat until sauce begins to boil. Add the shrimp and cook approximately 15 minutes. Add wine and cook another 10 minutes or until shrimp are done. Serve shrimp with sauce. Yield: 4 to 6 servings. *This is a shrimp dish to remember...a New Orleans favorite.*

**Nutritional Information Per Serving:**

| Calories | Cholesterol (mg) | Fat (g) | % Calories from Fat |
|---|---|---|---|
| 328 | 239 | 17.7 | 48.5% |

## Ⓕ BOILED SHRIMP

2 pounds shrimp, unpeeled
4 cups lite beer
4 bay leaves
¼ teaspoon pepper
1 clove garlic, minced

½ teaspoon garlic powder
¼ cup lemon juice
3 whole cloves
¼ teaspoon cayenne pepper
Salt as desired

Combine all ingredients in a large pot. Cover and bring to a boil over medium heat. Boil 2 minutes, then remove from heat. Let stand, covered, until shrimp are pink and firm, about 5 to 10 minutes depending on size of shrimp. Stir occasionally. Drain well. Serve chilled or at room temperature. Yield: 4 to 6 servings.
*The secret ingredient in this recipe makes it a real success.*

**Nutritional Information Per Serving:**

| Calories | Cholesterol (mg) | Fat (g) | % Calories from Fat |
|---|---|---|---|
| 152 | 239 | 2.4 | 14.4% |

## Ⓕ SHRIMP CLEMANCEAU

2 large baking potatoes,
  cubed (about 5 cups)
¼ cup light margarine
4 tablespoons minced garlic
2 bunches green onions,
  chopped
½ pound mushrooms, sliced
3 pounds shrimp, peeled

2 tablespoons finely chopped
  parsley
¼ cup white wine
1 tablespoon lemon juice
1 tablespoon Worcestershire
  sauce
Dash cayenne
1 (10-ounce) package frozen
  green peas

Place cubed potatoes on baking sheet coated with no stick cooking spray. Bake at 400 degrees, stirring occasionally, for about 30 to 40 minutes or until browned and tender. In large skillet, melt margarine and sauté garlic, green onion, and mushrooms until tender, stirring frequently. Add remaining ingredients except potatoes and peas. Stir until shrimp are done. Cook peas according to directions on package; drain. In 2-quart oblong casserole, combine cooked potatoes, peas, and shrimp mixture removed from skillet with slotted spoon. Reduce liquid in pan by half and pour over shrimp-potato mixture. Toss gently and serve. Yield: 8 servings.
*This different combination is one that will quickly become your favorite.*

**Nutritional Information Per Serving:**

| Calories | Cholesterol (mg) | Fat (g) | % Calories from Fat |
|---|---|---|---|
| 280 | 190 | 5.1 | 16.3% |

## ⓕ QUICK SHRIMP

1 bunch green onions, thinly
  sliced
3 large cloves garlic, minced
3 tablespoons light
  margarine

1 pound medium shrimp,
  peeled and deveined
1 cup white wine
Hot sauce to taste
Salt and pepper to taste

In pan, sauté onion and garlic in margarine until tender. Add shrimp, stirring constantly, cooking for 3 minutes or until shrimp turns pink. Add wine and simmer over low heat until half the liquid has been reduced. Add seasonings. Yield: 2 servings.
*Great served over rice or pasta.*

**Nutritional Information Per Serving:**

| Calories | Cholesterol (mg) | Fat (g) | % Calories from Fat |
|---|---|---|---|
| 335 | 250 | 11.2 | 30.1% |

## ⓕ DELICIOUS SHRIMP

¼ cup light margarine
½ cup chopped onion
4 cloves garlic, minced
2 pounds raw shrimp, peeled
2 tablespoons chopped
  parsley
1 teaspoon paprika

¼ teaspoon red pepper
2 tablespoons flour
⅓ cup water
4 tablespoons white wine
2 tablespoons green onion
  stems

In saucepan, melt margarine and sauté onion and garlic until tender. Add shrimp, parsley, paprika, and red pepper, cooking until shrimp are done. Stir in flour and then gradually add water and wine. Cook, stirring, until mixture comes to a boil. Lower heat and cook until sauce thickens. Add green onions. Serve over rice or noodles. Yield: 6 to 8 servings.
*If you need something quick in a pinch, try this one, and you will be a big success.*

**Nutritional Information Per Serving:**

| Calories | Cholesterol (mg) | Fat (g) | % Calories from Fat |
|---|---|---|---|
| 126 | 127 | 4.2 | 30.1% |

# Ⓕ SHRIMP SAUTÉ

2 tablespoons light
  margarine
1 bunch green onions,
  chopped
2 cloves garlic, minced

1 tablespoon Worcestershire
  sauce
1 teaspoon dried basil
2 pounds raw shrimp, peeled
2 cups non fat plain yogurt

In a large skillet, melt margarine and sauté green onions and garlic until tender. Add seasonings. Add shrimp and cook until shrimp are done (turn pink). Gradually stir in yogurt and heat thoroughly. DO NOT BOIL. Serve at once over fettuccine. Yield: 6 servings.
*This spectacular dish takes minutes to prepare.*

## Nutritional Information Per Serving:

| Calories | Cholesterol (mg) | Fat (g) | % Calories from Fat |
|----------|------------------|---------|---------------------|
| 178 | 171 | 3.8 | 19.2% |

# Ⓕ SCAMPI ITALIAN STYLE

2 tablespoons light
  margarine
1 pound large shrimp, peeled
1 teaspoon minced garlic
2 green onions, chopped
3 tablespoons dry sherry
1 tomato, (peeled and
  seeded) diced

1 teaspoon Worcestershire
  sauce
½ teaspoon hot pepper sauce
¼ teaspoon white pepper
⅛ teaspoon dried oregano
⅛ teaspoon dried thyme
2 tablespoons chopped
  parsley

Heat margarine in large skillet and sauté shrimp until it begins to turn pink. Add garlic and green onion, sautéing for 1 minute longer. Add sherry, tomatoes, and seasoning. Cook about 5 minutes or until shrimp are fully cooked and sauce has thickened slightly. Yield: 4 servings.
*Scampi lovers will be attracted to this delicious dish. Great served over rice.*

## Nutritional Information Per Serving:

| Calories | Cholesterol (mg) | Fat (g) | % Calories from Fat |
|----------|------------------|---------|---------------------|
| 152 | 156 | 4.5 | 27.0% |

# SHRIMP SCAMPI

1 pound medium shrimp,
   peeled
4 tablespoons lemon juice
2 tablespoons light
   margarine, melted

4 cloves garlic, minced
½ teaspoon salt
½ teaspoon pepper
½ teaspoon paprika

In a 13x9x2-inch baking dish arrange shrimp. In small bowl, combine remaining ingredients. Pour mixture over shrimp tossing to coat well. Broil four inches from heat until shrimp are golden brown. Watch carefully. Yield: 4 servings.
*Simple and delightful!*

**Nutritional Information Per Serving:**

| Calories | Cholesterol (mg) | Fat (g) | % Calories from Fat |
|---|---|---|---|
| 114 | 125 | 4.2 | 33.0% |

# Ⓕ SHRIMP ETOUFFÉE

2 tablespoons flour
1 tablespoon light margarine
1 cup finely chopped onion
1 bunch green onions,
   chopped
3 cloves garlic, minced
⅓ cup chopped parsley

2 pounds shrimp, peeled
¼ cup tomato paste
1 tablespoon Worcestershire
   sauce
Dash hot sauce
Dash crushed pepper

In a no stick skillet, brown flour over medium heat. After flour is brown, set aside. In a pot, melt margarine and sauté onion, green onion, garlic, parsley, and shrimp until done. Add tomato paste and stir until mixed. Add browned flour, stirring, until mixture thickens. If necessary, add water to reach desired consistency. Add remaining seasonings and cook over low heat for 15 minutes. Serve over rice. Yield: 8 servings.

**Nutritional Information Per Serving:**

| Calories | Cholesterol (mg) | Fat (g) | % Calories from Fat |
|---|---|---|---|
| 116 | 127 | 2.2 | 16.8% |

## Ⓕ SHRIMP AND CRAB PICANTE

4 tablespoons light
  margarine
3 cloves garlic, minced
1 large onion, chopped
1 bunch green onions,
  chopped
1 large green bell pepper,
  chopped
2 (10-ounce) cans tomatoes
  and green chilies

1 (14½-ounce) can tomatoes
  with no salt
1 teaspoon Worcestershire
  sauce
1 pound peeled shrimp,
  cooked
1 pound lump crabmeat
4 green onions, finely sliced

In large pot, melt margarine, and sauté garlic, onions, and green onions, and green pepper until tender. Put cans of tomatoes in food processor and blend until smooth. Add to vegetable mixture. Reduce heat and simmer for about 30 minutes. Add Worcestershire sauce. Add shrimp and crabmeat and continue cooking for 20 minutes. If needed, water can be added if mixture is too thick. Before serving, sprinkle with chopped green onions. Yield: 8 servings.
*Great served over rice.*

**Nutritional Information Per Serving:**

| Calories | Cholesterol (mg) | Fat (g) | % Calories from Fat |
|---|---|---|---|
| 182 | 156 | 5.2 | 25.7% |

## Ⓒ Ⓕ SALMON FRAMBOISE

1 cup dry white wine
¼ cup raspberry preserves

1 tablespoon green
  peppercorns
4 (6-ounce) salmon fillets

Combine wine, preserves, and green peppercorns. Pour over salmon fillets and refrigerate for 4 hours. Bake at 375 degrees for 20 minutes. Yield: 4 servings.

**Nutritional Information Per Serving:**

| Calories | Cholesterol (mg) | Fat (g) | % Calories from Fat |
|---|---|---|---|
| 302 | 60 | 6.4 | 19.0% |

# ⓒⒻ SALMON FILLETS WITH LEMON SAUCE

¾ cup lemon juice
1 tablespoon light margarine
3 tablespoons finely chopped
   onion
Salt and pepper as desired
1½ tablespoons light brown
   sugar

1 teaspoon dry mustard
1 pound salmon fillet,
   skinned and cut into 4
   pieces
2 tablespoons chopped
   parsley

In saucepan, combine the lemon juice, margarine, onion, salt and pepper, brown sugar, and mustard. Bring to boil. Place salmon fillets on foil lined pan. Pour sauce mixture over fish. Broil about 15 minutes, basting frequently with sauce. When done, sprinkle with parsley; serve. Yield: 4 servings.

*This recipe is fine dining — it is spectacular!*

**Nutritional Information Per Serving:**

| Calories | Cholesterol (mg) | Fat (g) | % Calories from Fat |
|---|---|---|---|
| 202 | 40 | 5.7 | 25.3% |

# Ⓕ CRAWFISH ETOUFFÉE

1½ cups finely chopped
   onion
⅓ cup finely chopped green
   bell pepper
2 cloves garlic, minced
2 tablespoons light
   margarine
2 tablespoons flour

1 pound peeled crawfish
   tails, rinsed and drained
1 cup water
Dash red pepper
Dash Worcestershire sauce
Salt and pepper to taste
Juice of lemon
1 bunch green onion tops
   only, finely sliced

In large skillet, sauté onion, green pepper, and garlic in margarine until tender. Stir in flour and cook 1 minute. Add crawfish tails and water. Cover and simmer over low heat for 15 minutes. Add seasonings. Add green onion stems and cook for 5 minutes longer. If mixture is too thick, add more water. Serve over cooked rice. Yield: 4 servings.

*This is so easy and will become your favorite etouffée recipe.*

**Nutritional Information Per Serving:**

| Calories | Cholesterol (mg) | Fat (g) | % Calories from Fat |
|---|---|---|---|
| 204 | 202 | 4.6 | 20.1% |

# Ⓕ CRAWFISH ELEGANTE

3 tablespoons light
  margarine
1 bunch green onions,
  chopped
½ cup chopped parsley
3 tablespoons flour

1 (12-ounce) can evaporated
  skimmed milk
3 tablespoons sherry
1 pound crawfish tails,
  rinsed and drained
Salt and pepper to taste
Dash cayenne pepper

In small skillet, melt margarine and sauté green onions and parsley. Blend in flour. Gradually add evaporated skimmed milk, stirring constantly until sauce thickens. Add sherry and crawfish tails, stirring gently. Season to taste. Serve over toast points. Yield: 6 to 8 servings. *Yes, an old favorite is made just a little bit better. Also, this recipe can be served in chafing dish as dip.*

**Nutritional Information Per Serving:**

| Calories | Cholesterol (mg) | Fat (g) | % Calories from Fat |
|---|---|---|---|
| 145 | 103 | 3.0 | 18.6% |

# Ⓕ SPICY CRAWFISH STEW

1 cup flour
2 onions, chopped
2 green bell peppers,
  chopped
2 stalks celery, chopped
6 cloves garlic, minced
½ cup chopped parsley
1 bunch green onions,
  chopped

4 bay leaves
1 (15-ounce) can no salt
  tomato sauce
2 (10-ounce) cans chopped
  tomatoes and green
  chilies
5 cups water
1 lemon, juiced
2 pounds crawfish tails

Place flour on cookie sheet and bake at 350 degrees for 30 minutes. Stir occasionally and watch closely until flour browns. In a large cooking pot coated with no stick cooking spray, sauté vegetables until tender. Add browned flour and cook one minute. Add bay leaves, tomato sauce, tomatoes, water, and lemon juice. Stir well and bring to a boil, lower heat, and cook for 1 hour. Add crawfish tails, cooking for an additional 15 minutes. Season to taste. Yield: 12 servings.
*Serve over rice. Freezes well. (The browned flour gives this dish a nice color as well as flavors it).*

**Nutritional Information Per Serving:**

| Calories | Cholesterol (mg) | Fat (g) | % Calories from Fat |
|---|---|---|---|
| 162 | 135 | 1.3 | 7.4% |

## Ⓕ CRAWFISH CASSEROLE

| | |
|---|---|
| 1 tablespoon light margarine | 3 cups cooked rice |
| 1 cup chopped onions | 1½ tablespoons lemon juice |
| ⅔ cup chopped green bell pepper | Salt and pepper as desired |
| 2 cloves garlic, minced | Dash red pepper |
| 1 pound crawfish tails, rinsed | 1 (10-ounce) can chopped tomatoes and green chilies |
| 1 (10¾-ounce) can 99% fat-free cream of mushroom soup | ½ cup shredded reduced fat sharp Cheddar cheese |

In large pan coated with no stick cooking spray, melt margarine. Add onions, green pepper and garlic, cooking until tender. Stir in crawfish, soup, rice, lemon juice, seasonings, tomatoes and green chilies. Mix well. Turn mixture into a shallow 2-quart casserole dish coated with no stick cooking spray. Bake at 350 degrees for 25 minutes. Sprinkle with cheese and return to oven for an additional 5 minutes. Yield: 6 servings. *Substitute shrimp for crawfish, if desired.*

**Nutritional Information Per Serving:**

| Calories | Cholesterol (mg) | Fat (g) | % Calories from Fat |
|---|---|---|---|
| 281 | 136 | 4.8 | 15.2% |

## CRAWFISH CREOLE

| | |
|---|---|
| ¼ cup canola oil | 1 pound peeled crawfish tails |
| ¼ cup flour | 1 teaspoon lemon juice |
| 1 onion, chopped | 1 teaspoon Worcestershire sauce |
| 2 stalks celery, chopped | 1 teaspoon sugar |
| 3 cloves garlic, minced | ¼ teaspoon red pepper |
| 1 green bell pepper, chopped | ½ teaspoon paprika |
| 1 cup (natural with ⅓ less salt) chicken broth | ½ teaspoon dried thyme |
| 2 cups fresh puréed tomatoes | ½ teaspoon dried basil |

In a heavy 5-quart pot, heat the oil and gradually add the flour. Cook over low heat, stirring constantly, until a light roux is formed. Add onion, celery, garlic, and green pepper, sautéing until tender. Gradually add chicken broth and tomatoes, stirring. Add crawfish and seasonings. Reduce heat and simmer for about 20 minutes. Yield: 4 servings. *Fresh tomatoes make this a light sauce. Great over rice.*

**Nutritional Information Per Serving:**

| Calories | Cholesterol (mg) | Fat (g) | % Calories from Fat |
|---|---|---|---|
| 334 | 83 | 15.1 | 40.6% |

## ⒸⒻ BROILED SCALLOPS

¼ cup mustard
¼ cup honey
1 teaspoon curry

1 teaspoon lemon juice
2 pounds sea scallops

Combine all ingredients except scallops, mixing well. Add scallops and marinate 15 minutes. Broil in oven for 10 to 15 minutes, basting and turning as needed. Yield: 8 servings.

*Use to make shish kabobs: skewer mushroom caps, cherry tomatoes, onion pieces, and green bell peppers. Broil, basting with sauce. Also, serve as appetizer with toothpicks for scallop lovers.*

**Nutritional Information Per Serving:**

| Calories | Cholesterol (mg) | Fat (g) | % Calories from Fat |
|---|---|---|---|
| 138 | 37 | 1.2 | 8.0% |

## ⒸⒻ TUNA NOODLE CASSEROLE

¾ cup sliced fresh
  mushrooms
¼ cup chopped red bell
  pepper
2 tablespoons finely chopped
  onion
3 tablespoons light
  margarine
3 tablespoons flour
2 cups skim milk

4 cups cooked medium
  noodles (cooked
  according to directions
  on package omitting salt
  and oil)
1 cup frozen green peas,
  thawed
Salt and pepper, if desired
1 (12¼-ounce) can solid white
  tuna in water, drained
½ cup shredded reduced fat
  sharp Cheddar cheese
¼ cup dry breadcrumbs

Coat a saucepan with no stick cooking spray and sauté mushrooms, red pepper, and onion until tender. Remove from saucepan and set aside. Add margarine to saucepan and add flour, cooking for 1 minute, stirring constantly. Gradually add milk, stirring constantly, and cook until thickened and bubbly. Pour sauce into a bowl. Stir in mushroom mixture, noodles, peas, salt and pepper, and tuna. Spoon mixture into a 2-quart casserole dish coated with no stick cooking spray. Sprinkle with cheese and breadcrumbs. Cover and bake at 350 degrees for 30 minutes. Yield: 8 servings.

**Nutritional Information Per Serving:**

| Calories | Cholesterol (mg) | Fat (g) | % Calories from Fat |
|---|---|---|---|
| 261 | 37 | 4.4 | 15.2% |

M. HANSBROUGH

# CAKES & COOKIES

## ⓒ BLUEBERRY POUND CAKE

1 (18½-ounce) package light
   yellow cake mix
1 (8-ounce) package light
   cream cheese
2 eggs

1⅓ cups water
1½ teaspoons vanilla
2 cups blueberries
⅔ cup chopped pecans

In large mixing bowl, mix all ingredients together except blueberries and pecans. Fold in blueberries and pecans. Pour batter into a 10-inch bundt pan coated with no stick cooking spray and dusted with flour. Bake at 350 degrees for 40 minutes or until done. Cool in pan for 20 minutes, invert, and sprinkle with powdered sugar, if desired. Do not overcook. Yield: 20 servings.
*Quick and great during blueberry season.*

### Nutritional Information Per Serving:

| Calories | Cholesterol (mg) | Fat (g) | % Calories from Fat |
|---|---|---|---|
| 174 | 28 | 6.8 | 35.0% |

## ⓒⒻ BLUEBERRY STREUSEL CAKE

1 cup blueberries
1 tablespoon lemon juice
1 cup flour
1½ teaspoons baking powder
¼ teaspoon salt

½ cup sugar
1 egg white
½ cup skim milk
¼ cup light margarine,
   melted

Sprinkle blueberries with lemon juice; set aside. Combine flour, baking powder, salt, and sugar in bowl. Add egg white, milk, and melted margarine to dry ingredients; mix well. Pour batter into an 8-inch square pan coated with no stick cooking spray and dusted with flour. Sprinkle blueberries over batter and sprinkle with Topping (see recipe below). Bake at 375 degrees for 40 to 45 minutes. Yield: 9 servings.
*This is great for breakfast or brunch.*

### Topping

½ cup sugar
¼ cup flour
¼ teaspoon cinnamon

2 tablespoons light
   margarine, melted.

Mix together all ingredients.

### Nutritional Information Per Serving:

| Calories | Cholesterol (mg) | Fat (g) | % Calories from Fat |
|---|---|---|---|
| 205 | <1 | 4.0 | 17.7% |

# ⓒⓕ CARROT CAKE

1¾ cups flour
⅔ cup whole wheat flour
1 teaspoon cinnamon
1 teaspoon baking soda
1 cup light brown sugar
3 tablespoons canola oil

1 egg
2 egg whites
3 cups shredded carrots
⅔ cup skim milk
1 teaspoon vanilla

In bowl, combine flours, cinnamon and baking soda; set aside. In another bowl, beat sugar and oil with whisk. Add egg and egg whites, one at a time, beating well after each addition. Stir in carrots, milk, and vanilla. Add flour mixture, stirring well. Pour batter into a 13x9x2-inch baking pan coated with no stick cooking spray and dusted with flour. Bake at 350 degrees for 25 minutes. Cool and frost with Cream Cheese Frosting (see recipe below). Yield: 24 servings.

**Cream Cheese Frosting**
½ cup sugar
2 tablespoons water
1 egg white
1 (8-ounce) package light
    cream cheese, softened

½ teaspoon grated orange
    rind
½ teaspoon vanilla

In small saucepan, combine sugar and water; stir well. Bring to a boil and cook for 2 minutes; sugar will be dissolved and form syrup. In mixing bowl, beat egg white until soft peaks form. While mixer is going, gradually add hot syrup in a thin stream to egg white. Continue beating until mixture is thick and glossy (about 4 minutes). In another bowl, combine cream cheese, orange rind, and vanilla, beating until light and fluffy. Add ⅓ of egg white mixture; beat at low speed just until blended. Fold in remaining egg white mixture. Frost cake.

*This might be a little more trouble than you like, however, it is worth the trouble; and you will want to use this frosting on your favorite cakes.*

**Nutritional Information Per Serving:**

| Calories | Cholesterol (mg) | Fat (g) | % Calories from Fat |
|----------|------------------|---------|---------------------|
| 134 | 14 | 3.8 | 25.3% |

## ©Ⓕ CREAM CHEESE COFFEE CAKE

2½ cups flour
¾ cup sugar, divided
½ cup light margarine
½ teaspoon baking powder
½ teaspoon baking soda
¼ teaspoon salt

1 cup non fat plain yogurt
1 teaspoon almond extract
4 egg whites, divided
1 (8-ounce) package light
   cream cheese, softened
¼ cup sliced almonds

In a large bowl, combine flour and ½ cup sugar. Cut in margarine until mixture resembles coarse crumbs. Reserve 1 cup crumb mixture. To remaining crumb mixture, add baking powder, baking soda, salt, yogurt, almond flavoring, and 2 egg whites. Spread batter over bottom and up sides of a 9-inch springform pan coated with no stick cooking spray. In small bowl, combine cream cheese, remaining ¼ cup sugar, and remaining 2 egg whites. Mix well and pour into batter lined pan. Sprinkle with sliced almonds and reserved crumb mixture. Bake at 350 degrees for 45 minutes or until cheese is set and crust is golden brown. Serve warm or cold. Refrigerate leftovers. Yield: 12 servings. *Coffee cake and cheesecake lovers will enjoy this rich creamy cake.*

**Nutritional Information Per Serving:**

| Calories | Cholesterol (mg) | Fat (g) | % Calories from Fat |
|---|---|---|---|
| 263 | 11 | 8.9 | 30.5% |

## © ALMOST BETTER THAN SEX CAKE

1 (18½-ounce) yellow cake
   mix
½ cup skim milk
¼ cup water
⅓ cup canola oil
2 eggs
2 egg whites
1 cup non fat plain yogurt

1 (3¾-ounce) box instant
   vanilla pudding
1 (4-ounce) bar German
   chocolate, grated
⅓ cup semi-sweet chocolate
   chips
½ cup chopped pecans

Combine all ingredients except chocolate chips and pecans in large mixing bowl. Beat slightly, only until mixture is combined. Stir in chocolate chips and pecans. Pour batter into a 10-inch fluted bundt pan coated with no stick cooking spray and dusted with flour. Bake at 350 degrees for 50 to 55 minutes. Do not overbake. Yield: 20 servings. *This is a lighter version of one of my favorite cakes.*

**Nutritional Information Per Serving:**

| Calories | Cholesterol (mg) | Fat (g) | % Calories from Fat |
|---|---|---|---|
| 246 | 22 | 12.4 | 45.4% |

 **COFFEE CAKE**

1 (8-ounce) tub light
   margarine
1¼ cups sugar
2 cups non fat plain yogurt
3 egg whites

1 teaspoon vanilla
1 teaspoon butter flavoring
3 cups flour
1½ teaspoons baking powder
1 teaspoon baking soda

In mixing bowl, beat margarine and sugar until fluffy. Add yogurt, egg whites, vanilla, and butter flavoring, mixing well. Combine flour, baking powder, and baking soda together. Gradually add to yogurt mixture, mixing well. Pour one third of the batter into a 10-inch bundt pan coated with no stick cooking spray and dusted with flour. Sprinkle with half the Nut Filling (see recipe below). Repeat layers, ending with batter. Bake at 350 degrees for 55 minutes or until toothpick inserted in center of cake comes out clean. Yield: 24 servings.

*This cake will definitely be a hit for all those coffee cake lovers.*

**Nut Filling**
½ cup light brown sugar
1½ teaspoons cinnamon

½ cup chopped pecans

In small bowl, combine all ingredients. Mix with fork until crumbly.

**Nutritional Information Per Serving:**

| Calories | Cholesterol (mg) | Fat (g) | % Calories from Fat |
|----------|------------------|---------|---------------------|
| 167 | <1 | 5.4 | 29.0% |

## CHOCOLATE CREAM CHEESE CAKE

1 (18.25-ounce) light Devil's
   Food cake mix
1 (8-ounce) package light
   cream cheese

1½ cups powdered sugar
1 egg white
1 teaspoon vanilla

Prepare cake mix according to directions on package using water and eggs. Pour batter into a 13x9x2-inch baking pan coated with no stick cooking spray and dusted with flour. In mixing bowl, beat remaining ingredients until creamy. Drop by tablespoonfuls on top of chocolate batter. Bake at 350 degrees for 35 minutes. Yield: 28 to 35 pieces.

*This is a super recipe — definitely try it!*

**Nutritional Information Per Piece:**

| Calories | Cholesterol (mg) | Fat (g) | % Calories from Fat |
|----------|------------------|---------|---------------------|
| 104 | 22 | 2.6 | 22.6% |

# ©Ⓕ CRANBERRY CAKE

½ cup light margarine
1 cup sugar
1 egg
2 egg whites
½ teaspoon almond extract
2 cups flour

3 teaspoons baking powder
1 cup non fat plain yogurt
1 cup whole berry cranberry
  sauce
½ cup sliced almonds

In a mixing bowl, cream margarine. Gradually add sugar beating until light and fluffy. Add egg and egg whites beating after each addition. Add almond extract. Combine flour and baking powder in measuring cup. Add to sugar mixture alternately with yogurt beginning and ending with flour mixture. Pour batter into a 13x9x2-inch pan coated with no stick cooking spray and dusted with flour. Spoon cranberry sauce evenly over batter; spread slightly, but do not try to cover batter. Sprinkle with almonds. Bake at 350 degrees for 35 minutes or until cake slightly pulls away from sides of pan. Drizzle with Glaze (see recipe below). Yield: 16 servings.

*This cake is delicious and can be made year round.*

**Glaze**
1 cup powdered sugar
2 tablespoons skim milk

½ teaspoon vanilla

In small bowl, combine all ingredients stirring until smooth.

**Nutritional Information Per Serving:**

| Calories | Cholesterol (mg) | Fat (g) | % Calories from Fat |
|---|---|---|---|
| 232 | 14 | 5.7 | 22.1% |

 **FRESH PEAR CAKE**

¾ cup sugar
¼ cup light margarine,
   softened
1 teaspoon vanilla
3 egg whites
1¾ cups flour

1 teaspoon baking powder
½ teaspoon baking soda
1 cup non fat plain yogurt
2 cups chopped pears, skin
   removed

In large mixing bowl, beat sugar, margarine, vanilla, and egg whites for 2 minutes. In another bowl, combine all dry ingredients. Gradually add dry ingredients to sugar mixture alternately with yogurt, beating on low speed. Fold in pears. Spread batter in a 13x9x2-inch baking pan coated with no stick cooking spray and dusted with flour. Sprinkle with Streusel (see recipe below). Bake at 350 degrees for 30 minutes or until toothpick in center comes out clean. Drizzle with Glaze (see recipe below). Yield: 16 squares.

**Streusel**
⅓ cup light brown sugar
2 tablespoons flour
½ teaspoon cinnamon

2 tablespoons light
   margarine

In small bowl, combine sugar, flour, and cinnamon. Cut in margarine until mixture is crumbly.

**Glaze**
½ cup powdered sugar
2 tablespoons skim milk

¼ teaspoon almond extract

Mix all ingredients until smooth.

**Nutritional Information Per Square:**

| Calories | Cholesterol (mg) | Fat (g) | % Calories from Fat |
|---|---|---|---|
| 160 | <1 | 2.4 | 13.3% |

# Ⓒ Ⓕ ORANGE COCONUT CAKE WITH WHITE FROSTING

½ cup shortening
1¼ cups sugar
1 tablespoon grated orange rind
2¼ cups flour
2 teaspoons baking powder

¼ teaspoon salt
1 cup orange juice
1 teaspoon coconut extract
⅓ cup flaked coconut
3 egg whites

In mixing bowl, cream shortening and sugar until fluffy. Add orange rind. Combine dry ingredients and add to creamed mixture alternately with orange juice. Add coconut extract. Stir in coconut. In another bowl, beat egg whites until stiff peaks form. Fold egg whites into orange batter. Pour batter into two 9-inch round cake pans that have been coated with no stick cooking spray and dusted with flour. Bake at 375 degrees for 25 minutes. Cool 10 minutes and remove to cool on wire racks. Frost cooled cake with White Frosting (see recipe below). Yield: 16 slices.

*Coconut lovers, here is a cake for you.*

## White Frosting

1 cup sugar
½ cup boiling water
Dash salt

2 egg whites
½ teaspoon vanilla
1 tablespoon flaked coconut

Combine sugar, boiling water, and salt in saucepan. Stir only until sugar dissolves. Cover and cook 2 minutes. Uncover and cook until mixture reaches 242 degrees on candy thermometer. While sugar mixture is cooking, beat egg whites in bowl until stiff peaks form. While mixer is going, gradually pour cooked syrup over beaten egg whites, beating until spreading consistency. Add vanilla and ice cake. Sprinkle top of cake with 1 tablespoon coconut.

## Nutritional Information Per Slice:

| Calories | Cholesterol (mg) | Fat (g) | % Calories from Fat |
|---|---|---|---|
| 263 | 0 | 7.9 | 27.2% |

# ♡ POPPY SEED CAKE WITH LEMON FILLING

## Cake

6 egg whites, room
   temperature
1 teaspoon cream of tartar
1¾ cups flour
¾ cup powdered sugar
2 teaspoons baking powder

2 teaspoons poppy seeds
1 teaspoon grated lemon rind
½ cup canola oil
½ cup water
1 teaspoon vanilla
1 teaspoon lemon extract

Beat egg whites in mixing bowl until foamy. Add cream of tartar, and beat at high speed of mixer until stiff peaks form. Combine flour, powdered sugar, baking powder, poppy seeds, and lemon rind in bowl. In another bowl, combine oil and water. Add to dry ingredients. Mix at low speed until blended. Stir in vanilla and lemon extract. Gently fold in beaten egg whites. Pour batter into two 9-inch round cake pans coated with no stick cooking spray and dusted with flour. Bake at 350 degrees for 20 to 25 minutes or until toothpick inserted comes out clean. Cool 10 minutes and remove to cool on wire racks. Spread Lemon Filling (see recipe below) between layers. Frost top and sides of cake with Lemon Frosting (see recipe below). Yield: 16 servings.

*A light lovely dessert to serve at a luncheon or tea.*

## Lemon Filling

¼ cup sugar
2 tablespoons cornstarch
Dash salt
1 cup skim milk

1 egg yolk, lightly beaten
½ teaspoon grated lemon
   rind
2 tablespoons lemon juice

Combine sugar, cornstarch, and salt in saucepan. Gradually add milk. Cook over medium heat, stirring constantly, until mixture thickens. Remove from heat. Gradually stir about one-fourth hot mixture into egg yolk. Return all to hot mixture. Cook over medium heat for a few minutes, stirring. Remove from heat; cool slightly. Stir in lemon rind and lemon juice. Cover and refrigerate until chilled.

## Lemon Frosting

1 egg white, room
   temperature
⅓ cup light corn syrup

1 tablespoon lemon juice
½ teaspoon lemon extract

Beat egg white at high speed until soft peaks form. Bring corn syrup and lemon juice to boil in small saucepan. While mixer continues to beat egg white, slowly pour boiling syrup mixture over egg white in slow steady stream. Beat at high speed for 5 minutes or until light and fluffy. Beat in lemon extract.

## Nutritional Information Per Serving:

| Calories | Cholesterol (mg) | Fat (g) | % Calories from Fat |
|----------|------------------|---------|---------------------|
| 194 | 14 | 7.4 | 34.5% |

## Ⓒ Ⓕ BOSTON CREAM PIE

2 egg yolks
¼ cup sugar
4 egg whites
½ teaspoon cream of tartar

¼ cup sugar
⅔ cup flour
2 tablespoons light
   margarine, melted

Combine egg yolks and ¼ cup sugar in large bowl. Beat with mixer until thick and lemon colored. Beat egg whites and cream of tartar in mixer until foamy. Gradually add ¼ cup sugar, 1 tablespoon at a time, beating until stiff peaks form. Gently fold egg whites into yolk mixture. Carefully fold flour and margarine alternately into egg mixture. Spoon batter into a wax paper-lined 9-inch round cake pan that has been coated with no stick cooking spray and dusted with flour. Bake at 325 degrees for 30 minutes. Cool in pan 10 minutes; remove from pan and peel off wax paper. Cool on wire rack. Split cake horizontally into two layers. Spread Filling (see recipe below) between layers. Spread Glaze (see recipe below) over top of cake. Refrigerate until ready to serve. Yield: 10 to 12 servings.

### Filling

3 tablespoons sugar
1 tablespoon cornstarch
1 cup skim milk

1 egg yolk, beaten
1 teaspoon vanilla

In saucepan, combine sugar and cornstarch. Gradually stir in milk and egg yolk. Cook over medium heat, stirring constantly, until mixture comes to a boil. Boil 1 minute or until thickened. Remove from heat; stir in vanilla. Transfer to bowl, cover with plastic wrap, and chill thoroughly.

### Glaze

½ cup powdered sugar
3 tablespoons cocoa
2 tablespoons boiling water

1 tablespoon light margarine
½ teaspoon vanilla

Combine sugar and cocoa; stir until well blended. Add remaining ingredients; stir until smooth.

### Nutritional Information Per Serving:

| Calories | Cholesterol (mg) | Fat (g) | % Calories from Fat |
|---|---|---|---|
| 137 | 55 | 2.9 | 19.2% |

#  STRAWBERRY CUSTARD CAKE

**Cake**

| | |
|---|---|
| 4 eggs, separated | ¼ teaspoon salt |
| 2 tablespoons water | 1½ tablespoons cornstarch |
| 1 cup sugar | 1 teaspoon vanilla |
| 1 cup flour | 1 (8-ounce) carton frozen |
| 1 teaspoon baking powder | whipped lite topping |

Beat egg yolks with 2 tablespoons water in large mixing bowl. Add sugar gradually and beat well. Combine remaining dry ingredients and add to sugar mixture. Add vanilla. In another bowl, beat egg whites until stiff. Fold into batter. Pour batter into two 9-inch round cake pans coated with no stick cooking spray and dusted with flour. Bake at 325 degrees for 40 to 45 minutes. Remove from pans and cool on wire racks. To assemble cake, put bottom layer on serving plate. Top with Strawberry Mixture (see recipe below). Spread all Custard Filling (see recipe below) on top. Top with second layer. Frost sides and top with whipped topping. Yield: 16 slices.
*This will definitely be a summer favorite.*

**Strawberry Mixture**

| | |
|---|---|
| ¼ cup water | 1 pint strawberries |
| ¼ cup sugar | |

In small saucepan, bring water and sugar to a boil, boiling just until sugar dissolves. Hull and cut strawberries in half and place in bowl. Pour prepared syrup over strawberries and refrigerate until chilled. Toss to keep strawberries covered with syrup. Let strawberries marinate in syrup for 2 hours if possible.

**Custard Filling**

| | |
|---|---|
| 3 tablespoons sugar | 1½ cups skim milk |
| 2 tablespoons cornstarch | 1 egg |
| ⅛ teaspoon salt | 2 teaspoons vanilla |

Combine sugar, cornstarch, and salt in saucepan. Gradually add milk, stirring until blended. Cook over medium heat, stirring constantly, until mixture thickens and comes to a boil. Boil 1 minute, stirring. Remove from heat. Beat egg at high speed of mixer until thick and lemon colored. Gradually stir in one-fourth hot mixture into beaten egg; return to remaining hot mixture. Cook, stirring constantly, for several minutes. Remove from heat; add vanilla. Cover and chill in refrigerator.

**Nutritional Information Per Slice:**

| Calories | Cholesterol (mg) | Fat (g) | % Calories from Fat |
|---|---|---|---|
| 153 | 67 | 2.6 | 15.4% |

 **PINEAPPLE CAKE**

**Cake**

¾ cup tub margarine
1⅛ cups sugar, divided
1 teaspoon vanilla
1 teaspoon almond extract

1 cup skim milk
2¾ cups flour
4 teaspoons baking powder
4 egg whites

In a large mixing bowl, cream margarine and 1 cup sugar until light. Add vanilla and almond extract to milk. Combine flour and baking powder; add alternately with milk to creamed mixture. Beat well. In another mixing bowl, beat egg whites until fluffy. Gradually add ⅛ cup sugar, beating until stiff peaks form. Fold egg whites into batter. Pour batter into three 9-inch round cake pans coated with no stick cooking spray and dusted with flour. Bake at 350 degrees for 15 to 20 minutes. Cool cake in pans and remove to cooling rack. Put Filling (see recipe below) in between layers. Frost sides and top with Pineapple Frosting (see recipe below). Yield: 16 servings.
*This is a good old fashioned pineapple cake.*

**Pineapple Filling**

⅓ cup sugar
3 tablespoons cornstarch

1 (20-ounce) can crushed
  pineapple in its own
  juice, undrained
½ cup pineapple juice

Combine all ingredients in a small heavy saucepan and cook, stirring, over a low heat until thickened. Set aside to cool. Spread between layers.

**Pineapple Frosting**

3 tablespoons tub margarine
3 cups powdered sugar
1 tablespoon lemon juice

2 to 3 tablespoons pineapple
  juice

In mixing bowl, cream margarine and powdered sugar. Add lemon juice. Add pineapple juice to make spreading consistency, beating until smooth. Frost cake.

**Nutritional Information Per Serving:**

| Calories | Cholesterol (mg) | Fat (g) | % Calories from Fat |
|---|---|---|---|
| 254 | <1 | 5.5 | 19.3% |

## ⓒⒻ QUICK PINEAPPLE CAKE

1 (20-ounce) can crushed
    pineapple in its own juice
    (undrained)

2 cups flour
1 cup sugar
1 teaspoon baking soda

Mix all ingredients in large bowl. Pour into a 13x9x2-inch baking pan coated with no stick cooking spray and dusted with flour. Bake at 350 degrees for 30 to 40 minutes. Frost with Icing (see recipe below) while cake is hot.

**Icing**

4 ounces light cream cheese
1 tablespoon light margarine

1 teaspoon vanilla
1⅔ cups powdered sugar

In mixing bowl, combine cream cheese and margarine until light. Add vanilla and powdered sugar, mixing until well combined. Yield: 24 servings.

**Nutritional Information Per Serving:**

| Calories | Cholesterol (mg) | Fat (g) | % Calories from Fat |
|---|---|---|---|
| 133 | 3 | 1.2 | 8.1% |

## ⓒⒻ PINEAPPLE SNACK CAKE

1 (8-ounce) can unsweetened
    crushed pineapple,
    undrained
1½ cups flour
½ cup sugar
2 teaspoons baking powder
¼ teaspoon salt

¼ cup skim milk
3 tablespoons light
    margarine, melted
1 egg, beaten
1 teaspoon vanilla
⅓ cup light brown sugar

Drain pineapple, reserving ¼ cup juice; set aside. In bowl, combine flour, sugar, baking powder, and salt. Make a well in center. In another bowl, combine reserved pineapple juice, milk, margarine, egg, and vanilla. Add to dry ingredients, stirring, just until dry ingredients are moistened. Pour batter into a 9x9x2-inch baking pan coated with no stick cooking spray and dusted with flour. Top with crushed pineapple and sprinkle with brown sugar. Bake at 350 degrees for 20 to 25 minutes or until toothpick inserted comes out clean. Yield: 9 servings.

**Nutritional Information Per Serving:**

| Calories | Cholesterol (mg) | Fat (g) | % Calories from Fat |
|---|---|---|---|
| 200 | 24 | 2.7 | 12.1% |

# ©Ⓕ PINEAPPLE DREAM CAKE

1 (18.25-ounce) package light
yellow cake mix
2 eggs

2 egg whites
1⅓ cups water

Combine cake mix, eggs, egg whites, and water in mixing bowl. Mix at low speed until blended and mix at high speed 2 minutes. Pour batter into two 9-inch round cake pans coated with no stick cooking spray and dusted with flour. Bake at 350 degrees for 25 minutes or until top springs back when touched. Cool and remove from pans to wire racks. Frost cake with Pineapple Frosting (see recipe below). Refrigerate until chilled. Yield: 16 servings.

**Pineapple Frosting**

1 (4-serving) package instant
vanilla pudding
1 (15¼-ounce) can crushed
pineapple in its own
juice, undrained

1 envelope dry whipped
topping mix

Stir pudding mix into crushed pineapple. Prepare whipped topping mix according to directions on package substituting skim milk; fold in pineapple mixture. Frost between layers and on sides and top of cake.

**Nutritional Information Per Serving:**

| Calories | Cholesterol (mg) | Fat (g) | % Calories from Fat |
|---|---|---|---|
| 196 | 27 | 3.8 | 17.6% |

## ⓒⒻ PINEAPPLE CHIFFON CAKE

1½ cups flour
1 cup sugar
2 teaspoons baking powder
¼ teaspoon salt
½ cup canola oil
½ cup frozen pineapple juice
   concentrate, at room
   temperature

1 teaspoon vanilla
6 egg whites, at room
   temperature
2 tablespoons powdered
   sugar
1 (20-ounce) can
   unsweetened crushed
   pineapple, well drained

Combine flour, sugar, baking powder, and salt into a large mixing bowl. Make a well in center of dry ingredients and add oil, ½ cup pineapple juice concentrate, and vanilla. Mix only until well blended. In another mixing bowl, beat egg whites until foamy. Add powdered sugar and continue beating until whites are stiff. In fourths, gently fold the flour/oil mixture into egg whites, adding a quarter of the crushed pineapple with each addition. Pour batter in to a bundt pan coated with no stick cooking spray and dusted with flour. Bake at 350 degrees for 35 to 40 minutes or until the cake top springs back to touch. Cool cake 10 minutes. With a knife, loosen sides and center; invert to serving plate. Spread warm cake with Pineapple Glaze (see recipe below). Yield: 16 servings.

### Pineapple Glaze

3 tablespoons frozen
   pineapple juice
   concentrate

1 cup powdered sugar
1 teaspoon lemon juice

Combine all ingredients in bowl, mixing well until smooth.

### Nutritional Information Per Serving:

| Calories | Cholesterol (mg) | Fat (g) | % Calories from Fat |
|---|---|---|---|
| 238 | 0 | 7.0 | 26.4% |

## Ⓒ Ⓕ PINEAPPLE OATMEAL CAKE

¾ cup light brown sugar
¼ cup safflower oil
¼ cup light margarine
4 egg whites
½ cup non fat plain yogurt
1 teaspoon vanilla
2 cups flour
1 teaspoon baking soda
1 teaspoon baking powder

1 teaspoon grated orange
   rind
1 teaspoon cinnamon
1½ cups old fashioned
   oatmeal
1 cup crushed pineapple,
   packed in its own juices,
   undrained

In large bowl, combine sugar, oil, and margarine; beat well. Add egg whites, yogurt, and vanilla; mix well. Combine flour, baking soda, baking powder, orange rind, and cinnamon. Add half the flour mixture and all of the oatmeal. Mix well. Alternately add remaining flour mixture and pineapple, mixing well after each addition. Pour batter into a 13x9x2-inch baking pan coated with no stick cooking spray and dusted with flour. Bake at 350 degrees for 25 minutes or until cake is done. Yield: 24 pieces.
*The longer it sits, the better it gets. Very moist snack cake.*

**Nutritional Information Per Serving:**

| Calories | Cholesterol (mg) | Fat (g) | % Calories from Fat |
|---|---|---|---|
| 128 | <1 | 3.7 | 25.9% |

## Ⓒ Ⓕ APPLE CAKE

½ cup flour
½ cup sugar
1 teaspoon baking powder
1 teaspoon cinnamon
⅛ teaspoon salt

2 tart apples, cored, peeled
   and chopped
1 egg, lightly beaten
1 teaspoon vanilla

Combine dry ingredients in bowl; mix well. Add apple, stirring to coat. Combine egg and vanilla; add to apple mixture, stirring just until dry ingredients are moistened. Pour batter into a 9-inch round pie plate coated with no stick cooking spray. Bake at 350 degrees for 25 minutes or until lightly browned. Yield: 8 servings.
*This snack cake would be good for breakfast.*

**Nutritional Information Per Serving:**

| Calories | Cholesterol (mg) | Fat (g) | % Calories from Fat |
|---|---|---|---|
| 109 | 27 | 0.8 | 6.7% |

# CHOCOLATE PUDDING CAKE

**Cake**

½ cup sugar
1 cup flour
2 teaspoons baking powder
2 tablespoons unsweetened
    cocoa

½ cup skim milk
1 teaspoon vanilla
1 tablespoon light margarine,
    melted
1½ cups boiling water

Combine sugar, flour, baking powder, and cocoa together into a 9x9x2-inch square baking pan. Stir in milk, vanilla, and margarine. Spread batter in pan. Mix Topping (see recipe below) and sprinkle over batter. Pour boiling water over all and bake at 350 degrees for 25 to 30 minutes. Yield: 16 servings.
*Surprise! A pudding forms on the bottom of the cake.*

**Topping**

¾ cup light brown sugar

¼ cup unsweetened cocoa

Combine all ingredients and sprinkle evenly over batter.

**Nutritional Information Per Serving:**

| Calories | Cholesterol (mg) | Fat (g) | % Calories from Fat |
|---|---|---|---|
| 89 | <1 | 0.7 | 7.1% |

# CHOCOLATE CHESS BARS

1 (18.25-ounce) package lite
    Devil's Food cake mix
1 egg
½ cup light margarine,
    melted
1 tablespoon water

1 (8-ounce) package light
    cream cheese
1 (16-ounce) box powdered
    sugar
3 egg whites
1 teaspoon vanilla

In large mixing bowl, combine cake mix, 1 egg, melted margarine, and water. Beat by hand until well blended. Pat batter into bottom of a 13x9x2-inch baking pan coated with no stick cooking spray. In mixing bowl, beat cream cheese, powdered sugar, and 3 egg whites until mixture is smooth and creamy. Add vanilla. Pour over batter in pan. Bake at 350 degrees for 45 minutes or until top is golden brown. Cool and cut into squares. Yield: 48 squares.
*You will get requests for this bar cookie.*

**Nutritional Information Per Square:**

| Calories | Cholesterol (mg) | Fat (g) | % Calories from Fat |
|---|---|---|---|
| 103 | 7 | 2.6 | 22.8% |

 **HEAVENLY HASH**

2 cups flour
1½ cups sugar
½ cup light margarine
¼ cup cocoa
1 cup water
½ cup skim milk
1½ teaspoons vinegar

1 teaspoon baking soda
1 egg
2 egg whites
1 teaspoon vanilla
1 (10-ounce) package
    miniature marshmallows

Combine flour and sugar in bowl. Heat margarine, cocoa and water in saucepan over low heat until boiling. Remove from heat and pour over dry ingredients in bowl. Combine skim milk and vinegar with baking soda, egg, egg whites, and vanilla; add to chocolate mixture. Mix well. Pour into a 15x10x1-inch jelly roll pan coated with no stick cooking spray and dusted with flour. Bake at 400 degrees for 15 minutes. Top with miniature marshmallows. Slowly pour hot Chocolate Icing (see recipe below) on top of marshmallows. Be careful because Chocolate Icing will run off sides. Yield: 48 pieces.
*It is hard to pass these brownies without eating one.*

**Chocolate Icing**

6 tablespoons light
    margarine
¼ cup cocoa
½ cup skim milk

1 (16-ounce) box powdered
    sugar
1 teaspoon vanilla
1 cup chopped pecans

Combine margarine, cocoa, and milk in saucepan; bring to a boil. Add other ingredients, stirring well.

**Nutritional Information Per Piece:**

| Calories | Cholesterol (mg) | Fat (g) | % Calories from Fat |
|----------|------------------|---------|---------------------|
| 136 | 5 | 3.5 | 22.8% |

 **BROWNIES**

| | |
|---|---|
| 6 tablespoons light margarine | 1 cup light brown sugar |
| 4 tablespoons cocoa | 1 cup flour |
| ½ cup sugar | 4 egg whites |
| | 1 teaspoon vanilla |

In cup, melt margarine and cocoa together in microwave. Combine with remaining ingredients, stirring until well mixed. Pour batter into a 9x9x2-inch baking pan coated with no stick cooking spray and dusted with flour. Bake at 350 degrees for approximately 30 minutes. Yield: 25 squares.

**Nutritional Information Per Square:**

| Calories | Cholesterol (mg) | Fat (g) | % Calories from Fat |
|---|---|---|---|
| 85 | 0 | 1.5 | 16.0% |

 **OATMEAL COOKIES**

| | |
|---|---|
| 1½ cups flour | ¼ cup skim milk |
| ½ cup light brown sugar | 2 egg whites |
| ½ cup sugar | 1 teaspoon vanilla |
| 1 teaspoon cinnamon | 1½ cups old fashioned oatmeal |
| ½ teaspoon baking powder | |
| ¼ teaspoon baking soda | ½ cup raisins |
| ½ cup canola oil | ½ cup chopped pecans |

In large bowl, combine flour, brown sugar, sugar, cinnamon, baking powder, and baking soda; set aside. In another bowl, combine oil, milk, egg whites, and vanilla. Stir into dry ingredients, mixing well. Stir in oatmeal, raisins, and pecans. Drop by rounded spoonfuls 1-inch apart on baking sheet coated with no stick cooking spray. Bake at 400 degrees for 10 to 12 minutes. Remove cookies to waxed paper to cool. Yield: 4 dozen cookies.

*Attention all oatmeal cookie lovers — this one is for you!*

**Nutritional Information Per Cookie:**

| Calories | Cholesterol (mg) | Fat (g) | % Calories from Fat |
|---|---|---|---|
| 75 | <1 | 3.2 | 38.7% |

 **CRISPY OATMEAL COOKIES**

½ cup light margarine
½ cup sugar
½ cup light brown sugar
½ cup molasses
1 teaspoon vanilla
2 egg whites

3 cups flour
1 teaspoon baking soda
2 cups old fashioned oatmeal
1 cup crisp rice cereal
½ cup chopped pecans

In mixing bowl, cream margarine with sugar and brown sugar until light and fluffy. Add molasses, vanilla, and egg whites. Combine flour and baking soda; gradually add to creamed mixture, beating well. Stir in oatmeal, cereal, and pecans, mixing well. Drop dough on a cookie sheet coated with no stick cooking spray. Bake at 350 degrees for 8 to 10 minutes. Yield: 5 dozen cookies.

**Nutritional Information Per Cookie:**

| Calories | Cholesterol (mg) | Fat (g) | % Calories from Fat |
|---|---|---|---|
| 70 | 0 | 1.6 | 20.7% |

**OATMEAL MELTIES**

¼ cup light margarine
½ cup canola oil
¾ cup sugar
¾ cup light brown sugar
2 egg whites
1 teaspoon vanilla

2½ cups flour
1 teaspoon baking soda
½ teaspoon salt
2¼ cups old fashioned
   oatmeal
½ cup chopped pecans

In mixing bowl, cream margarine, oil, sugars, egg whites, and vanilla until light and fluffy. In another bowl, combine flour, baking soda, and salt. Add to creamed mixture. Stir in oatmeal and pecans. Place spoonfuls of dough on an ungreased cookie sheet and bake at 350 degrees for 12 to 15 minutes. Yield: 48 cookies.

**Nutritional Information Per Cookie:**

| Calories | Cholesterol (mg) | Fat (g) | % Calories from Fat |
|---|---|---|---|
| 98 | 0 | 3.8 | 35.0% |

#  STRUDEL

| | |
|---|---|
| 2¼ cups flour | 1 (15.5-ounce) jar low sugar |
| 1 tablespoon sugar | apricot spread or apricot |
| ½ teaspoon salt | preserves |
| ½ cup light margarine, | 2 tablespoons powdered |
| melted | sugar |
| 1 cup non fat plain yogurt | |

Combine all ingredients except apricot spread and powdered sugar in bowl and stir until mixture form a ball. Wrap dough in waxed paper; refrigerate 1 hour. Remove from refrigerator and divide into four equal parts. Roll each piece of dough out on floured waxed paper to form a rectangle. Spread apricot spread over entire rectangle. Sprinkle Filling (see recipe below) over apricot spread. Roll each rectangle up lengthwise to form a roll. Place roll on baking sheet coated with no stick cooking spray and dusted with flour. Repeat with remaining dough and filling. Bake at 350 degrees for 40 minutes to 1 hour. Sprinkle with powdered sugar. Let cool and slice into 1-inch slices. Yield: 48 slices. *Strudel is always a favorite and this is an easy recipe.*

**Filling**

| | |
|---|---|
| ½ cup light brown sugar | ⅔ cup chopped walnuts |
| 1 tablespoon cinnamon | ½ cup white raisins |

Combine all ingredients in a bowl; mix well.

**Nutritional Information Per Slice:**

| Calories | Cholesterol (mg) | Fat (g) | % Calories from Fat |
|---|---|---|---|
| 56 | <1 | 2.1 | 33.2% |

#  CHOCOLATE MERINGUE KISSES

| | |
|---|---|
| 2 egg whites, at room | ½ cup semi-sweet chocolate |
| temperature | mini-morsels |
| ⅓ cup sugar | ½ teaspoon vanilla |

In a large mixing bowl, beat egg whites at high speed of an electric mixer one minute. Gradually add sugar, 1 tablespoon at a time, beating until stiff peaks form and sugar is dissolved (approximately 3 minutes). Gently fold in chocolate chips and vanilla. Drop by heaping teaspoonfuls onto a cookie sheet lined with wax paper. Bake at 300 degrees for 35 minutes. Cool slightly on cookie sheets before removing. Cool completely on wire racks. Yield: 3 dozen kisses.

**Nutritional Information Per Kiss:**

| Calories | Cholesterol (mg) | Fat (g) | % Calories from Fat |
|---|---|---|---|
| 20 | 0 | 0.8 | 37.7% |

## ⓒ PRALINE MERINGUES

½ cup dark brown sugar
¼ cup sugar
3 egg whites
½ teaspoon cream of tartar

¼ teaspoon lemon juice
½ teaspoon vanilla
½ cup finely chopped pecans

Combine both sugars together. In mixer, beat egg whites and cream of tartar until stiff. Beat in 1 tablespoon sugar mixture at a time, alternately with drops of lemon juice and vanilla. Beat until stiff and glossy. Fold in pecans. On baking sheets lined with brown paper, drop by heaping teaspoons. Bake at 250 degrees for 45 minutes. (Meringue will spread during baking). Yield: 36 meringues.

**Nutritional Information Per Meringue:**

| Calories | Cholesterol (mg) | Fat (g) | % Calories from Fat |
|---|---|---|---|
| 28 | 0 | 1.0 | 32.3% |

## ⓒ NO BAKE COOKIES

½ cup graham cracker
   crumbs
2½ cups old fashioned
   oatmeal
1½ cups sugar

2 tablespoons cocoa
½ cup skim milk
½ cup light margarine
½ cup peanut butter
1 teaspoon vanilla

In bowl, combine graham cracker crumbs and oatmeal. Set aside. In saucepan, stir sugar, cocoa, milk, and margarine over medium heat until dissolved. Bring mixture to boil and cook for 2 minutes. Remove from heat. Stir in peanut butter and vanilla until well combined. Quickly blend in cracker mixture. Beat by hand until thickens (few minutes). Drop by teaspoon onto waxed paper. Refrigerate until firm and store in refrigerator. Yield: 5 dozen.
*These ingredients are always in the pantry. It is a quick cure for a sweet tooth and they are nourishing too.*

**Nutritional Information Per Cookie:**

| Calories | Cholesterol (mg) | Fat (g) | % Calories from Fat |
|---|---|---|---|
| 56 | <1 | 2.2 | 35.1% |

# Ⓒ Ⓕ LEMON SQUARES

**Crust**
**2 cups flour**
**½ cup powdered sugar**
**4 ounces light cream cheese**

**2 tablespoons light**
**margarine**

In bowl, stir together flour and powdered sugar. Cut in cream cheese and margarine with pastry blender until crumbly. Press into bottom of a 13x9x2-inch baking pan coated with no stick cooking spray and dusted with flour. Bake at 350 degrees for 20 minutes. Pour Lemon Filling (see recipe below) over hot pastry and continue baking for 20 minutes longer or until top is light golden and set. Cool and cut into bars. Yield: 4 dozen bars.
*This is one of my favorite recipes.*

**Lemon Filling**
**5 egg whites**
**1½ cups sugar**
**1½ tablespoons grated lemon**
**rind**

**⅓ cup flour**
**1 teaspoon baking powder**
**½ cup fresh lemon juice**

In mixing bowl, beat egg whites and sugar. Combine lemon rind, flour, and baking powder. Stir into egg mixture. Add lemon juice; mixing well.

**Nutritional Information Per Bar:**

| Calories | Cholesterol (mg) | Fat (g) | % Calories from Fat |
|---|---|---|---|
| 61 | 1 | 0.7 | 10.5% |

# Ⓒ CHEWY CHOCOLATE CHIP COOKIES

**2 cups powdered sugar**
**¾ cup flour**
**½ teaspoon baking powder**
**½ cup egg whites (about 3 or**
**4 eggs)**

**1 teaspoon vanilla**
**⅔ cup miniature semi-sweet**
**chocolate chips**
**⅔ cup chopped walnuts**

In large mixing bowl, beat sugar, flour, baking powder, and egg whites until well combined. Add vanilla. Stir in chocolate chips and walnuts. Drop by rounded teaspoonfuls on cookie sheet coated with no stick cooking spray and dusted with flour. Bake at 325 degrees for 15 minutes. Yield: 36 cookies.
*Cookies spread during baking so place apart on baking sheet.*

**Nutritional Information Per Cookie:**

| Calories | Cholesterol (mg) | Fat (g) | % Calories from Fat |
|---|---|---|---|
| 69 | 0 | 2.5 | 33.4% |

## ⓒ ORANGE BALLS

1 (12-ounce) box vanilla
   wafers, crumbled fine
2 cups powdered sugar
1 (6-ounce) can frozen orange
   juice, thawed

½ cup finely chopped pecans,
   toasted
Powdered sugar

Combine all ingredients together except powdered sugar for rolling. Form into small balls and roll in powdered sugar. Yield: 3 to 4 dozen. *Freezes well. Serve in miniature muffin papers for a fancy occasion.*

**Nutritional Information Per Ball:**

| Calories | Cholesterol (mg) | Fat (g) | % Calories from Fat |
|---|---|---|---|
| 80 | 7 | 3.2 | 36.4% |

## ⓒⒻ APRICOT OATMEAL BARS

½ cup light margarine
⅔ cup light brown sugar
1½ cups flour
½ teaspoon salt, if desired

1½ teaspoons vanilla
2 cups old fashioned oatmeal
1 (16-ounce) jar apricot
   preserves

In mixing bowl, combine the ingredients above in order listed except for the preserves. Press half of the mixture into the bottom of a 13x9x2-inch baking pan coated with no stick cooking spray. Spread preserves over top. Crumble other half of oatmeal mixture over preserves. Bake at 350 degrees for 30 to 35 minutes. Yield: 3 to 4 dozen squares.
*Oatmeal lovers will like this tart cookie.*

**Nutritional Information Per Square:**

| Calories | Cholesterol (mg) | Fat (g) | % Calories from Fat |
|---|---|---|---|
| 85 | 0 | 1.4 | 14.6% |

M. HANSBROUGH

# DESSERTS & PIES

ⒸⒻ **MOCK CHOCOLATE ÉCLAIR**

2 wrapped packages graham
   crackers from 16-ounce
   box
2 (4-serving) packages
   vanilla instant pudding

3 cups skim milk
4 ounces frozen light
   whipped topping

Layer bottom of 13x9x2-inch baking dish with one-third of graham crackers. In mixing bowl, beat pudding mix with milk until thickens; set aside for several minutes. Fold in whipped topping. Spread half of pudding mixture over graham crackers. Repeat layers, ending with graham crackers on top (three layers graham crackers). Spread with Chocolate Topping (see recipe below). Yield: 15 to 20 servings.
*Is this really an imitation? It is so good.*

**Chocolate Topping**

¼ cup cocoa
⅔ cup sugar
¼ cup skim milk

1 tablespoon vanilla
1 tablespoon margarine

Combine cocoa, sugar, and milk in saucepan. Bring to a boil for 1 minute. Remove from heat and add vanilla and margarine. Cool slightly and pour over graham crackers. Refrigerate until ready to serve (can be made night before).

**Nutritional Information Per Serving:**

| Calories | Cholesterol (mg) | Fat (g) | % Calories from Fat |
|---|---|---|---|
| 164 | <1 | 2.9 | 16.0% |

# ⓒ CHOCOLATE LAYERED DESSERT

**Crust**
1 cup flour                     ½ cup chopped pecans
7 tablespoons light
    margarine

Mix all ingredients and press into ungreased 13x9x2-inch pan. Bake at 350 degrees for 20 minutes. Cool and then top with Cream Cheese Layer (see recipe below).

**Cream Cheese Layer**
¾ cup frozen light whipped     1 (8-ounce) package light
    topping                         cream cheese
                               ⅔ cup powdered sugar

Combine ingredients in mixer and beat only until well blended. Spread on top of first layer. Top with Pudding Layer (see recipe below).

**Pudding Layer**
1 (4-serving) package instant  3 cups skim milk
    vanilla pudding            1 teaspoon vanilla
1 (4-serving) package instant  1¼ cups frozen light whipped
    chocolate pudding              topping

Mix pudding with milk and beat according to directions on package. After thickens, add vanilla. Spread on top of Cream Cheese Layer. Cover dessert with frozen whipped topping. Yield: 16 servings.
*Easy and a favorite of everyone.*

**Nutritional Information Per Serving:**

| Calories | Cholesterol (mg) | Fat (g) | % Calories from Fat |
|----------|------------------|---------|---------------------|
| 214 | 9 | 8.8 | 36.8% |

## ©Ⓕ BREAD PUDDING

8 cups French bread, cut into
  small pieces
½ cup raisins
¼ cup light brown sugar
½ cup sugar
1½ cups skim milk

1 (12-ounce) can evaporated
  skimmed milk
1 teaspoon vanilla
1 egg yolk
4 egg whites

Spread French bread in a 3-quart baking dish. Sprinkle raisins over bread. In bowl, combine remaining ingredients except egg whites. In mixing bowl, beat egg whites until stiff peaks form and fold into sugar mixture. Pour over bread and raisins in pan. Let sit 5 minutes. Bake at 350 degrees for 30 to 40 minutes and serve hot with Rum Sauce (see recipe below). Yield: 12 servings.
*This is a lighter version of one of all of our favorites. Enjoy!*

**Rum Sauce**
2 tablespoons flour
2 tablespoons light
  margarine

½ cup sugar
1 cup skim milk
1 tablespoon dark rum

In small saucepan, combine flour, margarine, and sugar. Gradually add milk, stirring constantly. Cook until mixture comes to a boil and thickens. Remove from heat and stir in rum. Serve over hot bread pudding.

**Nutritional Information Per Serving:**

| Calories | Cholesterol (mg) | Fat (g) | % Calories from Fat |
|---|---|---|---|
| 253 | 20 | 2.1 | 7.6% |

## ©Ⓕ CHOCOLATE SAUCE

1½ cups sugar
⅔ cup cocoa
1 cup skim milk

1 cup light corn syrup
1 tablespoon light margarine
1 teaspoon vanilla

In large saucepan bring sugar, cocoa, milk, and corn syrup to a boil; cook 5 minutes. Add vanilla. Yield: 3 cups.
*Great served over frozen yogurt. Use a large pot as sauce bubbles when cooking.*

**Nutritional Information Per Tablespoon:**

| Calories | Cholesterol (mg) | Fat (g) | % Calories from Fat |
|---|---|---|---|
| 49 | <1 | 0.2 | 4.1% |

 **TRIFLE**

12 ounces light cream cheese
⅔ cup sugar
⅔ cup evaporated skimmed
    milk
1 (16-ounce) angel food cake,
    cubed

1 (20-ounce) can crushed
    pineapple, including
    juice
2 tablespoons cornstarch
1 (8-ounce) container frozen
    light whipped topping

In mixing bowl, beat cream cheese, sugar, and evaporated milk until creamy. Fold into cubed angel food cake. In small saucepan, combine pineapple and cornstarch. Cook over low heat until thick, stirring constantly; set aside. In trifle dish or glass bowl, layer half of angel food cake mixture, pineapple mixture, and whipped topping. Repeat again, ending with whipped topping. Refrigerate. Yield: 8 to 10 servings.
*Can be made ahead and this dessert is definitely one to try.*

**Nutritional Information Per Serving:**

| Calories | Cholesterol (mg) | Fat (g) | % Calories from Fat |
|---|---|---|---|
| 313 | 20 | 7.5 | 21.7% |

## ⓒⓕ **FANTASTIC TRIFLE**

1 (16-ounce) angel food cake
⅔ cup sugar
3 tablespoons cocoa
1 tablespoon cornstarch
⅔ cup evaporated skimmed
    milk
¼ cup coffee liqueur

3 (1³⁄₁₆-ounce) English toffee
    candy bars, crushed
3 (4-serving) packages
    instant vanilla pudding
3 cups skim milk
2 bananas, peeled and sliced
1 (12-ounce) container frozen
    light whipped topping

Cube cake and put in bowl. To make chocolate sauce: combine sugar, cocoa, cornstarch, and ⅔ cup evaporated milk. Cook over low heat until thickens. Remove from heat; add coffee liqueur. Cool. Pour chocolate mixture over cake in bowl. Add crushed candy to angel cake mixture. In mixer, beat pudding and 3 cups skim milk until thick. Pour over angel food cake mixture. Refrigerate 15 minutes. In trifle dish, layer cake mixture, banana, and whipped topping. Repeat layers, ending with whipped topping. Yield: 16 servings.
*This is spectacular, can be made ahead, and serves a crowd.*

**Nutritional Information Per Serving:**

| Calories | Cholesterol (mg) | Fat (g) | % Calories from Fat |
|---|---|---|---|
| 261 | 5 | 3.8 | 13.2% |

ⓒⒻ **ANGEL FOOD CAKE WITH MOCHA FILLING**

1 (14.5-ounce) box angel food
   cake mix
1 (4-serving) package
   chocolate pudding mix

2 teaspoons instant coffee
   powder
1⅓ cups skim milk
1 (8-ounce) container frozen
   lite whipped topping

Prepare angel food cake according to directions on package in a 10-inch tube pan. Invert and cool thoroughly. In saucepan, mix pudding mix and instant coffee. Prepare pudding according to directions on package using only 1⅓ cups milk; cool. Beat until smooth and fold in half of whipped topping. Split cake in three layers with serrated knife. Spread half the just-prepared pudding mixture between the layers only. Then to remaining half of pudding mixture, add remaining half of whipped topping and frost sides and top of cake. Chill. Yield: 12 servings.
*It sounds complicated but it is easy and very good.*

**Nutritional Information Per Serving:**

| Calories | Cholesterol (mg) | Fat (g) | % Calories from Fat |
|---|---|---|---|
| 217 | <1 | 2.8 | 11.8% |

ⓒⒻ **CHOCOLATE TORTE**

2 envelopes unflavored
   gelatin
½ cup cool water
1½ cups boiling water
¾ cup cocoa

¼ cup light margarine, room
   temperature
1 teaspoon vanilla
6 egg whites
½ cup sugar
1 (12-ounce) angel food cake

In a large bowl, combine gelatin and cool water. Allow to stand 5 minutes. Add boiling water and stir until gelatin has completely dissolved. Add cocoa and margarine, stirring until margarine has melted. Add vanilla. Set aside to cool. In another mixing bowl, beat egg whites until foamy. Gradually add sugar, a little at a time, beating until soft peaks form. Fold egg whites into cooled cocoa mixture. Tear up angel food cake into ½-inch pieces and gently mix with cocoa mixture. Pour into a 9-inch springform pan coated with no stick cooking spray. Refrigerate overnight. To serve, remove outer rim and slice. Yield: 10 slices.
*A chocolate lover will love this rich, yet light dessert. Hint: If in a hurry, place in freezer for 2 hours and serve.*

**Nutritional Information Per Slice:**

| Calories | Cholesterol (mg) | Fat (g) | % Calories from Fat |
|---|---|---|---|
| 176 | 0 | 2.8 | 14.4% |

 **COFFEE TOFFEE DELIGHT**

12 ounces angel food cake
1 tablespoon instant coffee
1 tablespoon boiling water
4 (1.4-ounce) chocolate-
   covered toffee candy bars

1 quart non fat vanilla frozen
   yogurt
1 (8-ounce) container light
   frozen whipped topping
3 tablespoons crème de cacao

Cut angel food cake to fit in a 9-inch springform pan. Dissolve coffee in boiling water. Cool. Crush candy bars in food processor or by pounding with mallet. Combine crushed candy and dissolved coffee with softened yogurt. Spoon mixture on top of angel food cake; freeze until firm. Mix whipped topping with crème de cacao and spread over yogurt layer. Freeze. Cut into wedges to serve. Yield: 16 slices.
*For a spectacular ending you will want to serve this dessert. Great because it can be made ahead.*

**Nutritional Information Per Slice:**

| Calories | Cholesterol (mg) | Fat (g) | % Calories from Fat |
|---|---|---|---|
| 198 | 6 | 5.4 | 24.6% |

 **TORTONI**

1 egg white
½ teaspoon salt
1 tablespoon instant coffee,
   dissolved
3 tablespoons powdered
   sugar

1 cup light frozen whipped
   topping
¼ cup powdered sugar
1 teaspoon vanilla
⅛ teaspoon almond extract
¼ cup sliced almonds,
   toasted

Beat egg white in mixing bowl until stiff. Fold in salt and coffee. Gradually add 3 tablespoons powdered sugar. In another bowl, combine whipped topping, ¼ cup powdered sugar, vanilla, and almond extract. Fold both mixtures together. Fold in toasted almonds. Pour mixture in champagne glasses and keep in freezer until ready to serve. Yield: 6 servings.
*This is a favorite from my other cookbook that is too good not to include. It's light and delicious.*

**Nutritional Information Per Serving:**

| Calories | Cholesterol (mg) | Fat (g) | % Calories from Fat |
|---|---|---|---|
| 99 | <1 | 4.8 | 43.9% |

# ♡Ⓒ MOCHA PIE

3 egg whites
½ cup sugar
12 saltine soda crackers,
    finely crushed
1 teaspoon baking powder
½ cup chopped pecans

1 teaspoon vanilla
1 teaspoon instant coffee
1 teaspoon water
1 (8-ounce) container frozen
    light whipped topping
1 teaspoon vanilla

In mixing bowl, beat egg whites until almost stiff. Gradually add sugar beating until thick and glossy. Mix crackers, baking powder, pecans, and vanilla. Fold into beaten egg whites. Spoon mixture into a 9-inch glass pie plate coated with no stick cooking spray. Bake at 350 degrees for 30 minutes. Remove and cool thoroughly. Dissolve coffee in water. Fold into whipped topping with vanilla. Spread on top of pie. Refrigerate several hours before serving. Yield: 8 servings.

**Nutritional Information Per Serving:**

| Calories | Cholesterol (mg) | Fat (g) | % Calories from Fat |
|---|---|---|---|
| 135 | 0 | 6.6 | 44.3% |

# Ⓒ Ⓕ CHOCOLATE ICE CREAM DELIGHT

1 (18.5-ounce) 97% fat free
    Devil's Food cake mix
3 eggs
1⅓ cups water
1 cup chocolate syrup,
    divided

⅔ gallon frozen non fat
    vanilla yogurt
1 (8-ounce) container frozen
    light whipped topping

Combine cake mix, eggs, and water and follow directions on box of cake mix. Divide batter into three 9-inch round cake pans coated with no stick cooking spray and dusted with flour. Bake at 350 degrees for 15 minutes. Remove and cool on racks. With a fork, poke lots of holes in top of each layer. Drizzle ⅓ cup chocolate syrup over each layer allowing to soak in. Place first layer on serving plate and spread with yogurt. Top with remaining layer and yogurt. End with third cake layer and frost with whipped topping. Yield: 16 servings.
*A delightful dessert that everyone will enjoy.*

**Nutritional Information Per Serving:**

| Calories | Cholesterol (mg) | Fat (g) | % Calories from Fat |
|---|---|---|---|
| 303 | 42 | 4.7 | 13.9% |

# ©Ⓕ ICE CREAM PIE

1 cup chocolate wafer
  crumbs
1 cup graham cracker
  crumbs

¼ cup light margarine,
  melted
½ gallon frozen non fat
  vanilla yogurt

In bowl, combine chocolate wafer crumbs and graham cracker crumbs with melted margarine, stirring until combined. Pat into bottom of 13x9x2-inch pan and chill. Soften frozen vanilla yogurt and spread on top of crust. Chill in freezer. Top with Chocolate Sauce (see recipe below) and return to freezer. Yield: 12 servings.
*Great because it can be made ahead and will please everyone.*

**Chocolate Sauce**
⅔ cup sugar
3 tablespoons cocoa
1 tablespoon cornstarch

⅔ cup evaporated skimmed
  milk
1 tablespoon light margarine
1 teaspoon vanilla

In saucepan, combine sugar, cocoa, and cornstarch. Gradually add evaporated milk. Cook over low heat, stirring, until mixture thickens. Add margarine and vanilla. Cool slightly before spreading on top of yogurt.

**Nutritional Information Per Serving:**

| Calories | Cholesterol (mg) | Fat (g) | % Calories from Fat |
|----------|------------------|---------|---------------------|
| 279 | 6 | 5.8 | 18.8% |

# ©Ⓕ FROZEN PINK ANGEL FOOD CAKE

1 (16-ounce) round angel
  food cake
½ gallon non fat frozen
  vanilla yogurt

1 (6-ounce) can frozen
  concentrated pink
  lemonade, thawed
12 drops red food coloring

Split angel food cake horizontally into three layers with serrated knife. Let yogurt soften until it can be easily mixed with lemonade and food coloring. (If you want a pinker icing, just add more food coloring). Lay bottom layer of angel food cake on serving platter. Working quickly, ice layer and inside hole with yogurt mixture. Repeat with next layer making sure to ice hole in center. Ice filled cake with remaining yogurt. Immediately put in freezer. Yield: 16 servings.
*Make ahead and serve when you need a light refreshing dessert.*

**Nutritional Information Per Serving:**

| Calories | Cholesterol (mg) | Fat (g) | % Calories from Fat |
|----------|------------------|---------|---------------------|
| 189 | 2 | 0.2 | 1.0% |

# © STRAWBERRY DESSERT

1¾ cups crushed graham
cracker crumbs
4 tablespoons sugar, divided
¼ cup light margarine,
melted
4 egg whites

4 tablespoons sugar
1 teaspoon vanilla
1 quart fresh strawberries,
hulled and sliced
1 (8-ounce) container frozen
light whipped topping

In bowl, combine crumbs, 2 tablespoons sugar, and margarine. Stir until well blended and press into a 9x9x2-inch square baking pan. In large mixing bowl, beat egg whites until soft peaks form. Gradually add 4 tablespoons sugar, beating until stiff peaks form. Add vanilla. Spread meringue over crumb layer. Bake at 350 degrees for 15 minutes; cool completely. In another bowl, sprinkle strawberries with remaining 2 tablespoons sugar. Let stand 15 minutes; drain. Top cooled meringue with whipped topping and top with strawberries. Refrigerate. Yield: 9 servings.

*When strawberries are in season, do not pass this dessert by.*

**Nutritional Information Per Serving:**

| Calories | Cholesterol (mg) | Fat (g) | % Calories from Fat |
|----------|------------------|---------|---------------------|
| 170 | 0 | 5.8 | 30.9% |

# ©⑤ PEACH MOUSSE

6 large peaches
4 tablespoons honey
1 tablespoon lemon juice
1 teaspoon almond extract
1 tablespoon plain gelatin

5 egg whites
⅛ teaspoon cream of tartar
¼ cup sugar
1 teaspoon vanilla

Dip peaches into boiling water for one minute. Remove; cool, and peel. Slice and place in food processor with honey and lemon juice, blending until very smooth. Pour into saucepan; stir in almond extract. Sprinkle gelatin over top of mixture and stir over low heat until gelatin dissolves. Cool to room temperature. In mixing bowl, beat egg whites with cream of tartar until soft peaks form. Gradually beat in sugar and continue beating until whites are stiff. Beat in vanilla. Carefully fold peach mixture into egg whites. Pour into a soufflé dish or glass bowl. Refrigerate for 2 to 3 hours. Yield: 6 to 8 servings.

*A light summer dessert to use those fresh peaches.*

**Nutritional Information Per Serving:**

| Calories | Cholesterol (mg) | Fat (g) | % Calories from Fat |
|----------|------------------|---------|---------------------|
| 100 | 0 | 0.1 | 0.6% |

 **FRUIT PARFAIT**

2 medium oranges, peeled
    and sectioned
1 pint fresh strawberries,
    stemmed and halved

1 cup fresh blueberries
1 large banana, sliced
⅓ cup coconut, toasted

Combine oranges, strawberries, and blueberries. Set in refrigerator. Prepare Orange Cream Topping (see recipe below). At serving time, slice banana and add to fruit. Alternate layers of fruit with coconut and Orange Cream Topping in six (4-ounce) parfait glasses. Yield: 6 servings.

*Great summer dessert!*

**Orange Cream Topping**
¾ cup non fat plain yogurt
2 tablespoons light brown
    sugar

1 teaspoon grated orange
    rind

Combine ingredients in chilled mixing bowl. Beat until topping doubles in volume, about 5 minutes.

**Nutritional Information Per Serving:**

| Calories | Cholesterol (mg) | Fat (g) | % Calories from Fat |
|---|---|---|---|
| 158 | <1 | 4.7 | 26.6% |

## ⓒ CHEESECAKE

3 tablespoons light
    margarine, melted
1 cup graham cracker
    crumbs
2 tablespoons sugar
1 (15-ounce) carton part-skim
    ricotta cheese

1 cup low fat vanilla yogurt
3 egg whites
⅓ cup sugar
1 teaspoon vanilla
½ teaspoon almond extract

Combine margarine, graham cracker crumbs, and sugar in small bowl. Press firmly into a 9-inch round pie plate; set aside. In medium mixing bowl, combine all remaining ingredients. Beat at high speed of electric mixer until smooth. Pour into prepared crust. Bake at 350 degrees for 40 to 45 minutes. Filling will firm as it cools. Chill at least 6 hours and garnish with fresh strawberries if desired.

**Nutritional Information Per Serving:**

| Calories | Cholesterol (mg) | Fat (g) | % Calories from Fat |
|---|---|---|---|
| 171 | 14 | 6.2 | 32.4% |

##  ⓒ HEAVENLY CHEESECAKE

½ cup graham cracker
   crumbs
1 tablespoon light margarine,
   melted
1 (8-ounce) package light
   cream cheese

1 (8-ounce) container part-
   skim ricotta cheese
½ cup sugar
1 teaspoon vanilla
3 egg whites

In a small bowl combine graham cracker crumbs and margarine. Pat into bottom of a 9-inch round pie plate coated with no stick cooking spray. In a mixing bowl, combine cream cheese and ricotta until well blended. Add sugar and vanilla, mixing well. In another mixing bowl, beat egg whites until soft peaks form. Fold egg whites gradually into cheese mixture until well combined. Pour batter into pie shell. Bake at 350 degrees for 45 to 55 minutes. Remove from oven to cool. Cool and spread with Topping (see recipe below). Yield: 8 to 10 servings.

**Topping**
½ cup non fat plain yogurt
¼ cup sugar

½ teaspoon vanilla

In small saucepan, combine yogurt, sugar, and vanilla. Stir constantly over low heat with whisk until smooth. Cool.

**Nutritional Information Per Serving:**

| Calories | Cholesterol (mg) | Fat (g) | % Calories from Fat |
|---|---|---|---|
| 177 | 20 | 6.8 | 34.5% |

## ⓒ Ⓕ CHOCOLATE FONDUE

2 cups sugar
¾ cup unsweetened cocoa
2 tablespoons cornstarch
¼ teaspoon salt
4 cups cold skim milk

3 tablespoons light
   margarine
1 teaspoon vanilla
¼ teaspoon butter flavoring

Mix sugar, cocoa, cornstarch, and salt together in saucepan. Add skim milk, stirring well. Cook over medium heat to a boil. Lower heat, and simmer 20 minutes. Add margarine, vanilla, and butter flavoring. Use angel food cake cut into squares, marshmallows, or fresh fruit for dipping. Yield: 5 cups.
*Great for cocktail parties.*

**Nutritional Information Per Tablespoon:**

| Calories | Cholesterol (mg) | Fat (g) | % Calories from Fat |
|---|---|---|---|
| 28 | <1 | 0.3 | 10.8% |

# ⓒⒻ MOCHA FUDGE MOUSSE PIE

**Brownie Crust**

⅓ cup warm water
1 teaspoon instant coffee
1 (19.85-ounce) box 93% fat
    free fudge brownie mix

2 egg whites
1 teaspoon vanilla
⅓ cup chopped pecans

In small cup, stir together water and coffee until dissolved. In large bowl, combine brownie mix, egg whites, and vanilla stirring with spoon until well mixed. Stir in pecans. Pour batter into a 9-inch pie plate coated with no stick cooking spray. Bake at 350 degrees for 25 minutes or until done. Do not overbake. Cool pie with crust on wire rack. Spread with Chocolate Mousse (see recipe below). Top with Whipped Topping (see recipe below). Refrigerate. Yield: 10 servings.
*This easy pie will get rave reviews! (Don't tell you just opened boxes).*

**Mousse and Topping**

¾ cup skim milk
2 tablespoons coffee liqueur,
    divided
1 teaspoon instant coffee

1 (3.9-ounce) package
    chocolate flavored
    instant pudding and pie
    filling mix
1 (8-ounce) container frozen
    light whipped topping,
    divided

In bowl, stir together milk, 1 tablespoon coffee liqueur, and coffee until coffee is dissolved. Add the pudding mix and beat at high speed of mixer for 1 minute. Gently fold in half of the whipped topping. Spread mixture evenly over brownie crust. Combine remaining 1 tablespoon coffee liqueur with remaining half of whipped topping, mixing gently. Spread over pudding mixture in pie.

**Nutritional Information Per Serving:**

| Calories | Cholesterol (mg) | Fat (g) | % Calories from Fat |
|----------|------------------|---------|---------------------|
| 378 | .4 | 10.8 | 25.8% |

## ⓒⓕ GLAZED BANANAS

2 tablespoons light
   margarine
¼ cup light brown sugar
⅛ teaspoon cinnamon

¼ cup fresh orange juice
3 firm bananas, peeled, split
   lengthwise, and halved

In pan, heat margarine, brown sugar, cinnamon, and orange juice until bubbly. Add banana slices, cooking for 5 minutes, turning as needed. Serve immediately. Yield: 6 servings.
*Serve over frozen vanilla yogurt, and you will have a sensational dessert.*

### Nutritional Information Per Serving:

| Calories | Cholesterol (mg) | Fat (g) | % Calories from Fat |
|---|---|---|---|
| 96 | 0 | 2.1 | 19.8% |

## ⓒⓕ BLUEBERRY COBBLER

¾ cup water
2 tablespoons cornstarch

½ cup sugar
4 cups fresh blueberries

In saucepan, combine water, cornstarch, and sugar; bring to boil. Cook for 1 minute, stirring constantly. Add berries and mix; remove from heat. Pour into a 10-inch pie plate. Cover with Topping (see recipe below). Bake at 425 degrees for 25 to 30 minutes or until topping is lightly browned. Yield: 6 servings.

**Topping**
1 cup flour
½ teaspoon salt
1½ teaspoons baking powder
⅓ cup skim milk

3 tablespoons canola oil
1 teaspoon sugar
¼ teaspoon cinnamon

Combine flour, salt, and baking powder. Mix milk with oil; add to flour. Using a fork, mix until dough forms a ball. Drop by spoonfuls onto cobbler. Combine sugar and cinnamon; sprinkle over dough.
*Serve hot with frozen vanilla yogurt and you will have a hit!*

### Nutritional Information Per Serving:

| Calories | Cholesterol (mg) | Fat (g) | % Calories from Fat |
|---|---|---|---|
| 280 | <1 | 7.4 | 23.9% |

# ⓒⓕ STRAWBERRY CUSTARD BRÛLÉE

1½ cups fresh strawberries
2 tablespoons sugar
1½ tablespoons cornstarch
1 egg, lightly beaten
1 cup skim milk

2 tablespoons non fat plain
  yogurt
½ teaspoon vanilla
1 tablespoon light brown
  sugar

Gently rinse and drain strawberries. Divide among five 4 to 6-ounce ramekins or custard cups; set aside. In saucepan, combine sugar and cornstarch; stir well. Add egg; mix. Gradually stir in milk. Cook over low heat until thickened, stirring constantly. Remove from heat; cool 5 minutes. Add yogurt and vanilla, mixing well. Spoon custard mixture evenly over strawberries. Place ramekins on baking sheet. Sprinkle top with brown sugar. Broil 4 inches from heat about 2 minutes or until sugar melts. Serve immediately. Yield: 5 servings.
*Raspberries or any fruit can be substituted.*

**Nutritional Information Per Serving:**

| Calories | Cholesterol (mg) | Fat (g) | % Calories from Fat |
|---|---|---|---|
| 84 | 43 | 1.3 | 13.5% |

# ⓒⓕ PEACH COBBLER

⅓ cup sugar
1 tablespoon cornstarch
¾ cup orange juice
3 cups sliced peaches
  (peeled)
½ cup flour

½ cup whole wheat flour
1½ teaspoons baking powder
⅓ cup skim milk
3 tablespoons canola oil
1 teaspoon sugar
¼ teaspoon cinnamon

In small saucepan, stir ⅓ cup sugar and cornstarch; add orange juice. Cook until bubbly. Add peaches and cook until hot; keep warm. Stir together flours and baking powder. Add milk and oil; stir until mixture forms a ball. On floured surface, pat into an 8-inch circle. Cut into 8 wedges. Spoon hot peach mixture into a 9-inch pie plate and top with pastry wedges. Combine sugar and cinnamon; sprinkle on top of pastry. Bake at 425 degrees for 25 to 30 minutes or until pastry is brown. Yield: 8 servings.
*For a real treat, serve with frozen vanilla yogurt.*

**Nutritional Information Per Serving:**

| Calories | Cholesterol (mg) | Fat (g) | % Calories from Fat |
|---|---|---|---|
| 194 | <1 | 5.5 | 25.4% |

## ⓒⓕ NECTARINE AND RASPBERRY CRUMBLE

4 ripe nectarines
6 tablespoons light brown
   sugar, divided
2½ tablespoons flour, divided
½ teaspoon cinnamon
½ pint raspberries

1 cup old fashioned oatmeal
2 tablespoons light
   margarine
2 tablespoons fresh orange
   juice

Peel, pit, and slice nectarines about ½-inch thick. In a small bowl, combine 2 tablespoons brown sugar, 1½ tablespoons flour, and cinnamon. Toss with nectarines. Gently stir in raspberries. Coat a 9-inch pie plate with no stick cooking spray and place fruit mixture in it. Combine remaining 4 tablespoons brown sugar, oatmeal, and 1 tablespoon flour with margarine and orange juice, mixing until crumbly. Crumble over fruit. Bake at 425 degrees for 25 to 30 minutes or until fruit is bubbly. If topping begins to burn, cover loosely with foil. Yield: 6 to 8 servings.

### Nutritional Information Per Serving:

| Calories | Cholesterol (mg) | Fat (g) | % Calories from Fat |
|---|---|---|---|
| 148 | 0 | 2.7 | 16.2% |

## ⓒⓕ CUSTARD PIE

3 cups skim milk
1 cup sugar
½ cup flour

2 eggs
1 teaspoon vanilla
1 9-inch crust

In saucepan, heat milk on low heat. In bowl, mix sugar, flour, and eggs. Beat well and pour into heated milk. Cook over medium heat until mixture boils. Remove from heat and add vanilla. Pour custard filling into prepared crust. Bake at 350 degrees for 20 minutes. Yield: 8 servings.
*A true custard lover's delight.*

### Nutritional Information Per Serving:

| Calories | Cholesterol (mg) | Fat (g) | % Calories from Fat |
|---|---|---|---|
| 295 | 55 | 9.6 | 29.3% |

# ⓒ Ⓕ APPLE CRUMBLE PIE

**Crust**

12 graham cracker squares, crushed

¼ teaspoon cinnamon

3 tablespoons light margarine, melted

Combine all ingredients, mixing until crumbs are moistened. Press crumbs onto bottom and sides of 9-inch pie plate. Fill crust with Filling (see recipe below). Sprinkle Topping (see recipe below) over filling. Bake at 350 degrees for approximately 1 hour or until apples are done and pie is bubbly. Yield: 8 servings.

*An outstanding apple pie!*

**Filling**

5 cups tart apples, peeled, cored, and sliced

⅔ cup sugar

¼ cup flour

1 teaspoon vanilla

Combine all ingredients in large bowl and mix well. Spoon into crust.

**Topping**

¾ cup flour

⅓ cup light brown sugar

1 teaspoon cinnamon

6 tablespoons light margarine

Combine flour, sugar and cinnamon together in small bowl. Blend in margarine until mixture is crumbly.

**Nutritional Information Per Serving:**

| Calories | Cholesterol (mg) | Fat (g) | % Calories from Fat |
|---|---|---|---|
| 302 | 0 | 7.7 | 23.0% |

 **PEAR CRUMBLE PIE**

**Pie Crust**

¾ cup flour

¼ teaspoon salt

3 tablespoons canola oil

1 tablespoon cold water

2 teaspoons lemon juice

Combine flour and salt; mix well. Combine oil, cold water, and lemon juice; add to dry ingredients. Stir with fork until dry ingredients are moistened. Pat into a 9-inch pie plate. Prepare Filling (see recipe below) and top with Crumble Topping (see recipe below). Bake at 375 degrees for 1 hour or until pie is bubbly. If topping browns too quickly, cover with foil and continue baking. Yield: 8 to 10 servings.

**Filling**

4½ cups peeled, cored, and
   sliced pears

½ cup sugar

¼ cup flour

2 tablespoons lemon juice

Toss pears with sugar, flour, and lemon juice. Spoon mixture into unbaked pie crust.

**Crumble Topping**

1 cup flour

½ cup light brown sugar

1 teaspoon cinnamon

¼ teaspoon salt, optional

5 tablespoons light
   margarine

Combine all ingredients except margarine. Cut in margarine with fork until crumbly.

**Nutritional Information Per Serving:**

| Calories | Cholesterol (mg) | Fat (g) | % Calories from Fat |
|----------|------------------|---------|---------------------|
| 286 | 0 | 7.5 | 23.6% |

## ⓒ Ⓕ BLUEBERRY MERINGUE PIE

½ cup water
½ cup sugar
2 tablespoons cornstarch
¼ teaspoon cinnamon

4 cups blueberries,
approximately
(1 container)
1 tablespoon lemon juice
2 egg whites
3 tablespoons sugar

Combine water, ½ cup sugar, and cornstarch in saucepan, stirring well. Cook over medium heat, stirring constantly, until smooth, thickened, and transparent. Add blueberries, and continue cooking over low heat about 15 minutes. Remove from heat; add lemon juice. Pour mixture into Pastry (see recipe below). In mixer, beat egg whites until stiff. Gradually add 3 tablespoons sugar and continue beating until stiff glossy peaks form. Spread meringue over blueberries in pie. Bake at 350 degrees for 10 to 15 minutes or until well browned. Yield: 8 servings.

*This is an excellent choice for blueberry pie lovers.*

**Pastry**
1 cup flour
1 tablespoon light brown
  sugar

3 tablespoons canola oil
2 tablespoons cold water

Combine flour and sugar in bowl. Add oil, stirring with fork until crumbly. Add cold water, and stir until ingredients are moistened. Press dough evenly over bottom and up sides of a 9-inch pie plate. Bake at 350 degrees for 15 minutes.

**Nutritional Information Per Serving:**

| Calories | Cholesterol (mg) | Fat (g) | % Calories from Fat |
|---|---|---|---|
| 233 | 0 | 5.6 | 21.5% |

## ⓒⒻ OPEN PEACH PIE

1½ cups flour
½ teaspoon salt
¼ cup canola oil
3 tablespoons skim milk
⅓ cup sugar
3 tablespoons cornstarch

½ teaspoon cinnamon
¼ teaspoon nutmeg
4 cups peeled, sliced fresh
  ripe peaches
1 tablespoon lemon juice
¼ teaspoon almond extract

Combine flour and salt in a bowl; add oil and milk, tossing with a fork until mixture resembles coarse meal. Gently press dough into a 4-inch circle on wax paper, wrap, and chill 15 minutes. Roll dough to a 12-inch circle, still covered. Remove paper and fit dough into a 9-inch pie plate coated with no stick cooking spray. Press dough into pie plate and prick with fork; set aside. Combine sugar and next 3 ingredients in a bowl; stir well and set aside. Combine peaches, lemon juice, almond extract, and sugar mixture in a large bowl; toss gently. Pour into prepared pie shell. Bake at 425 degrees for 40 minutes or until bubbly. If crust browns too quickly, cover edges with foil during last 10 minutes of baking. Yield: 8 servings.

### Nutritional Information Per Serving:

| Calories | Cholesterol (mg) | Fat (g) | % Calories from Fat |
|----------|------------------|---------|---------------------|
| 254      | <1               | 7.2     | 25.7%               |

## HOLLY B. CLEGG
13431 Woodmont Court
Baton Rouge, Louisiana 70810

Please send me the following copies of each book:

*From A Louisiana Kitchen* _____ copies @ $14.95 = _____
*A Trim and Terrific Louisiana*
   *Kitchen* _____ copies @ $16.95 = _____

SUBTOTAL $ _____
(Louisiana residents add 8% sales tax) **TAX** _____
**POSTAGE AND HANDLING** ($3.25) _____
**TOTAL** $ _____

Name _____

Address _____

City _____ State ____ Zip Code _____

Telephone Number ( ____ ) _____

Please charge to my ☐ Mastercard ☐ Visa

Card # _____ Expiration Date _____

Signature of Cardholder _____

OR CHARGE BY PHONE 1-800-88HOLLY

*Make checks payable to Holly B. Clegg*

---

## HOLLY B. CLEGG
13431 Woodmont Court
Baton Rouge, Louisiana 70810

Please send me the following copies of each book:

*From A Louisiana Kitchen* _____ copies @ $14.95 = _____
*A Trim and Terrific Louisiana*
   *Kitchen* _____ copies @ $16.95 = _____

SUBTOTAL $ _____
(Louisiana residents add 8% sales tax) **TAX** _____
**POSTAGE AND HANDLING** ($3.25) _____
**TOTAL** $ _____

Name _____

Address _____

City _____ State ____ Zip Code _____

Telephone Number ( ____ ) _____

Please charge to my ☐ Mastercard ☐ Visa

Card # _____ Expiration Date _____

Signature of Cardholder _____

OR CHARGE BY PHONE 1-800-88HOLLY

*Make checks payable to Holly B. Clegg*

**Reorder Additional Copies**